Why You Need This New Edition?

1. Reworked and updated chapters improve the presentation of various philosophical positions throughout the book.

2. The discussion of free will in Chapter Four now includes a discussion of the Consequence Argument, as well as an updated version of various compatibilist theories of freedom.

3. In Chapter Seven, the presentation of the cosmological argument is completely revised as well as the presentation of the problem of evil.

4. Several new graphic representations of various philosophical positions are included.

5. In Chapter Five, an overview of the various questions that might fall under the problem of personal identity has been added.

6. *Food for Thought* exercises have been updated by incorporating recent events. In Chapter Eight, for instance, the advantages of utilitarianism are illustrated with the help of events that took place in Afghanistan in 2005.

7. New short essay reflection questions have been added at the end of each chapter.

8. Several photographs have been added throughout the book to illustrate philosophical concepts.

PEARSON

Ultimate
Questions

Ultimate Questions

Thinking About Philosophy

Third Edition

Nils Ch. Rauhut
Coastal Carolina University

Prentice Hall

Boston   Columbus   Indianapolis   New York   San Francisco   Upper Saddle River
Amsterdam   Cape Town   Dubai   London   Madrid   Milan   Munich   Paris   Montreal
Toronto   Delhi   Mexico City   Sao Paulo   Sydney   Hong Kong   Seoul
Singapore   Taipei   Tokyo

Meiner Mutter
Hanna Therese Wilhelmine Auguste Rauhut (geb.Dusi) gewidmet.

Editor in Chief: Dickson Musslewhite
Acquisitions Editor: Nancy Roberts
Editorial Project Manager: Kate Fernandes
Director of Marketing: Brandy Dawson
Senior Marketing Manager:
  Laura Lee Manley
Operations Specialist: Christina Amato
Manager, Cover Visual Research &
  Permissions: Karen Sanatar
Cover Research Coordinator:
  Cathy Mazzucca
Cover Credit: Andromeda Constellation
  Stocktrek Images/Corbis

Manager: Jayne Conte
Cover Designer: Suzanne Behnke
Manager, Visual Research: Beth Brenzel
Manager, Rights and Permissions:
  Zina Arabia
Media Editor: Rachel Comerford
Full-Service Project Management:
  Sudip Sinha/Aptara®, Inc.
Composition: Aptara®, Inc.
Printer/Binder: Courier Companies, Inc.
Cover Printer: Courier Companies, Inc.
Text Font: 10/12 Sabon

Credits and acknowledgments borrowed from other sources and reproduced, with permission, in this textbook appear on appropriate page within text or on pages.

Library of Congress Cataloging-in-Publication Data
Rauhut, Nils Ch.
  Ultimate questions: thinking about philosophy / Nils Ch. Rauhut.—3rd ed.
    p. cm.
  ISBN-13: 978-0-205-73197-8
  ISBN-10: 0-205-73197-X
  1. Philosophy—Textbooks.   I. Title.
  BD21.R36 2011
  100—dc22

                                                    2010027104

10 9 8 7 6 5 4 3
Prentice Hall
is an imprint of

www.pearsonhighered.com

ISBN-10:   0-205-73197-X
ISBN 13: 978-0-205-73197-8

Contents

Preface

An introductory philosophy class confronts both students and teachers with unique challenges. For many students, philosophy is mystifying because they have learned to associate any field of study with remembering the currently accepted answers to a set of easily understood questions. When they are told that the practice of philosophy produces multiple and conflicting responses to the same questions, students tend to be confused. How, many ask, is anybody supposed to identify the right answers to these great philosophical questions, and how is it possible to be graded fairly on that effort? When teachers reply that nearly any response might be accepted as long as it is well supported by arguments, they have done little to ease students' concerns.

On the other hand, teaching introductory philosophy classes is equally as challenging as taking them. Teachers who ask students to read a well-known piece of philosophical writing often discover that the students struggle to comprehend. As a consequence, students ask teachers to explain the writings and the ideas of famous philosophers to them. The result is all too familiar: professors lecture to passive student audiences. Unfortunately, lecturing and listening to lectures have very little to do with learning how to practice and appreciate philosophy.

In this book I have tried to be sensitive to these concerns. I do not presuppose that philosophical problems are naturally fascinating to students; instead, I try to show that the great problems of Western philosophy arise within our ordinary ways of thinking and being. In this way I hope to help students see why philosophical problems have meaning. Moreover, in the chapter *Philosophical Tools*, I provide an introduction to philosophical terminology and methodology that is often presupposed but rarely explicitly described to students. And in my exposition of the various problems, I provide many opportunities for readers to think actively on their own about philosophical questions. These *Food for Thought* exercises are designed to make students active thinkers. The exercises have grown out of my own experience of teaching introductory philosophy classes and hopefully will lead to lively discussions and more active learning.

The main changes in the third edition are the following: First, I have reworked and updated every chapter with an eye to improving the presentation of various philosophical positions. For example, my discussion of free will in Chapter 4 now includes a discussion of the consequence argument, as well as an updated version of various compatibilist theories of freedom. In Chapter 7, I have completely revised the presentation of the cosmological argument and the problem of evil. Second, I have included several new graphic representations of various philosophical positions. In Chapter 5, for instance, I give a new overview of the various questions that might fall under the problem of personal identity. Third, I have updated several *Food for Thought* exercises by incorporating recent events into the presentation. In Chapter 8, for example, I illustrate the advantages of utilitarianism with the help of events that took place in Afghanistan in 2005. Finally, I have added short Study and Reflection Questions at the end of each chapter.

Acknowledgments

I would like to thank those readers who have provided me with helpful feedback. Of special importance was the advice of Chris Blakey, Preston McKever-Floyd, Ron Green, Will Heusser, Basil Smith, and Bruce Suttle. Special thanks are also due to Sarah Holle, Maggie Barbieri, Mary Benis, Nancy Roberts, and Kate Fernandes from Prentice Hall. In addition, several reviewers have provided helpful suggestions: Mimi Marrinucci, Eastern Washington University; Chris Bauer, Sierra College; Jeremy Kirkby, Albion College; David McNaron, Nova Southeastern University; Ilya Gofman, Southern Connecticut State University; Robert Thomason, Point Loma Nazarene University; Walter Riker, University of West Georgia. Last but not least, I would like to thank my wife, Karin, whose support and love have made this book possible.

Nils Ch. Rauhut

Support for Instructors and Students

- **myphilosophylab** is an interactive and instructive multimedia site designed to help students and instructors save time and improve results. It offers access to a wealth of resources geared to meet the individual teaching and learning needs of every instructor and student. Combining an ebook, video, audio, multimedia simulations, research support and assessment, MyPhilosophyLab engages students and gives them the tools they need to enhance their performance in the course. Please see your Pearson sales representative or visit **www.myphilosophylab.com** for more information.

- **Instructor's Manual with Tests (0-205-15676-2)** For each chapter in the text, this valuable resource provides a detailed outline, list of objectives, discussion questions, and suggested readings and videos. In addition, test questions in essay and short answer formats are available for each chapter. For easy access, this manual is available within the instructor section of MyPhilosophyLab for *Ultimate Questions: Thinking About Philosophy*, or at **www.pearsonhighered .com/irc.**

• **PowerPoint Presentation Slides (0-205-15677-0)** These PowerPoint slides for each chapter help instructors convey philosophical principles in a clear and engaging way. For easy access, they are available within the instructor section of MyPhilosophyLab for *Ultimate Questions: Thinking About Philosophy*, or at **www.pearsonhighered.com/irc.**

About the Author

Nils Ch. Rauhut studied philosophy and history at the University of Regensburg (Germany). He received an M.A. degree in philosophy from the University of Colorado at Boulder, and a Ph.D. in philosophy from the University of Washington in Seattle. He taught at Weber State University in Ogden, Utah, and he is currently teaching at Coastal Carolina University in Conway, South Carolina.

Ultimate
Questions

CHAPTER ONE

WHAT IS PHILOSOPHY?

Making Sense of the World

Although not everyone has an interest in physics, psychology, geography, or economics, most people have a pretty clear idea of what these academic disciplines are about. The same is not true for philosophy. It is quite common to meet educated people who have only a foggy idea of what philosophy is and what philosophers do. Let us therefore begin with a brief explanation of the nature and scope of philosophy.

One way to clarify the nature of philosophy is to explore an imaginary scenario. Suppose that you are a member of a typical nomadic tribe living, say, four thousand years ago. Life is tough for your tribe; most of your time is spent hunting for food and shelter. However, there are also good days, especially during the summers when food is plentiful and temperatures are comfortable. Suppose that during one summer evening your fifteen-year-old daughter sits down next to you, points at the star-filled sky, and says, "I am amazed at the beauty of the sky. I have the feeling that this whole universe is an incredible place. But looking at these stars also makes me feel very small and insignificant. Tell me: Do these stars care about us? Do they take an interest in what we do down here?" At this point you probably wish that your daughter would be more like the other teenage girls in your tribe, who worry only about who will ask them to dance at the next sacred hunting celebration. But since it is such a fine summer evening, you sit back and try to respond to her questions as well as you can.

In order to answer your daughter's questions, you need to provide what one might call a big-picture view of the universe, which always involves some kind of story that attempts to make sense of the world in which we live. There are several ways to tell such a story. A natural way is the use of mythology.[1] Every culture has developed powerful mythological stories to make sense of the world. In the Western world, one of the oldest surviving mythologies is

Homer's *Iliad*. Homer's poem of the battle for Troy not only tells us something about history and cosmology, but also explores the nature of the underworld and the world of the gods. Mythologies provide an effective way to understand the cosmos and the role we humans play within it. So in our imaginary scenario, you might tell your daughter a mythological story similar to Homer's *Iliad* or Hesiod's *Theogony*. Aside from merely entertaining your daughter by the campfire, you would be instilling in her a sense of how the heavens came to be and what interest the gods take in our deeds and actions. It is, however, apparent that mythological stories leave something to be desired. Imagine that you have a critical-minded daughter. After listening politely to your mythological story, she might very well respond, "Wow, that was a great story, but how do you know that it is actually true?"

Food for Thought

It might seem as if mythology is a thing of the past. Who would base his or her understanding of the world on simple, powerful stories? Upon closer examination, however, it becomes clear that our understanding of the world is still shaped by invented stories. List some examples of how invented stories still influence and affect our understanding of the world.

At this point you have several options. You might either point to the long tradition of your tribe and try to convince your daughter that your tribe would not have survived for so long if these traditional stories were all bogus, or else you can try to provide additional support to show that the story you have told is true. There are several ways to offer such additional support. One way consists of the claim that one of your ancestors was very close to the gods (or God), and that a god revealed the truth of this story to him or her. When mythological stories are combined with divine revelations, mythology has a tendency to turn into religion.[2]

Religion is the second widely established means through which we can provide a big-picture view of the universe. Religion resembles mythology in that most religions contain stories that—at first glance—have the sound and look of mythological stories. However, religious stories, unlike mythologies, contain a reason that we should believe that they are true: divine revelation. Divine revelation can take very different forms. It might come as a dream, as it did for the Bible's Abraham; or it might come during meditations, as it did for the prophet Muhammad in the cave Hira; or it might consist of the discovery of holy texts, as occurred with the founder of the Mormon religion, Joseph Smith. No matter what form these divine revelations take, they offer a reason that religious stories are true.

Let us go back to our imaginary scenario. Suppose you defend your story with the claim that the gods revealed the story to some of your ancestors. Your daughter might respond to this defense as follows: "Oh, I do not doubt that our great ancestors were closer to the gods than we are now, but what makes me curious is this: I recently met a wandering medicine man from a tribe far away. He told me about the religious beliefs that have guided his tribe for centuries. Guess what? Their religious beliefs support completely different stories about the world and the gods. What reason do I have to believe our own religious stories, while I reject those of other tribes?"

This response shows that religion, as a method of understanding the world, is challenged by the fact that not all divine revelations are compatible. When different religious systems come into contact with one another, it becomes rather difficult to decide which revelation is more trustworthy. Although some individuals (especially if they have had religious experiences) may be convinced that a particular revelation is true while all others are misguided, not everybody can justify such strong convictions.

At this point philosophy enters the picture; it is a third major way of providing a big-picture view of reality. The word *philosophy* derives from the Greek words *philia* ("love") and *sophia* ("wisdom"). Philosophy can therefore be understood as love of wisdom. But what does this mean? We can understand the nature of philosophy better if we clarify the relationship among philosophy, mythology, and religion. Philosophy is related to mythology insofar as philosophers also try to provide a comprehensive, big-picture view of reality. Philosophy resembles religion in that philosophers provide reasons that their picture of reality is true. However, philosophers never appeal to divine revelation or to tradition in order to show that their theories are true; instead, they appeal to the power of reason. In a broad sense, **philosophy** can therefore be understood as an attempt to develop a big-picture view of the universe with the help of **reason**.

How Do We Make Sense of the World?

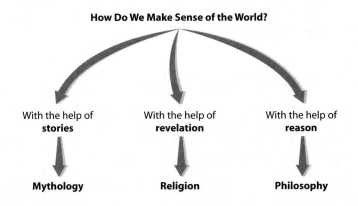

With the help of **stories**	With the help of **revelation**	With the help of **reason**
Mythology	**Religion**	**Philosophy**

Let us go back to our imaginary situation. What would it mean to explain the cosmos to your daughter with the help of reason? Well, you might say something along the following lines: "You have asked me, among other things, whether stars take an interest in what we are doing. In order to answer this question, we need to clarify the nature of stars. I believe that stars are balls of fire. You might not believe me, but here is the reason I think this is a plausible idea. Look at this campfire. It is a source of light. I have walked through many dark nights, and I can tell you that whenever I have seen light, it had something to do with fire. Consider lightning, for example. It causes trees to burn and is also a kind of fire. So it seems to me that wherever there is light, there must be fire. Since stars are a source of light, they too must be a kind of fire. Moreover, since fire does not seem to be able to perceive anything, I do not believe that stars are aware of what we are doing."

What you have just done is use an argument to defend your belief that stars are not aware of our actions. This is a key element in philosophy. Philosophers not only try to explain the world with the help of claims and stories, but also try to defend their claims with the help of arguments. We start to philosophize when we present arguments in defense of our big-picture view of reality.[3]

Although our understanding of philosophy is still incomplete, it is already possible to point to four key elements of philosophical reflections. First, in order to philosophize, we need to know more about arguments. We need to know how to construct arguments and how to evaluate them. We will do this in the next chapter. Second, the hypothetical situation that I described here illustrates that philosophy emerges as a response to persistent questioning. If your daughter had not been so reluctant to accept traditional stories, there would not have been any reason to present arguments in defense of your beliefs. Philosophy therefore comes most easily to us when we are in a critical state of mind, questioning whether our standard picture of the universe is really accurate. As long as we are absolutely convinced that our beliefs about the world are correct, we feel little need to justify them with the help of arguments. However, many people encounter situations in their lives when they begin to question their beliefs and convictions. It is during these times that philosophy emerges most naturally.

Food for Thought

Philosophy emerges most naturally in situations when we question whether our ordinary beliefs about the world are really true. The Russian writer Leo Tolstoy (1828–1910) described in his *Confessions* how he started to question everything in his life:

> So I lived; but five years ago something very strange began to happen to me. At first I experienced moments of perplexity and arrest of life, as though I did not know what to do or how to live; and I felt lost and became dejected. But this passed and I went on living as before. Then these moments of perplexity began to recur oftener and oftener, and always in the same form. They were always expressed by the questions: What is it for? What does it lead to?[4]

In normal everyday life we tend not to be as reflective and critical as Tolstoy was when he wrote his *Confessions*. However, it has been suggested that we all become self-doubting and perplexed at certain points in our lives. Is that true? If yes, what kinds of experiences or situations typically undermine our confidence that we understand the world correctly?

Third, doing philosophy is a social activity. It requires that we present our ideas and arguments to other people and that we are willing to listen to what others have to say about our claims. Philosophy thus takes a bit of courage. You will discover quickly that an argument that sounds brilliant to you might strike others as problematic. Being a good philosopher involves listening to the questions others have and modifying our ideas in the light of these questions. The British philosopher John Stuart Mill (1806–1873) wrote that a person does not deserve to be confident in his opinions unless "he has kept his mind open to criticism of his opinions and conduct. Because it has been his practice to listen to all that could be said against him."[5] What is important to realize in this context is that somebody who questions your ideas does not—in normal circumstances—aim to attack you as a person. Anyone who thinks in that way becomes defensive and brings a quick end to all philosophical dialogue. Philosophy flourishes when people feel comfortable to question each other in an atmosphere of mutual trust and respect.

Finally, the hypothetical conversation with your fifteen-year-old daughter also shows that philosophy has a tendency to lead to a plurality of different answers. I can defend my claim that stars are balls of fire with the help of an argument, but there are also arguments in defense of the claim that stars are unchanging, perfect entities. For most complex questions there are different answers that appear—at least for a while—equally reasonable. There are, of course, also some thoroughly misguided answers that one can show to be quite unreasonable. Although philosophy has the goal of producing one truthful picture of the universe, in practice it generates many different accounts of the world, which stand in opposition to each other. It often takes hundreds of years before some arguments are recognized to be mistaken. Progress in philosophy is a slow process; those of us who like immediate results and absolute certainty tend to be annoyed by philosophical reflection. However, studying questions that lead to opposing answers has the benefit of showing us new possibilities. The philosopher Bertrand Russell (1872–1970) wrote in this context:

> Philosophy, though unable to tell us with certainty what is the true answer to the doubts which it raises, is able to suggest many possibilities which enlarge our thoughts and free them from the tyranny of custom. Thus, while diminishing our feeling of certainty as to what things are, it greatly increases our knowledge as to what they might be; it removes the somewhat arrogant dogmatism of

those who have never traveled into the region of liberating doubt, and it keeps alive our sense of wonder by showing familiar things in an unfamiliar aspect.[6]

Philosophy introduces us to multiple ways of seeing the world, thus enriching our perspective but at the same time exposing us to risks. Once we are able to see many different points of view, we are in danger of losing a firm orientation. Ideas that are central to the way in which we live our lives can suddenly appear to be shallow conjectures. For this reason, philosophy is often accused of being subversive. Is it then beneficial to pursue philosophy and to risk undermining the most fundamental beliefs that shape our lives? This question cannot be answered universally. Studying philosophy can lead us to new knowledge and to a new outlook on life. But reflecting on the most fundamental questions in life can also result in perpetual doubt—or a reconfirmation of what we have believed since childhood. What the study of philosophy will do to you and your beliefs is not clear until you have considered it on your own. The following pages give you an opportunity to do just that.

Food for Thought

The Ancient Greek philosopher Socrates (469–399 BCE) was famous for wandering the streets of Athens, questioning people until they admitted that they did not know as much as they thought they knew. As you might imagine, this upset many Athenians—especially those in influential positions. They considered Socrates' questioning to be a danger to the city and eventually brought charges against him. In 399 BCE Socrates was condemned to death for corrupting young people and undermining the traditional religious beliefs of the city. Plato's *Apology* purportedly presents Socrates' famous defense speech, in which Socrates claimed that his questioning was beneficial to the Athenians and that they should have rewarded him instead of condemning him. Socrates claimed that it is better to be aware of one's ignorance than to go on believing dubious and unjustified ideas. He concluded that "the unexamined life is not worth living." Do you agree with Socrates? Is questioning one's beliefs a good thing, even if one ends up being perplexed?

The Relationship Between Science and Philosophy

In the last section, we defined philosophy as an attempt to explain the world with the help of reason. Some of you may find this definition puzzling. If philosophy is an attempt to explain the world with the help of reason, how then does philosophy differ from science? Scientists obviously also use reason when they explain the features of this world.

It is important to realize that what we call science was initially a part of philosophy. Aristotle (384–322 BCE), one of the greatest philosophers of antiquity, was a very influential physicist and biologist. Physics was historically described as natural philosophy. It is only during the last several hundred years that we distinguish more sharply among the various academic disciplines. Philosophy has given birth to natural science, psychology, sociology, and linguistics. In today's world we seem to learn most of the things that we can reasonably claim about the universe not from philosophers, but from physicists, astronomers, biologists, or psychologists. Consider the example from the previous section: What is the nature of stars? In order to answer this question we would turn to an astrophysicist, not a philosopher.

This raises a crucial question: If philosophy has prepared the grounds for modern science, and if modern science currently is our best tool to explain the universe with the help of reason, what role does philosophy play in the world today? Can philosophy tell us something about the world beyond what the sciences tell us? Would we lose anything if we closed all philosophy departments and directed the money saved into the various science departments?

In order to answer this question, we need to know a bit more about scientific disciplines such as physics or chemistry. Each scientific discipline deals with a specific subject matter. A physicist can tell you why you see lightning before you hear the thunder, but a physicist cannot explain to you whether going to law school will make you happy. Similarly, economists can explain the macroeconomic consequences of a low savings rate but cannot explain to you why your cholesterol level is so high. Thus, each scientific discipline deals with only a part of reality, but not with the whole. The Austrian philosopher Ludwig Wittgenstein (1889–1951) wrote: "[E]ven when all possible scientific problems have been answered, the problems of life have not been put to rest."[7]

Let me illustrate this with an example. I have always been curious as to whether or not I have a soul. Souls, if they exist, are entities that we cannot see, measure, or weigh. Souls are not like rocks, fingernails, or other physical objects. Since science obtains information about the world predominantly by measurements and experimentation, science can tell us a lot about rocks, clouds, and planets. However, science has a much harder time telling us about souls or a possible afterlife. Finding the answer to the question of whether we have souls requires not only observations and experiments but also a good deal of conceptual analysis; that is, we need to clarify what we mean by the term *soul* before we can make any progress in determining whether souls exist. Analyzing and clarifying complex concepts is an integral part of philosophy; it often involves testing definitions and analyzing hypothetical situations. The question of whether we have souls is therefore a good example of a philosophical question, which involves conceptual analysis and requires more than observations and experimentation.

Philosophical questions are "open" in the sense that we cannot easily predict what would constitute satisfactory answers. No scientific procedure can produce a quick answer to a philosophical question. Moreover, philosophical questions often deal with foundational matters that are not addressed within any science. Mathematicians, for example, can tell us lots of things about numbers. They can prove, for instance, that there are infinitely many prime numbers or that the square root of two is an irrational number. However, mathematicians very rarely address the fundamental question of what kind of things numbers actually are. Are numbers abstract entities that exist on their own, independent of any human cognition, or are numbers dependent on our minds? These kinds of foundational questions are left for philosophers to investigate, and they form an integral part of the philosophy of mathematics. What is interesting to note is that every science involves foundational questions that are not directly addressed by the science itself. We thus can speak of a philosophy of biology, a philosophy of physics, or a philosophy of science in general. Philosophy offers a home for foundational questions that fall outside the scope of ordinary scientific investigations.

It is worthwhile to stress that the line between philosophy and science is not fixed. Some philosophical questions have eventually turned into scientific questions once the appropriate scientific methodology was developed. For example, the question Is there life on Mars? is now clearly a scientific question, but it used to be a philosophical one. Similarly, the question Are computers able to think? is currently a philosophical question, but it might turn into a scientific question for cognitive scientists. This understanding clarifies why scientific investigations can have an important impact on philosophy. Although science by itself cannot answer philosophical questions, it can help philosophers to see open questions in a new light. Philosophers are, therefore, obligated to pay close attention to scientific results.

However, most classical philosophical questions, like the question of whether God exists, appear to be such that it is difficult to imagine (in principle) that they can be answered with the help of any scientific procedure. As a result, some people find philosophy frustrating; they have the feeling that philosophers do not get anywhere, since they have been exploring some of the same open questions for thousands of years without arriving at final answers. This is not a silly complaint, but before one concludes that philosophy is inherently a fruitless and frustrating activity, it is worthwhile to keep the following considerations in mind: Although it is probably impossible to answer open questions so that every reasonable person agrees with a given answer, it is very well possible to answer such questions satisfactorily in light of your experiences and observations of the world.

Food for Thought

Take a look at the following questions, and decide whether they are predominantly scientific or philosophical questions. Keep in mind that some questions might have scientific as well as philosophical components.

1. How many chromosomes does a human being have?
2. Is it morally permissible to remove chromosomes from an embryo?
3. What is required for beliefs to be rational?
4. What caused the extinction of the dinosaurs?
5. Is homosexual love unnatural?
6. Did extraterrestrials visit Earth in the past?
7. Are quarks the smallest particles in the universe?
8. Can we know that there are particles that are too small to be observed?
9. What caused the universe to exist?
10. Are economic theories genuine scientific theories?

Philosophy, unlike science, has a personal component. The purpose of philosophical activity is to clarify in your own mind which solution to an open question seems most reasonable. This does not mean that you can assert whatever strikes your fancy. Philosophy, as we have seen, is not mythological fantasy; philosophers are committed to adopt the solution that appears most reasonable in light of the best arguments available. It is, however, quite possible that different rational persons answer the same open question differently, because they have different experiences or because they make different background assumptions. One person, for example, might come to the conclusion that near-death experiences are all hogwash and the product of wishful thinking, whereas another person, who actually has had an after-death experience, is convinced that we will continue to exist after we die. Both positions might appear to be the most reasonable in the light of the best arguments available to these two thinkers. Thus, the point of your philosophical activity is, in part, to determine which solutions to open questions are the most reasonable in the light of your own experiences and thoughts about the world.

It will, of course, not always be possible for you to select one solution to an open question as the most reasonable. You might conclude, for example, that you really do not know whether you are always responsible for your actions or whether you will survive your death. But this, too, can constitute progress. Many students who start a philosophy class with the firm conviction that they know the answers to most open questions later come to realize that their arguments weren't as convincing and reasonable as they initially thought. This awareness of the limits of our knowledge makes the world a more mysterious place. But perhaps mysteries are not only a key feature of good movies, but also a key ingredient of a stimulating life.

Food for Thought

What Is Your Philosophy?

Engaging in philosophical activity frequently causes us to change our attitudes toward fundamental questions. In order to see whether your attitudes change during this class, it might be useful for you to record your positions at the beginning of the class. Answer the following questions with Yes, No, or I don't know, and discuss the questions with the rest of the class.

1. After bodily death a person continues to exist in a nonphysical form.
2. The ultimate goal in life is to live as pleasurably as possible.
3. Democracy is the best form of government.
4. God exists.
5. I am now the same person that I was when I was five years old.
6. I am always responsible for my actions.
7. To allow an innocent child to suffer needlessly when one could easily prevent it is morally reprehensible.
8. Ghosts exist.
9. One day there may be computers that understand Shakespeare better than I do right now.
10. It is wrong to impose the death penalty.
11. There are universal moral standards that apply to all human beings regardless of where they live.
12. The best way to treat depression is to inject chemicals into the brain.
13. If I had been born into a different environment, I might have become a professional killer.
14. It is impossible to know anything with absolute certainty.
15. The future is fixed; how one's life unfolds is a matter of destiny.
16. The life of a young child is more valuable than the life of a twenty-two-year-old college student.
17. If God does not exist, then there are no moral obligations, and no action is right or wrong.
18. It is impossible to be truly happy if one is an immoral person.
19. The possession of drugs for personal use should be decriminalized.

The Main Branches of Philosophy

Traditionally, philosophical questions can be divided into five different fields of study: **metaphysics, epistemology, ethics, aesthetics,** and **logic.** It is useful to be familiar with these different areas of inquiry in order to obtain an overview of the major questions studied in philosophy.

Metaphysics is usually defined as the study of ultimate reality; however, this definition is not the most insightful. One way to get a better understanding of this field of study is to list everything that we think exists in the universe. Can you imagine making such a list? Most of us would probably start our lists with familiar things such as cars, trees, cats, and people we know. However, after a while, some of us would perhaps also include items like angels, souls, and God. If we compared our lists, certain questions would ultimately develop. For example, I could ask, "Do you really believe that angels exist in the world?" This is a typical metaphysical question. As we will see later on, philosophers frequently wonder whether souls, God, time, numbers, or colors really exist, and all of these questions are part of metaphysics. In addition, metaphysics is concerned with clarifying how various entities are related to each other. Many people have thought, for instance, that every event has a cause. But how is this compatible with freedom? If everything we do is caused by events in the past, how is it possible to be free? Clarifying the relationship between causality and freedom is part of the problem of free will, and this question, too, belongs to the field of metaphysics.

Epistemology, the study of knowledge, is important for philosophers because it sometimes happens that in the process of exploring a question, we come to the conclusion that we cannot possibly know what answer to a question is correct. Many people believe, for instance, that we can never know whether God exists or not. People who deny that we can know answers to certain questions are called **skeptics**. It is an important part of philosophy to determine under what conditions skepticism is a reasonable position to adopt. This determination of the scope and limits of knowledge is the main part of epistemology.

The fields of **ethics** and **aesthetics** both deal with questions of value. Ethics is concerned with clarifying how people ought to act. Most people think, for example, that it is wrong to steal. But why exactly is stealing wrong? Could there be situations in which stealing could be morally justified? What about murder? Is murder always wrong, or are we sometimes permitted to take the life of another human? Is it even possible to answer questions like these in an objective way? The study of ethics deals with all of these questions.

Aesthetics is the study of art and beauty. When you listen to your favorite song on the radio or when you attend a performance of your favorite artist, you undergo aesthetic experiences. These experiences are pleasant and important. Can you imagine how bland the world would be without art? However, it is far from clear what kinds of factors are involved in aesthetic experiences and judgments. Is there something universal in aesthetic experiences that transcends cultural traditions and personal tastes? Are legitimate aesthetic judgments possible? These and related questions are central to the study of aesthetics.

The final—and in some sense most fundamental—area of philosophy is the field of **logic**. We have seen that philosophy requires that we defend our claims about the world with arguments. However, it is obvious that not all arguments are equally good. Many arguments are actually quite misleading and weak. Logic is the field of study that clarifies how we can distinguish good arguments from bad ones. We will start our exploration of philosophy with a brief excursion into the field of logic. The following chart should be useful for remembering the major fields of philosophy.

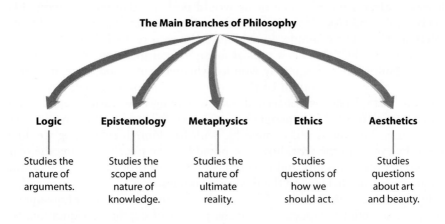

The Main Branches of Philosophy

Logic	Epistemology	Metaphysics	Ethics	Aesthetics
Studies the nature of arguments.	Studies the scope and nature of knowledge.	Studies the nature of ultimate reality.	Studies questions of how we should act.	Studies questions about art and beauty.

Although some fundamental questions have metaphysical, epistemological, and ethical aspects, most philosophical questions belong in one of these categories. Practice your grasp of these fundamental disciplines by completing the following exercise.

Food for Thought

Take a look at the following claims, and decide whether they are predominantly metaphysical, epistemological, ethical, aesthetic, or logical in nature.

1. It is better to suffer an injustice than to inflict one on others.
2. Vampires exist only in movies or books.
3. Nobody can know whether a fetus is a person or simply a collection of cells.
4. A valid argument can have false premises.
5. Everything that exists is a physical object.
6. Paris is the most beautiful city in the world.
7. Only doctors can know the causes of diseases.
8. There are more irrational numbers than rational numbers.
9. Don't pursue a major that will not make you rich.
10. It is impossible to predict the future.
11. Your stories are full of contradictions.
12. We will never understand why God lets innocent children suffer.
13. Those who think only about themselves lead unhappy lives.

Study and Reflection Questions

1. Religion and philosophy use different methods of explaining the world. Philosophy uses reason, and religion uses revelation to explain events. Does this mean that religion and philosophy have to be at odds with each other? Can the truths of reason be identical with the truths of revelation? Explain.

2. The practice of philosophy often means that we become unsure of whether all the things we used to believe are really true. Is this a good or bad situation? Do our lives become better if we question everything? Would it be better if we were to accept certain beliefs as truth, even if we could not justify them? Explain.

3. The study of mythology seems to be passé. But if you think about it, movie and television show themes have many similarities to myths. Is it fair to say that, if we still use myths as plots in television shows and movies, we are using mythology to make sense of our world? Provide pros and cons to this argument in your answer.

4. Science is not able to answer every question that we have about our lives. For example, no scientific discipline can answer the question What is the meaning of life? In your opinion, are such open questions meaningful? Should we assume that only questions easily answered by science are meaningful, and that all remaining open questions are of no value without clear meaning? If we follow this line of thought, we arrive at the conclusion that science—although not able to answer all questions—can answer all meaningful questions. Do you agree with this conclusion? Why or why not?

5. What philosophical question is most important to you? State the question, and give reasons that it is important at this stage in your life.

For Further Reading

Bontempo, Charles J., and S. Jack Odell, eds. *The Owl of Minerva: Philosophers on Philosophy.* New York: McGraw-Hill, 1975.

Bunnin, Nicholas, and E. P. Tsui-James, eds. *The Blackwell Companion to Philosophy.* Malden, MA: Blackwell, 2003.

Grayling, A. C., ed. *Philosophy 1: A Guide Through the Subject.* Oxford: Oxford University Press, 1998.

Greetman, Bryan. *Philosophy.* London: Palgrave Macmillan, 2006.

Hollis, Martin. *Invitation to Philosophy.* Oxford: Blackwell, 1985.

Melchert, Norman. *The Great Conversation.* 5th ed. Oxford: Oxford University Press, 2006.

Nagel, Thomas. *The View from Nowhere.* Oxford: Oxford University Press, 1989.

———. *What Does It All Mean?* Oxford: Oxford University Press, 1987.

Russell, Bertrand. *The Problems of Philosophy.* Oxford: Oxford University Press, 1912.

Solomon, Robert C. *Introducing Philosophy: A Text with Integrated Readings.* 9th ed. Oxford: Oxford University Press, 2007.

Yancy, George, ed. *The Philosophical I.* Lanham, MD: Rowman & Littlefield, 2002.

Endnotes

1. I understand the term *mythology* in a very general sense as referring to any invented story that has been transmitted orally over many generations within a given culture. I am grateful to Steven Duncan for pointing out that, from an anthropological point of view, it might very well be false to think that mythological stories stand in any direct competition with philosophical, religious, or scientific claims. However, my imaginary scenario is not designed to make any anthropological or historical claims about how mythology, religion, and philosophy have developed. Instead, I use the imaginary scenario simply to stress that there are relevant logical and epistemological differences among mythological, religious, and philosophical explanations of reality. An additional empirical question, which I would like to leave unanswered, is whether these logical and epistemological differences among mythology, religion, and science have had any actual historical significance.

2. I understand religion here predominantly as an epistemological phenomenon, that is, as a method of shaping beliefs about the world. It should be quite clear that not all religions have such an epistemological element, and that the term *religion* is typically used with a much broader meaning that includes a wide range of sociological and psychological phenomena as well. My goal here is not to say anything profound about religion; I want to stress instead that religion tends to provide types of explanations that differ from those of philosophical inquiry.

3. It is worth noting that not all philosophical traditions make argumentation the center of philosophical activity. Robert Abele pointed out to me that in Eastern philosophy, it is traditionally not arguments and concepts that take precedence. Rather, it is the experience of enlightenment that counts, through the use of various methods of meditation. However, even in the Eastern philosophical tradition, argumentation plays a significant role, and it is therefore not completely misleading to claim that arguments are an important ingredient of all philosophy.

4. Leo Tolstoy, *A Confession and Other Religious Writings* (Lawrence, KS: Digireads.com, 2010), p. 11.

5. John Stuart Mill, *On Liberty* (New York: Longman, 2006), p. 32.

6. Bertrand Russell, *The Problems of Philosophy* (Oxford: Oxford University Press, 1912), p. 156.

7. Ludwig Wittgenstein, *Tractatus Logico-Philosophicus*, trans. D. F. Pears and B. F. McGuinness (London: Routledge and Kegan, 1961), Proposition 6.52. Although Wittgenstein acknowledged that philosophical questions go beyond the limits of scientific investigations, he was very skeptical about whether our language allows us to express philosophical questions and possible answers to them. For Wittgenstein, philosophical questions cannot be clearly expressed and, therefore, push us into a nondiscursive mystical realm beyond language.

CHAPTER TWO

PHILOSOPHICAL TOOLS

At its heart, philosophy consists of exploring and assessing answers to open questions. This process—especially the assessment of arguments—demands that philosophers use certain logical tools and techniques that may be foreign to you. For example, let's consider the following quotation from an encyclopedia entry about the problem of evil:

> The argument from evil focuses upon the fact that the world appears to contain states of affairs that are bad, or undesirable, or that should have been prevented by any being that could have done so, and it asks how the existence of such states of affairs is to be squared with the existence of God. But the argument can be formulated in two very different ways. First, it can be formulated as a purely **deductive argument** that attempts to show that there are certain facts about the evil in the world that are **logically incompatible** with the existence of God. One especially ambitious form of this first sort of argument attempts to establish the very strong claim that it is **logically impossible** for it to be the case both that there is any evil at all, and that God exists. Alternatively, rather than being formulated as a **deductive argument** for the very strong claim that it is **logically impossible** for both God and evil to exist, (or for God and certain types, or instances, or a certain amount of evil to exist), the argument from evil can instead be formulated as an **evidential (or inductive/probabilistic) argument** for the more modest claim that there are evils that actually exist in the world that make it unlikely—or perhaps very unlikely—that God exists.[1]

Confused? Probably. Trained philosophers can read this encyclopedia entry without any problem, but for beginning students the text can be quite challenging. If you look closely, the text contains several terms that are important to philosophy, but that might not be familiar to you if you are encountering philosophy for the first time. This chapter will help you to become familiar with some important logical tools that philosophers frequently use in thinking and writing. The following chart will give you an overview of the concepts that we will discuss in this chapter.

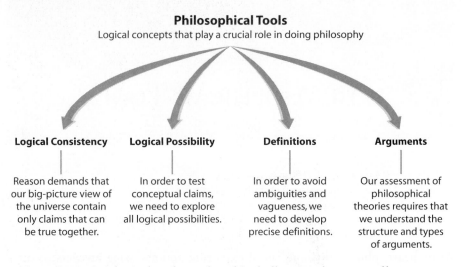

Philosophical Tools
Logical concepts that play a crucial role in doing philosophy

Logical Consistency	Logical Possibility	Definitions	Arguments
Reason demands that our big-picture view of the universe contain only claims that can be true together.	In order to test conceptual claims, we need to explore all logical possibilities.	In order to avoid ambiguities and vagueness, we need to develop precise definitions.	Our assessment of philosophical theories requires that we understand the structure and types of arguments.

Learning to use logical tools can be a bit challenging, but your efforts to master these techniques will pay off in later chapters when we explore and evaluate responses to significant philosophical problems. Don't get discouraged if you can't understand the usefulness of these tools immediately. The role that they play will become clearer as we explore more specific philosophical questions later on.

Logical Consistency

In everyday life we rarely step back and test whether all our beliefs about the world are compatible with each other. In philosophical investigation, on the other hand, the search for **logical consistency** becomes a driving force for innovation and philosophical progress. Philosophy is, as American philosopher William James (1842–1910) pointed out, "an unusually stubborn effort to think clearly."[2] But what precisely is logical consistency, and how is it related to thinking clearly about the world? Some examples will help to illustrate this important philosophical tool.

Suppose you meet somebody who holds the following two beliefs:

A. It is always morally wrong to take the life of another human being.

B. It is morally permissible to execute serious criminals.

It is clear that there is a logical tension between these two claims. If assertion A is true and it is always wrong to take the life of another human being, then it follows that it must also be wrong to execute serious criminals. So claims A and B cannot be true at the same time, and they are, therefore, logically inconsistent with each other. In general, we can say that a set of claims is **logically consistent** if and only if it is possible that all claims in the set are true at the same time; a set of claims is **logically inconsistent** if and only if it is impossible that all claims in the set are true at the same time.

Determine whether the following pairs of statements are logically consistent with each other.

1. Nobody knows the future. / God is omniscient.
2. The theory of evolution is true. / God exists.
3. It is always morally wrong to kill innocent persons. / Having an abortion is morally acceptable.
4. Nobody is perfect. / My father is flawless.
5. Humans are free. / The past determines the future.
6. I am the same person that I was when I was five years old. / Everything changes.
7. Stoning somebody to death is morally wrong/If a culture approves of stoning as a punishment then it is morally right to stone somebody.
8. No animal has a soul. / Humans are animals.
9. Democracy is the best form of government. / The majority of people in every society are stupid.
10. All birds can fly. / Penguins cannot fly.

As you can see from these examples, identifying logical inconsistencies may not be a trivial affair. Most inconsistencies are not easy to spot and require the discussion and analysis of additional beliefs. In order to illustrate this more clearly, consider the following example. Suppose you meet somebody who holds the following two beliefs:

A. Everything that exists is a physical entity.
B. Angels exist.

A and B together are not yet logically inconsistent with each other. However, we can ask whether the person also holds the following background belief:

C. Angels are nonphysical entities.

If it turns out that the person does hold belief C in addition to A and B, then we have shown that those beliefs are logically inconsistent with each other. This example illustrates that the search for logical consistency requires that we also investigate background beliefs. We are frequently not fully aware of what our background beliefs are and whether they are in conflict with the rest of our belief system. Philosophy helps us to unravel hidden aspects of our belief system. In this way we can discover that our own views of the universe are much more complex than we initially imagined them to be.

A Demand of Reason: Avoid Contradictions

Once we realize that some of our beliefs about the world are logically inconsistent with each other, we have found a reason to reevaluate and change our big-picture view of the world. Many of us, however, are not excited about the prospect of having to modify our beliefs; we want to hold on to that which is familiar and comforting. In an extreme case, one might imagine somebody who resists change in the following way: "All right, you have shown that my beliefs about the world are in conflict with one another. So what? I think that logical consistency is overrated. I am happy to have a logically inconsistent belief system. My thoughts are free, and I have the right to believe whatever I want."

A specific example might help us to illustrate the problematic nature of holding logically inconsistent beliefs. Suppose you meet Maria, who believes the following:

A. God loves all people.

B. If God loves somebody, then God makes sure that the person will be saved.

C. Some people will go to hell.

D. All people who go to hell are not saved by God.

This set of beliefs is logically inconsistent. Suppose Maria realizes this, but she is nevertheless unwilling to change her belief system. What is wrong with that? In this situation we can show Maria that her beliefs A and B commit her to believing that all people will be saved by God. Moreover, her beliefs C and D commit her to believing that some people will not be saved by God. Putting these two beliefs together, we can show Maria that she has to believe the following as well: All people will be saved by God, and some people will not be saved by God.

This last belief is very peculiar. Philosophers call this type of statement a **contradiction**, that is, a sentence that both denies and asserts that something is the case. Contradictions have a unique property in that no matter what the world is like, we can know right away that contradictions cannot be true. They are necessarily false statements and thus ought not to be part of a reasonable view of the world. It is a demand of reason that we eliminate logical inconsistencies in our big-picture view of the world and that we are willing to change our beliefs if they have been shown to entail logical inconsistencies or contradictions.

The good news is that there is always more than one way to make an inconsistent set of beliefs logically consistent again. In the case of Maria there are numerous ways for her to modify her beliefs. For example, she might decide to modify her belief A and believe that God loves most but not all people. Alternatively, she might modify her belief D and believe that people who go to hell (temporarily) can nevertheless be saved in the end. As you can see from these examples, there are endless possibilities. The more creative your mind the more options you will see. However, selecting the right adjustment of your big-picture view of the universe is often tricky. Any modification of one belief can lead to unforeseen consequences in other parts of your belief system.

Thinking through these consequences is a lot of fun and a natural by-product of doing philosophy.

Logical Possibility

Contradictions are statements that cannot possibly be true. But what exactly do we mean by the word *possible* here? Because it is used differently in different contexts, it is useful to distinguish various meanings of the word. Consider the following two sentences:

A. It is not possible for LeBron James to throw a basketball so hard that it will travel for more than a mile through the air.
B. It is not possible that LeBron James is both taller and shorter than Kobe Bryant.

Both of these sentences are true, but the meaning of the word *possible* differs between them. In the first sentence we are dealing with **causal possibility.** The reason LeBron James cannot throw a basketball that far has to do with physics and the laws of nature. In general, we can say that a state of affairs is causally possible if it does not violate the laws of nature. For example, it is causally possible that five different hurricanes will hit Florida this year or that the Philadelphia Phillies will win the World Series three times in a row. However, it is causally impossible for an airplane to travel faster than the speed of light or for a human being to live without oxygen.

Consider sentence A again: It is causally impossible for LeBron James to throw a basketball for more than a mile. Notice, however, that we can *imagine* LeBron throwing a basketball that far. Something like this will never happen (on Earth), since the laws of nature do not permit such a thing. But one can conceive of it happening. It is therefore **logically possible** that LeBron can throw a basketball more than a mile through the air. A good test of whether something is logically possible is to ask yourself whether you could make a movie about it. We can depict scenes in movies that violate the laws of nature; we can make movies about superheroes, talking toasters, or flying horses—all of which are logically possible.

When students are first introduced to the concept of logical possibility, they tend to think that everything is logically possible. But this is not the case. Notice that we cannot produce a movie that makes sentence B true; it is logically impossible that Lebron James is both taller and shorter than Kobe Bryant. If we assert both claims, we are involved in a contradiction. We can say, therefore, that a state of affairs is logically possible if it does not entail a contradiction.

But let us briefly return to the question that started our analysis of possibility. The crucial thing to remember is that in philosophy, when we test for consistency or search for contradictions, we check for logical and not causal possibility.

Food for Thought

It is important that you clearly understand the distinction between logical and causal possibility. Answer the following questions with True or False:

1. It is causally possible for water to turn into gold.
2. It is causally possible that an earthquake will destroy all buildings in New York City next week.
3. It is logically possible that a soccer ball can be completely red and completely green at the same time.
4. It is logically impossible that all faculty members at Yale are space aliens.
5. It is logically possible that a girl is taller than herself.
6. It is logically possible for Britney Spears to turn into a frog.
7. It is causally possible for the sun to rotate around the earth.
8. It is logically impossible that a turtle is the creator of this universe.
9. It is causally impossible that one person can rob all the banks in Boston during one day.
10. It is logically impossible that there are triangles with four sides.

In order to determine whether something is logically possible, we need to use our imaginations and explore what philosophers call "possible worlds." This can be a bit confusing at first, but after a while it should be a lot of fun to explore in your mind whether certain scenarios are indeed logically possible. When philosophers consider logically possible scenarios, they conduct thought experiments, which often have the sound and feel of science fiction because they deal with remote, though still logically possible, scenarios. It is perfectly all right if you are still a bit skeptical of whether the notion of logical possibility can be of much use. The benefits of the ability to conceive of logically possible scenarios will become more obvious in the following sections and in the context of studying concrete philosophical problems.

Definitions

Although philosophical thinking starts by reflecting on ordinary experiences, it quickly leads to more abstract questions. For instance, a philosopher might start by asking whether he is morally obligated to follow his country's laws, but in order to answer this question, he must clarify both the nature of morality and the nature of moral obligation. Similarly, another philosopher might wonder whether her future is already determined, but in order to answer this question, she has to think about time, causality, probability, and free will.

Although we may use terms like *causality, morality, time,* and *freedom* on a daily basis, we tend not to step back and ask, "What is time?" "What is causality?" or "What is freedom?" In everyday life we simply assume that we have a sufficiently clear understanding of what these terms mean. Philosophical reflection, however, forces us to take a closer look at these abstract terms. Sometimes this leads to the perhaps unpleasant revelation that we do not know how to explain them. As the medieval philosopher Augustine (354–430) once remarked, "What then is time? If no one asks me, I know: if I wish to explain it to one who asks, I know not."[3]

One way to clarify terms like these is to develop precise **definitions** of these terms. For this reason philosophers since the time of Socrates have thought very carefully about how to develop and test definitions. There are very different ways to approach definitions, and not all of them work very well in philosophy.

Lexical vs. Real Definitions

When you need to find out what a word means, what do you do? You might ask a friend with a good vocabulary or type the term into Web sites such as Google or Wikipedia. Or—like most beginning philosophers—you may think that definitions can simply be found in dictionaries. After all, if I do not know the precise meaning of the word *obfuscate,* for example, I can look it up in a good dictionary. Definitions that are stated in standard dictionaries are **lexical definitions**, which attempt to explain how particular words are generally used by native speakers of a given language. Although lexical definitions are helpful in everyday contexts, their usefulness in philosophy is limited.

In order to illustrate this reality, let us consider the example of the word *moral.* Suppose my dictionary tells me that the word *moral* means "conforming to accepted standards of behavior." This lexical definition might very well be true; that is, it is indeed true that the majority of all English speakers use the word *moral* with this meaning. However, it should be pretty clear that this lexical definition does not sufficiently explain what it is to be moral. It seems entirely possible, for instance, that some immoral acts may conform to accepted standards of behavior;[4] there is more to being moral than simply conforming to accepted standards of behavior. This example shows that lexical definitions do not offer much help with philosophical investigations. In philosophy we want to find out what morality and virtue really are and not just how the majority of English speakers use the words *moral* or *virtue.* Philosophers are interested in "real" definitions, that is, definitions that explain the essential nature of a thing or a phenomenon.[5]

A more useful method for developing real definitions goes back to Plato and Aristotle, and it consists of defining a term by stating **necessary and sufficient conditions** for the correct application of the term.[6] In order to illustrate this philosophical technique, let us consider an example. Suppose you meet someone who is confused about the term *vertebrate.* In order to help him, you can say, "A vertebrate is a kind of animal." What you have just done is to state a necessary condition for being a vertebrate; being an animal is a necessary condition for being a vertebrate because it is impossible for something to be a vertebrate if it is not an animal. In general, one can define necessary conditions as follows: *A* *condition q is necessary for p if it is impossible for something to be p without being q.* Specifying necessary conditions for the correct application of a term is a useful first step in clarifying a term; to know necessary conditions for the application of a term is often equivalent to knowing what kind of thing one is dealing with.

But more needs to be done before we arrive at a precise definition. Let us return to our term *vertebrate*. We have seen that being an animal is a necessary condition for being a vertebrate. What else do we need to know in order to state a precise definition? We need the specific conditions that distinguish vertebrates from other kinds of animals. Vertebrates are animals with a segmented spinal cord; thus, having a segmented spinal cord is a **sufficient condition** for being a vertebrate since it is impossible for something that has a segmented spinal cord to not be a vertebrate. In general, one can define a sufficient condition as follows: *A condition q is sufficient for p if it is impossible for something to be q and not p.* After clarifying necessary and sufficient conditions for the term *vertebrate,* we are in a position to develop a precise definition: Vertebrates are animals with a segmented spinal cord.

Let us look at another example. Suppose you encounter somebody who is confused about squares. In order to help her you want to develop a precise definition. You notice right away that there are some necessary conditions for being a square.

1. For anything to be a square, it is necessary that the thing have exactly four sides.
2. For anything to be a square, it is necessary that the thing be a closed figure that lies in a plane.
3. For anything to be a square, it is necessary that all of the thing's sides be of equal length.

Notice, too, that if we put all the necessary conditions together, we actually obtain a sufficient condition for the term to apply. We thus can obtain a good definition of the term *square*: A square is any closed figure that lies in a plane and has exactly four sides of equal length. In this case one says that the necessary conditions are together jointly sufficient.

In real philosophical investigations philosophers are often at odds about whether a certain list of necessary conditions is jointly sufficient for a term to apply. Take, for example, the case of the American philosopher Mary Anne Warren (1946–2010), who in her article "On the Moral and Legal Status of Abortion"[7] attempts to develop a precise definition of what we mean by the term *person*. She suggests, among other things, that the following two conditions are necessary and jointly sufficient for personhood:

1. Consciousness (of objects and events external and/or internal to the being and in particular the capacity to feel pain)
2. Reasoning (the developed capacity to solve new and relatively complex problems)

She concludes that we should understand a person as a being that has consciousness and an ability to reason. Such a clarification of personhood has significant ramifications. If we accept Warren's definition, it follows that fetuses are not persons and consequently have no moral and legal rights. If we want to reject Warren's analysis, we need to show that she has made a mistake in claiming that these two conditions are necessary and jointly sufficient for personhood. We will learn in the next section how definitions can be challenged.

Food for Thought

Complete the following sentences by filling in one of these phrases: (a) necessary condition, (b) sufficient condition, (c) necessary and sufficient condition, (d) condition that is neither necessary nor sufficient.

1. Being an animal is a _____ for being a monkey.
2. Being immortal is a _____ of being a superhero.
3. Being a grandfather is a _____ for being a father.
4. Being against the law is a _____ for being immoral.
5. Being born in New York City is a _____ for being a U.S. citizen.
6. Being a dog is a _____ for being a collie.
7. Being H_2O is a_____ for being water.
8. Being free is a _____ for being morally responsible.
9. Being rich is a _____ for being happy.

Food for Thought

Fill in the gaps in the following claims so that they form precise definitions.

1. *Daughter* means _____ offspring.
2. *Skyscraper* means very tall _____.
3. *Stallion* means _____ horse.
4. _____ means young sheep.
5. *Snack* means _____ meal.
6. Knowledge is _____ belief.
7. _____ is frozen water.

Challenging Definitions: Counterexamples and Thought Experiments

Suppose you are dissatisfied with how a philosopher has defined a term. What can you do? How can you challenge a proposed definition? Let us consider the case of Warren's definition of personhood. Is she right to claim that any being that is a person has to have consciousness and an ability to reason? In order to challenge her account, you can construct a counterexample. For example, you might say the following: Suppose my grandmother has a severe car accident. She is still breathing, but the doctors tell me that her brain has been so severely damaged by the accident that she is incapable of any higher brain functions. Her abilities to speak, think, and reason are gone. Does this mean that my grandmother is not a person any longer? If you answer this question with a no, then you have produced a counterexample to Warren's definition of personhood. Counterexamples very often involve descriptions of fantastic but logically possible scenarios. Philosophers call these scenarios thought experiments, many of which describe logically possible states of affairs that are designed to challenge definitions and other conceptual claims.

At first many students find it surprising that logically possible scenarios can refute theories. Many people tend to think that theories can be refuted only by facts, that is, by events that really happen. But philosophy is mostly concerned with clarifying the relationships among concepts. Conceptual relationships are logical in nature, and for this reason logically possible scenarios need to be taken into consideration. The ability to test and refute conceptual claims with the help of thought experiments is an important philosophical technique. With the help of the next exercise, practice your ability to find counterexamples to theories.

Food for Thought

Refute the following hypotheses by finding logically possible scenarios that constitute counterexamples to the claims.

1. In order to be completely happy, it is necessary to have shelter and some clothing.
2. Seeing an event take place with one's own eyes is a sufficient condition for knowing that the event occurred.
3. Having bad grades in college is a necessary condition for having lots of fun in college.
4. Performing actions that make the majority of people happy is a sufficient condition for performing morally good actions.
5. Believing strongly that something is true is a necessary condition for its being indeed true.
6. To be capable of self-motivated activities is a necessary condition for being a person.
7. Dreaming that something took place is a sufficient condition for knowing that the event did not take place.
8. Having a brain is a sufficient condition for having a mind.
9. Having a brain is a necessary condition for having a mind.

The Basic Structure of Arguments

Most beginning students associate the word *argument* with a verbal disagreement. In ordinary language use we frequently say things like the following: "I had a bad argument with my roommate yesterday." However, this use of the word *argument* has nothing to do with its use in philosophy. In philosophy we understand arguments to be reasons for thinking that an assertion is true. If I ask you to give me an argument in support of your belief that being famous is more important for happiness than being loved, I want you to give me your reasons for thinking that your claim about happiness is true.

In order to illustrate this further, consider the following example: "I believe that ghosts exist, because late at night I have heard strange noises in my room." This is an example of an argument. It is—as we can easily see—not a particularly strong argument, but let us ignore that fact for the moment. Every argument has two components: a claim that the argument tries to establish and reasons that are offered in support of that claim. The claim is called the **conclusion** of the argument, and the reasons offered in support are called **premises.** In our example the claim that ghosts exist is the conclusion of the argument, and the fact that strange noises have been heard is the premise of the argument. The presence of the word *because, since,* or *for* is a good indicator that the sentence or some part of it is used as a premise in an argument. When you see the word(s) *therefore, thus, hence,* or *it follows that,* you are normally dealing with the conclusion of an argument.

When you develop an argument yourself, it is always easy to know what the conclusion of your argument is going to be, because the conclusion is something you believe to be true and want others to believe as well. The claims "God exists," "All people are created equal," and "I know that I am not dreaming right now" can all function as the conclusion of an argument. It is, however, much more challenging to find good premises for these conclusions. The premises of an argument are the reasons you think your belief about the world is true. Good and reasonable premises for important claims are hard to come by, since we know what we believe, but we often are not quite sure why we do so.

Food for Thought

Construct arguments that provide support for the following conclusions:

1. Playing violent video games does not cause the player to act violently in real life.
2. All human beings have equal moral rights.
3. Getting a degree in finance is more useful than getting a degree in philosophy.
4. It is wrong to eat animals.
5. We have a moral obligation to pay our taxes.

Continued

Continued

6. Many commercially successful movies are not worth seeing.
7. Divorce has a negative impact on the affected children.
8. Women are superior to men.
9. Private property should be abolished.
10. Angels exist.
11. Marijuana should be legalized.
12. Pornography should not be legal.
13. Pornography should be legal.

Putting Arguments into Standard Form

The last exercise illustrates that arguments come in many forms and shapes, but not all arguments are worth our time. Many are fairly silly pieces of reasoning. In order to accurately assess the value of arguments, it is frequently useful to put them into so-called **standard form.** An argument in standard form lists all the premises in numbered, sequential order and then adds the conclusion at the end. Let us go back to our initial example: "I believe that ghosts exist, because late at night I have heard strange noises in my room." If we put this argument into standard form, we obtain the following:

```
1. I have heard strange noises late at night in my
   room.
```
Therefore: Ghosts exist.

The word *therefore* is sometimes also symbolized as ∴. Although arguments in ordinary discourse are rarely presented in standard form, it is useful to put them into this form since it becomes easier to determine whether the argument is reasonable or not. In philosophy it is an important skill to put arguments, which are sometimes presented in convoluted ways, into standard form. The following exercise should help you acquire this skill.

Food for Thought

Put the following arguments into standard form "In order to do so it will be useful to identify the conclusion of the argument first. Keep in mind that the conclusion does not have to be stated last."

1. God exists. I know this since the Bible tells us that God exists and the Bible contains only the truth.
2. Persons who smoke are irrational. This is clear since all rational people know that smoking is suicide and no rational person commits suicide.
3. It is wrong to take the life of a human being. A fetus is a human being, and to conduct an abortion is to take the life of a fetus. I conclude therefore that it is wrong to conduct an abortion.

4. If it is possible to know that God exists, then it must also be possible to know whether angels exist. I conclude therefore that it is not possible to know that God exists, for it is obviously not possible to know that angels exist.

5. Only those beings are free who can act in unpredictable ways. It is thus obvious that computers can never be free, for computers are programmed to act in predictable ways.

6. Only those who actually help to build the products should benefit from the sale of these products on the open market. I conclude therefore that the owners of factories should not receive any benefits, for the owners never help to build the products.

7. Either pacifism is crazy, or else we must dissolve our military. If pacifism were crazy, then Gandhi's philosophy should not be taken seriously. But Gandhi's philosophy is interesting and must be taken seriously. We must therefore dissolve our military.

8. Everyone who imposes his or her way of life on other human beings commits a moral wrong. It follows therefore that banning smoking in all restaurants is morally wrong, for banning smoking in all restaurants is a case in which nonsmokers impose their way of life on other human beings.

9. I am sure that I will die of a heart attack. This is highly likely since my father died of a heart attack, my grandfather died of a heart attack, and my brother died of a heart attack as well.

10. It is not wrong to kill spiders. But if spiders have eternal souls, then it is wrong to kill them. Thus, it is false that spiders have eternal souls.

As you can see from these exercises, it can be challenging to put an argument into standard form. Sometimes arguments in ordinary language contain surplus information that needs to be eliminated. Not every claim in an argument will function as a premise after we have put the argument into standard form. On the other hand, arguments in ordinary discourse sometimes imply premises that are not stated explicitly. In that case we need to supply additional premises that are not part of the original argument.

Food for Thought

Put the following arguments into standard form, and add the premise that is implied but not stated explicitly.

1. All free beings abuse their free will from time to time. Peter is therefore a sinner, since all people who abuse their free will from time to time are sinners.

Continued

Continued

2. Our proposals were not accepted, since all proposals in the green folder were rejected.
3. It is always irrational to believe a proposition on the basis of insufficient evidence. It follows therefore that belief in the existence of extraterrestrial beings is irrational.
4. Spending money on boring lectures is a waste of resources. It follows therefore that spending money on college is a waste of resources.
5. You will not do well in the upper-level English class, because the professor made it very clear that only students with strong writing skills have a chance to do well in that class.
6. Anybody who voluntarily decides to destroy his or her own body is irrational. This shows that smokers are irrational people.

To put an argument into standard form is, thus, not always a straightforward affair and often involves some degree of interpretation. When arguments get very complex, philosophers sometimes disagree about how best to present the argument in standard form. But in spite of these difficulties, it is always a good idea to try to put an argument into standard form. An argument in this form is much easier to evaluate, since all can see its logical structure in one glance.

Deductive and Inductive Arguments

To evaluate an argument, we first need to classify it; different types of arguments are evaluated according to different criteria. Arguments fall into two main classifications. Consider the following two examples:

Argument A
```
1. If my brain stops functioning, then it will not
   be possible for me to have any thoughts.
2. When I die, my brain will stop functioning.
```
```
Therefore: When I die, it will not be possible for
me to have any thoughts.
```

Argument B
```
1. Every new freshman I have talked to has been
   enrolled in a freshman success seminar.
```
```
Therefore: All new freshmen are enrolled in a
freshman success seminar.
```

It is easy to see that these two arguments belong in different categories. Argument A establishes its conclusion more firmly than argument B does. We call arguments of this type **deductive arguments**. In a deductive argument the premises aim to provide conclusive support for the truth of the conclusion. The goal of a deductive argument is to offer such strong support that, if the premises are true, the conclusion **must** be true as well. On the other hand, arguments like argument B, which establish their conclusions only to some degree of probability, are called **inductive arguments**. The goal of an inductive argument is to provide support for the conclusion such that, if the premises are true, then it is very likely that the conclusion is true as well.

We will see very soon that deductive and inductive arguments are evaluated in different ways. It is therefore useful to develop the ability to distinguish between these two types of arguments. The following exercise will help you to develop this ability.

Food for Thought

Put the following arguments into standard form, and determine whether they are inductive or deductive arguments.

1. All physical entities can be divided. A proton is a physical entity. Therefore: Protons can be divided.
2. While I am taking this test, I am experiencing the same feeling of doom I experienced during my last math test. I failed that last math test, so it follows that I will fail this test as well.
3. I cannot know that a belief is true if there is a chance that it might be false. There is a chance that my belief that I have a soul is false. It follows therefore that I cannot know that I have a soul.
4. Every scientific theory that we have developed in the past has eventually been shown to be false. So all scientific theories we develop in the future will eventually be shown to be false as well.
5. We have found a piece of hair on the victim that matches the sample of hair we took from Bob. Bob therefore is the killer.
6. If there are universal moral standards for all human beings, then all human beings agree on what is right or wrong. But human beings disagree on what is right or wrong. It is thus obvious that there are no universal moral standards.
7. Either human cloning is immoral, or it will be a blessing for humanity. Human cloning is certainly not a blessing for humanity. I conclude therefore that human cloning is immoral.
8. Either the defendant refuses to take the stand, or he confesses. If he refuses to take the stand, he must have something to hide. If he confesses, then he is guilty. So the defendant either has something to hide or he is guilty.

Continued

Continued

9. Every time I pray, I can feel God's presence, his eternal love, and his good will. These feelings are as vivid as the impressions I receive from my senses. When I see a cup of water in front of me, I am sure that there is indeed a cup of water in front of me. It follows, therefore, that just as I can know that the cup of water exists, I can also know that God exists.

Evaluating Deductive Arguments: Validity and Soundness

Deductive and inductive arguments are evaluated according to different standards. Let us start by taking a closer look at deductive arguments. A good deductive argument must be **valid;** that is, the following statement must apply: *If all the premises of the argument are true, then the conclusion must be true as well.* Please notice the "if" clause in this definition. Remember that an argument can be valid even if the premises are, in fact, false. Consider the following deductive argument:

```
1. All students have rich parents.
2. Peter is a student.
```
Therefore: Peter has rich parents.

This argument is valid, although premise 1 is obviously false. Notice that the argument has the necessary characteristic of validity: If the premises are true, then the conclusion must be true as well. It does not matter that premise 1 is actually false. Validity is a judgment about the logical relationship between the premises and the conclusion. If the relationship is *truth preserving*—that is, if the assumption that the premises are true guarantees that the conclusion is true as well—the argument is valid. In order to develop your ability to recognize valid arguments, complete the following exercise.

Food for Thought

Try to determine whether the following arguments are valid.

A.
```
1. Taking a human life is always morally wrong.
2. Aborting a fetus is taking a human life.
```
Therefore: Aborting a fetus is morally wrong.

B.
1. No government has the right to force people to pay taxes.

Therefore: The United States government has no right to force people to pay taxes.

C.
1. Many teenagers who watch violent movies act violently later on.

Therefore: Watching violent movies causes violent behavior.

D.
1. All successful people are happy.
2. Jill is happy.

Therefore: Jill is successful.

Beginning students tend to be confused by the concept of validity. What is the point in determining whether an argument is valid, if that does not guarantee that the argument has true premises? The reason is that it is frequently not possible to establish beyond all reasonable doubt whether a premise is true or false. But since we can establish whether an argument is valid without having to know whether the premises of the argument are true or false, we can criticize an argument as invalid simply by virtue of its logical structure. Demonstrating that a deductive argument is invalid is a powerful philosophical strategy to dismiss it. If I can show that an argument is invalid, I can say, "Well, I am not sure whether your premises are true or not, but even if they are true, it would not follow that the conclusion of your argument has to be true as well." Notice that in order to show that an argument is invalid, you have to use the concept of logical possibility; you must show that it is logically possible that the premises are true and yet the conclusion is false. Moreover, valid arguments help us to clarify the logical relation between ideas. If we find a valid argument but dislike the conclusion (perhaps because it conflicts with what we want to believe about the world), we know that we have to discard at least one of the premises. In order to understand this better, consider the following example:

1. If all events are caused, then we are not free.
2. All events are caused.

Therefore: We are not free.

This argument is valid, but most of us will find the conclusion hard to accept. We tend to think that we are free beings who are responsible for our actions. However, since the argument is valid, it shows us that if we want to reject the conclusion, we also have to reject at least one of its premises. For if both premises are accepted as true, the conclusion must be accepted as well. In this way valid arguments help us to clarify the logical relation between our ideas. If we want to reject one idea, we often have to reject other (much more innocent-looking) ideas as well.

Validity is, however, only a necessary condition for a deductive argument to be a good argument. When we explore the world with the help of arguments, not only do we want our deductive arguments to be valid, but in addition we want our arguments to have true premises. *Valid deductive arguments with true premises are called* **sound** *arguments.* The ultimate goal in philosophy is always to produce and find sound arguments.

Evaluating Deductive Arguments: Logical Form

Deductive arguments can be identified and classified according to their logical form. Take a look at the argument that follows, and compare it with the argument about free will in the previous section.

```
1. If Tony takes drugs, he is an irresponsible
   person.
2. Tony takes drugs.
```
Therefore: Tony is an irresponsible person.

It is easy to see that these two deductive arguments have the same form, that is, they follow the same pattern of thinking. This pattern can be expressed with the help of symbols to give a general argument schema:

```
1. If p, then q.
2. p.
```
Therefore: q.

This deductive argument form is well known among philosophers and has its own name: *modus ponens.* Every argument that is an instance of *modus ponens* must be valid. It does not matter what sentences are substituted for the placeholders p and q; as long as the form *modus ponens* is preserved, the resulting argument must be valid. Being able to recognize the logical form of an argument is therefore an excellent and quick way to determine whether arguments are valid.

Closely related to *modus ponens* is the deductive argument form called **modus tollens.** The following argument is an instance of *modus tollens:*

```
1. If the future is already determined, then I am
   not responsible for my actions.
2. I am responsible for my actions.
```
Therefore: The future is not already determined.

The logical form of *modus tollens* can be captured with the help of the following argument schema:

```
1. If p, then q.
2. Not q.
Therefore: Not p.
```

Another well-known deductive argument form is called **disjunctive syllogism.** The following is an example of a disjunctive syllogism:

```
1. Either Darwin's theory of evolution is wrong, or
   we humans are related to monkeys.
2. Humans are not related to monkeys.
Therefore: Darwin's theory of evolution is wrong.
```

The following argument schema expresses the general logical form of a disjunctive syllogism:

```
1. Either p or q.
2. Not q.
Therefore: p.
```

A further famous argument form is called **hypothetical syllogism.** The following argument is an instance of this logical form:

```
1. If materialism is false, then Marxism is a
   faulty philosophical system.
2. If Marxism is a faulty philosophical system, then
   one should not believe everything Marx writes.
Therefore: If materialism is false, then one should
not believe everything Marx writes.
```

The following argument schema expresses the logical form of hypothetical syllogisms:

```
1. If p, then q.
2. If q, then r.
Therefore: If p, then r.
```

There are many additional deductive argument forms, but to introduce all of them would go beyond the scope of an introductory textbook. Being familiar with *modus ponens, modus tollens, disjunctive syllogism,* and *hypothetical syllogism* should make you aware that many deductive arguments can quickly be identified and recognized as instances of well-known valid logical argument forms.

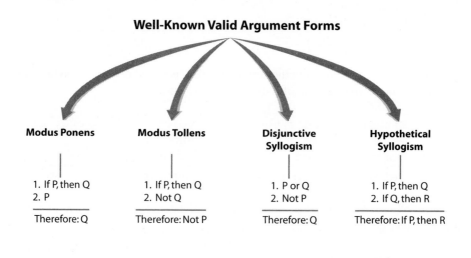

Well-Known Valid Argument Forms

Modus Ponens	Modus Tollens	Disjunctive Syllogism	Hypothetical Syllogism
1. If P, then Q 2. P	1. If P, then Q 2. Not Q	1. P or Q 2. Not P	1. If P, then Q 2. If Q, then R
Therefore: Q	Therefore: Not P	Therefore: Q	Therefore: If P, then R

Food for Thought

Put the following deductive arguments into standard form, and determine whether the arguments are of the form *modus ponens, modus tollens, disjunctive syllogism,* or *hypothetical syllogism.*

1. Either I will stop smoking right now, or I will suffer severe health problems in the next ten years. I know myself well enough to know that I will not stop smoking any time soon. It follows therefore that I will suffer severe health problems in the next ten years.
2. If it is true that all people act always with only their own interest in mind, then no one can truly be moral. But if no one can truly be moral, then studying moral theory is pointless. It follows therefore that if all people act always with only their own interest in mind, then studying moral theory is pointless.
3. In order to pass the class, I must score more than 90 percent on the final exam. I therefore did not pass the class, since I scored 85 percent on the final exam.
4. Either God is mad, or the creation of the universe was simply a cosmic accident. God is certainly not mad. We must conclude therefore that the creation of the world was simply a cosmic accident.
5. If it is logically possible that all my current beliefs are false, then I cannot refute global skepticism. Although I hate to admit it, it surely

is logically possible that all my beliefs are false. I conclude therefore that I cannot refute global skepticism.

6. If life on Earth is simply the result of natural processes, then we should not be surprised to find other forms of life on other planets. Life is the result of natural processes. It follows thus that we should expect to find other forms of life on other planets.

7. If my senses are reliable, then whatever I see or hear is in fact true. My senses are therefore not reliable, because sometimes I see or hear things that are not true.

8. Either studying philosophy is corrupting the soul of young people, or it is the path to true wisdom. Young people are corrupted by their desire for sex, money, or fame but certainly not by studying philosophy. So studying philosophy must indeed be the path to true wisdom.

Evaluating Inductive Arguments: Probability

As we have seen already, the premises of an inductive argument support its conclusion only to some degree of probability. Take a look at the following example of an inductive argument:

```
1. All people I have ever met have lied whenever it
   was convenient for them.
```
Therefore: All humans lie whenever it is convenient for them.

Let us suppose the premise of this argument is true; this certainly gives us a reason for thinking that the conclusion is true as well. If all people I know start to lie whenever it is convenient for them, I certainly have reason to believe that all humans do the same. Notice, however, that the conclusion does not have to be true. Given the truth of the premise, it is still logically possible that there are some humans who never lie. For this reason, inductive arguments, unlike deductive arguments, can never be valid. However, it would be silly to reject an inductive argument on this basis. In order to evaluate inductive arguments, we do not check to see whether they are valid or invalid; instead, we try to determine whether they establish their conclusion with a high or low degree of probability.

Inductive arguments that establish their conclusion to a high degree of probability are called **strong inductive arguments.** Those inductive arguments that establish their conclusion only to a low degree of probability are called **weak inductive arguments.** If an inductive argument is strong and if its premises are true then we classify the argument as cogent. It is relatively difficult to evaluate inductive arguments quickly. In philosophy inductive arguments do not play as central a role as they do in other more empirical disciplines like psychology or sociology. However, three types of inductive arguments are worth mentioning.

Probably the most widely used type of inductive argument is called an **enumerative inductive argument;** the previous argument is a good example. The basic idea behind this type of inductive argument can be expressed with the help of the following argument schema:

```
1. All observed A's have been B's.
```
```
Therefore: Probably all A's everywhere are B's.
```

Although enumerative inductive arguments are frequently used, it is difficult to evaluate them. An enumerative inductive argument is certainly stronger if we have observed a relationship between events of type A and events of type B to occur frequently (i.e., if the sample size is large). But even then, the resulting enumerative inductive argument can still be weak. To illustrate this, consider the following example:

```
1. All cars that I have observed have been red.
```
```
Therefore: Probably all cars everywhere are red.
```

Notice that this argument remains weak even if I have seen thousands of red cars. The problem is that the relationship between being red and being a car is an accidental one; there is no underlying connection between being a car and being red.

Enumerative inductive arguments are most successful when they are dealing with so-called lawlike relationships. For example, if I have observed that several metal bars have expanded when they were exposed to heat, then I am justified to conclude that probably all metal bars expand when heated. In this case there exists a lawlike relationship that explains why metal bars expand when heated. It is, however, far from clear to know when we are dealing with lawlike relationships. Fortunately, philosophers do not use enumerative inductive arguments as frequently as scientists do, and it is therefore sufficient to recognize the logical form of these arguments without yet knowing how to evaluate them properly. We will discuss the strength of these arguments in more detail when we discuss the classical epistemological problem of induction.

A second important type of inductive argument is called argument by analogy. Consider the following example:

```
1. Taking this philosophy class is similar to tak-
   ing an English class.
2. I always get low grades in my English classes.
```
```
Therefore: I conclude that I will also get a low
grade in this philosophy class.
```

The strength of this argument depends on the comparison between English classes and philosophy classes. Analogical arguments can be very powerful and are frequently used in philosophical writings; however, it is easy to see that the strength of an argument by analogy depends on the degree to which the two compared items are indeed similar to each other. In some respects English classes are just like philosophy classes; both classes normally involve reading and the writing of papers. But there are also some crucial differences; philosophical writing tends to be shorter and more argument driven than writing in English classes, and the reading materials in both classes are of course quite different. These differences between English classes and philosophy classes undermine the strength of the argument by analogy, which has to be classified as a weak inductive argument. Because there are no general rules to determine whether an analogy is appropriate, analogical arguments must be analyzed on a case-by-case basis. If the analogy is a strong one, the resulting inductive argument is strong. If the analogy is weak, the resulting argument is weak.

A final important type of inductive argument is called **inference to the best explanation, or abductive argument.** The key idea of this type of inductive argument can be explained with the help of the following—by now familiar—example:

```
1. I have heard strange noises late at night in my
   room.
```
Therefore: Ghosts exist.

As it stands right now, this inductive argument does not seem very strong. However, consider the following modification of the argument, which turns the argument into an inference to the best explanation.

```
1. I have heard strange noises late at night in my
   room.
2. The best explanation for these strange noises is
   that they are caused by ghosts.
```
Therefore: Ghosts probably exist.

If premise 2 is indeed true, and the hypothesis that ghosts cause these strange noises is the best explanation available, then the argument is much stronger than it was before.

This, however, raises a crucial question: How can we determine whether a given explanation of an event is better than all other explanations? Any event can be explained in many different ways; strange noises in the night might, for example, be caused by ghosts or by mice in the attic or by a roommate who is watching a horror movie. Our judgment of whether a given explanation is better than others depends on many factors, but two frequently play a prominent role and are therefore worth mentioning.

1. Explanation A is better than explanation B if (all other things being equal) explanation A is simpler than explanation B.

2. Explanation A is better than explanation B if (all other things being equal) explanation A fits together better with the rest of my beliefs about the world.

Principle 1 is often called **Ockham's razor** in recognition of the medieval philosopher William of Ockham (1285–1347), who praised simplicity as a virtue in theory construction. Principle 2 can be called the **principle of conservatism.** Both principles are somewhat controversial. The principle of Ockham's razor requires a clear understanding of the term *simplicity.* We normally think that an explanation is simpler if it requires us to make fewer independent assumptions. But it is not always clear how many independent assumptions are involved in a given explanation. As for the principle of conservatism, it is rather subjective; that is, an explanation that is compatible with the rest of my belief system might not fit well into your belief system. If I am a professional ghost hunter who has seen many ghosts in the past and who is spending a night in a haunted castle, the idea that strange noises are caused by ghosts might be the most conservative explanation available to me. On the other hand, if I am a person who has never seen ghosts and who is sleeping in a dorm room on campus, I will consider the idea that strange noises at night are caused by ghosts to be too outlandish (nonconservative) to be true. In this case it is easier to accept the idea that the noises are caused by a student in the next room who is watching a horror movie. This explanation is, in this situation, not only more conservative but also simpler and thus probably the best explanation available.

As you can see from this example, inferences to the best explanation must be evaluated very carefully. Deciding which explanation is indeed the best is often contentious, and reasonable people might come to different conclusions. However, this type of inductive argument plays an important role in philosophy, and we will encounter it frequently during our exploration of well-known philosophical problems.

Important Inductive Argument Forms

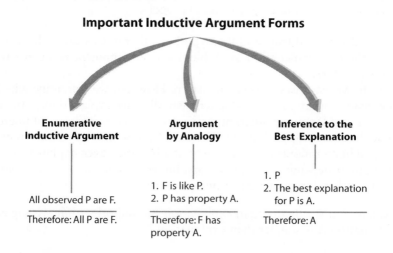

Enumerative Inductive Argument	**Argument by Analogy**	**Inference to the Best Explanation**
	1. F is like P.	1. P
	2. P has property A.	2. The best explanation for P is A.
All observed P are F.		
Therefore: All P are F.	Therefore: F has property A.	Therefore: A

Food for Thought

Take a look at the following arguments, and decide whether they are inductive or deductive arguments. If they are inductive, indicate what type of inductive argument they are, and decide whether they are weak or strong.

1. We humans love to think that we are special beings in this universe. However, if you really think about it, we humans are just like machines. Of course, we are rather complicated machines, but that doesn't change the fact that we are machines. It is clear, of course, that machines can never have free will. It follows therefore that we humans have no free will as well.

2. If God exists, then innocent beings would not be suffering in the world. However, innocent beings do suffer. It follows therefore that God doesn't exist.

3. I talked to Maja yesterday and found out that she doesn't believe in God. She also told me that she is very frustrated and unhappy. Billy and his brother Jim are frustrated and unhappy as well, and they, too, are atheists. I conclude therefore that atheists everywhere are frustrated and unhappy with their lives.

4. I went to Professor Hogan's office hours yesterday, but there was a long line of students waiting for him. I eventually gave up waiting. I think the best explanation of why so many students were waiting outside Professor's Hogan's office is that he must have given them bad grades. I conclude therefore that Professor Hogan is a hard grader.

5. If being an altruist is a necessary condition for being moral, I have to conclude that I am not moral, for it is clear to me that I am not an altruist.

6. The universe is really just like a complicated clock. But every clock has a maker. It follows therefore that the universe has to have a maker as well.

7. My first marriage ended when I told my wife about an affair. My second marriage ended when my wife found out that I had had a fling. I conclude therefore that my third marriage will end as well if my third wife ever finds out that I am cheating again.

8. How did the universe get started? Scientists tell us that it all started with the big bang. But what caused the big bang? I think the best explanation is that God caused the big bang. I conclude therefore that God probably exists.

Logical Evaluation of Arguments

Arguments are sets of statements (premises) that aim to provide support for one conclusion. The premises are the reasons why one should think that the conclusion is true.

Deductive Arguments

In a deductive argument the premises aim to provide conclusive support for the truth of the conclusion

Good deductive arguments must be valid and sound.

An argument is **valid** if it is logically impossible that the conclusion is false if the premises are true.

An argument is **sound** if it is valid and all the premises are true.

Inductive Arguments

Inductive arguments aim to show that the conclusion is likely to be true.

Good inductive arguments must be strong and cogent.

An argument is **strong** if it is very likely that the conclusion is true if the premises are true.

An argument is **cogent** if it is strong and all the premises are true.

Study and Reflection Questions

1. Many successful commercials are based on invalid or fallacious arguments. Describe a commercial that is based on a fallacious argument. Will the commercial be successful in spite of its logical deficiencies?

2. Some philosophers such as Kierkegaard have argued that those who put too much emphasis on reason might end up with a problematic worldview. What do you think? Is it possible to be influenced too much by reason?

3. Try to develop a good definition of the term *happiness*. Do this by identifying necessary and sufficient conditions for being happy. Do you think that your definition captures the essence of happiness?

4. Describe a person who has logically inconsistent beliefs. Will such an inconsistent belief system necessarily lead to disadvantages and problems?

5. Enumerative inductive arguments play a crucial role in science. However, we have seen that such arguments support their conclusions only with a high degree of probability. There is always the possibility that the conclusions of enumerative inductive arguments are false even if the premises are all true. Is that a problem for scientists?

For Further Reading

Law, Stephen. *The Philosophical Gym: 25 Short Adventures in Thinking*. London: Thomas Dunne Books, 2003.

Gensler, Harry. *Introduction to Logic*. New York: Routledge, 2001.

Howard-Snyder, Frances, Daniel Howard-Snyder, and Ryan Wasserman. *The Power of Logic*. 4th ed. Boston: McGraw-Hill, 2008.

Hurley, Patrick. *A Concise Introduction to Logic*. 10th ed. Belmont, CA: Wadsworth, 2008.

Rosenberg, Jay. *The Practice of Philosophy*. Englewood Cliffs, NJ: Prentice Hall, 1984.

Schick, Theodore, and Lewis Vaughn. *How to Think About Weird Things*. Boston: McGraw-Hill, 2004.

Weston, Anthony. *A Rulebook for Arguments*. 4th ed. Indianapolis, IN: Hackett, 2008.

Woodhouse, Mark B. *A Preface to Philosophy*. Belmont, CA: Wadsworth, 2003.

Endnotes

1. Michael Tooley, "The Problem of Evil," *Stanford Encyclopedia of Philosophy* (Spring 2010 Edition), Edward N. Zalta (ed.), URL = http://plato.stanford.edu/archives/spr2010/entries/evil/index.html#SomImpDis.
2. William James, "Review of *Grunzuge der Physiologischen Psychologie* by Wilhelm Wundt, 1875," in *Essays, Comments, and Reviews,* (Cambridge, MA: Harvard University Press, 1987), p. 296.
3. Augustine, *Confessions* (London: Penguin, 1961), p. 273.
4. Take the example of segregation in the United States. Racial segregation was well established in the first part of the twentieth century in the southern part of the country. Black and white Americans had their own schools, buses, water fountains, and so on. To accept this racial segregation was to conform to accepted standards of behavior, but it was clearly not moral.
5. This distinction between nominal and real definitions goes back at least to Aristotle (*Posterior Analytics*) and has been accepted in one form or another by most philosophers throughout the ages. It is true that any kind of essentialism has been attacked by a number of prominent philosophers in the analytic tradition (e.g., Russell and Quine), but I think that the distinction between nominal and real definitions is clearly useful for students of philosophy, even if they should find out later on that the distinction might be challenged.
6. There is a great deal of confusion among philosophers about the precise analysis of "necessary and sufficient conditions." I understand the binary relations "x is necessary for y" and "x is sufficient for y" as conceptual relationship that holds between concepts. Hence, it follows that if x is necessary for y, then it is **logically necessary** that if y is the case, then x must be the case as well. Overall, I understand the method of defining a term by stating necessary and sufficient conditions as being a more general version of Aristotle's method of *genus and differentia*.
7. Mary Anne Warren, "On the Moral and Legal Status of Abortion," in *Monist* 1973, 57:1 pp. 43–61.

CHAPTER THREE

WHAT DO WE KNOW?

Why Knowledge Matters

Chapter 2 introduced a range of logical and conceptual tools. We are now in a better position to clarify abstract concepts, to test definitions, and to construct and evaluate different types of arguments. We have learned that good deductive arguments have two important features: They must be *valid*, and they must be *sound*. Logic can help us determine whether an argument is valid, but logic alone cannot establish whether an argument is sound. In order to do that, we need to **know** whether the premises of an argument are true; here we enter the realm of **epistemology**—the theory of knowledge. This chapter will introduce some fundamental concepts and theories in the study of knowledge. By becoming familiar with these ideas, you may better recognize under what conditions our beliefs can be considered to be instances of knowledge.

Food for Thought

The word *know* can be used in a variety of ways. Consider the following three examples:

A. I know that George Washington was the first American president.

B. I know how to speak French.

C. I know Woody Allen very well.

Example A can be called an instance of **propositional knowledge** because I know *that* something is the case. Example B can be called **"knowledge-how"** since it is concerned with how to do things like speaking French or fixing cars. Example C might be dubbed **"knowledge by acquaintance"** since it implies that we are directly acquainted with something or someone. *In philosophy we are nearly exclusively* *concerned with propositional knowledge.* In order to practice your understanding of these different ways to use the word *know*, decide whether the following examples are instances of propositional knowledge, knowledge-how, or knowledge by acquaintance.

1. I know exactly how you feel about her death.
2. 2 + 2 = 4—I know that for a fact.
3. I used to know Peter very well, but in recent times we have grown apart.
4. I am not afraid to cheat on my exams because I know how to cheat without getting caught.
5. If only I knew more about the Vietnam War.
6. My father used to be the smartest man. Now, he has Alzheimer's, and he doesn't know anything anymore.
7. You might know everything that is in your accounting book, but this does not mean that you know anything about how to run an accounting firm.

Initially, you might wonder why it is necessary to develop a theory of knowledge at all. Can we not be satisfied with belief? Believing something is easy and comfortable; there are no rules for what you may choose to believe. If you are so inclined, you might believe that you are the reincarnation of Genghis Khan or that Elvis lives in the house next door. So why even bother with knowledge? A few examples might be helpful in illustrating why knowledge matters and why mere belief is often not sufficient. Suppose that you go to the hospital for surgery. Suppose you have a chance to talk to the surgeon before the operation. Doesn't it seem clear that you demand knowledge from the surgeon? You want him to *know* what is wrong with you, and you want him to *know* how to fix it. If the surgeon says to you, "I actually do not know whether you have a tumor, but I believe that you might have one and that surgery might be helpful," then it might be time to look for a different surgeon. We demand *knowledge* from our medical doctors and not mere belief. What is true for doctors is also true for tax accountants, lawyers, college professors, architects, house builders, and many other professionals. We are willing to pay money for their services because we think that they *know* and not simply because they have beliefs. It matters a great deal, therefore, whether and when we are entitled to call something an instance of knowledge.

Food for Thought

Some thinkers have argued that people who are very gullible are committing a moral wrong. The philosopher W. K. Clifford (1845–1879)

Continued

Continued

claimed that it is wrong always, everywhere, and for anyone to believe anything upon insufficient evidence. He wrote:

> If a man, holding a belief which he was taught in childhood or persuaded of afterwards, keeps down and pushes away any doubts which arise about it in his mind . . . and regards as impious those questions which cannot easily be asked without disturbing it—the life of that man is one long sin against mankind. . . .[1]

Do you agree with Clifford that those people who believe too easily are committing a moral wrong?

Searching for a Definition of Knowledge

But what exactly is knowledge? Although we use the word *knowledge* quite frequently in our everyday life, most of us would be hard pressed to state a precise definition of the term. In ordinary circumstances this lack of clarity about the nature of knowledge rarely comes to our attention. We seem to be able to recognize instances of knowledge even if we cannot say precisely what knowledge is. However, when we search for answers to philosophical questions, it becomes important to clarify the precise limits of our knowledge. This, in turn, requires that we develop a precise definition of knowledge.

Let us apply the logical tools that we learned in the last chapter to aid our search for a precise definition of knowledge. Although belief and knowledge are different from each other, there is nevertheless a relationship between them. Suppose, for example, that I utter this claim: "I know that the world is round." If this claim is true, it follows immediately that I also *believe* that the world is round. Knowledge presupposes belief. *Believing* that something is the case is, therefore, a necessary condition for *knowing* that something is the case. Finding one necessary condition for knowledge is a first step in our quest for an adequate definition. If we keep on searching, we might find other necessary conditions that together might be jointly sufficient for knowledge.

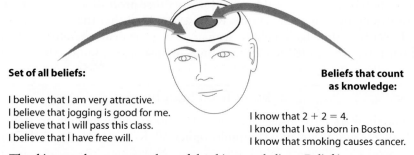

Set of all beliefs:

I believe that I am very attractive.
I believe that jogging is good for me.
I believe that I will pass this class.
I believe that I have free will.

Beliefs that count as knowledge:

I know that 2 + 2 = 4.
I know that I was born in Boston.
I know that smoking causes cancer.

The things we know are a subset of the things we believe. Belief is a necessary but not a sufficient condition for knowledge.

It is apparent that we trust some of our beliefs more than others. I believe, for instance, that I will still be alive in the year 2050. But this is a relatively weak belief. I would not be surprised if this belief turned out to be false. If someone were to ask me to bet on the belief, I would sensibly decline. There are, however, some beliefs on which I would be willing to wager. I believe, for example, that I am not going to be a millionaire by the end of this year. I believe this very strongly, and I am willing to bet on it. Since we hold some beliefs very dear to our hearts, we might suspect that the strength of a belief is the key to knowledge. If this were correct, we could say that strongly believing something to be true is sufficient for knowledge. Unfortunately, this does not lead to a satisfactory definition.

In order to illustrate the shortcomings of this definition, it is instructive to consider the following counterexample: Suppose you buy a lottery ticket, and suppose the chance of winning is 1:1,000,000. Given these odds, you probably believe very strongly that the ticket you bought is a dud. Nonetheless, would you feel justified in saying that you *know* that the ticket is a dud? Obviously not! It is only after the drawing, when you have compared the numbers on your ticket with the winning numbers, that you can claim to know that the ticket is a losing ticket. You did not know this all along, even if you believed it strongly all along; knowledge requires more than strong belief.

This lottery ticket example suggests a key insight: Truth is another necessary condition for knowledge. We can know something only if it is indeed true. Nobody can know, for instance, that $2 + 3 = 7$. You might believe it if you happen to be very confused about numbers, but you cannot know it. Similarly, you can believe that Boston lies south of New York City, or that Los Angeles is located by the Atlantic Ocean, but you cannot know those things. If we combine this new necessary condition with our first necessary condition, we arrive at the following definition: Knowledge is true belief. Is this definition adequate? Is truth together with belief jointly sufficient for knowledge? The following example should help to answer this question.

Consider the fictional case of Mike, who participates in the quiz show *Who Wants to Be a Millionaire?* He is asked the name of the Greek city-state that defeated the Persians in the battle of Marathon. Mike has never studied ancient Greek history, nor has he ever heard about the battle of Marathon. He nevertheless selects "Athens" as the right answer. In this situation Mike had the belief that Athens was the right answer, and the belief actually turned out to be true, but it is clear that Mike did not *know* the answer. He was simply guessing, and guessing—even if it turns out to be true—is not the same thing as knowing. Truth and belief are therefore not jointly sufficient to establish knowledge.

Food for Thought

This last example illustrates that having true beliefs is not sufficient for having knowledge. Can you think of other situations in which people hold true beliefs about something but fail to have knowledge?

In order to make further progress in our search for an adequate definition of knowledge, it is instructive to reflect on the example of Mike and the quiz show in more detail. Notice how different our impression of Mike would have been if he had responded to the question as follows: "I'm certain that either Sparta or Athens defeated the Persians in the battle of Marathon, since these were the two dominant Greek military powers in the fifth century BCE. The Persians attacked from the east, but Sparta was located on the Peloponnese, a bit more in the west. It seems more likely therefore that the Athenians fought and defeated the Persians in the battle of Marathon, since Athens is located on the eastern shore." Here Mike would have been providing a justification for his belief that Athens fought against the Persians in the battle of Marathon. If Mike could have justified his belief, we would naturally have assumed that he knew something about ancient Greek history. This example suggests that justification in addition to truth is a further crucial component of knowledge. Of course, it is not quite clear how strong the justification must be before we can count the belief as knowledge. Mike's justification for his belief about Athens, for example, is not terribly impressive. We will see later that different philosophers make different demands in this context. However, it is safe to say that knowing p requires some form of justification for the belief that p is likely to be true.

Together, these three criteria put us in a position to formulate the classical, tripartite definition of knowledge. According to this definition, belief, truth, and justification are three necessary conditions for knowledge, which together are jointly sufficient. In short, **knowledge is true, justified belief.** This classical definition has been around since Plato (ca. 428–ca. 347 BCE), who was the first philosopher to suggest it. In recent times some epistemologists have challenged this definition. They claim to have found cases in which this definition is not quite adequate and conclude that another condition is needed. Although this is an important concern, we cannot pursue it in the context of an introduction to epistemology. For our purposes the classical definition of knowledge is precise enough, and we will use it in the remainder of this chapter.

Food for Thought

Practice your understanding of the classical definition of knowledge by deciding whether the following sentences, uttered by you, are true or false. If you think that a sentence is true, provide a justification for thinking so.

1. I know that I have two hands.
2. I know that my parents will never get divorced.
3. I know that other people experience the smell of coffee just as I do.
4. I know that Joe Montana was a better quarterback than John Elway.
5. I know that water is H_2O.
6. I know that killing people is wrong.
7. I know that all people are created equal.

8. I know that dinosaurs have existed on Earth in the past.
9. I know that there are nine planets in our solar system.
10. I know that Michael Jackson was an emotionally troubled man.

Food for Thought

Situations seem to exist—so-called Gettier cases—in which true, justified beliefs do not amount to genuine knowledge. Can you think of such situations?

Three Different Theories of Knowledge

The discussion in the last section has given us a better idea of what knowledge is, but we have yet to answer the most essential question in epistemology: What do we know? It would be ideal if we could answer this question once and for all, but the question is—as are all philosophical questions—an open one, meaning that there is more than one way in which we can answer it. The key objective is to develop a satisfactory theory of epistemic justification. We have seen that knowledge is true, justified belief; therefore, if we can clearly determine when and how our beliefs are justified, we can also determine the scope and limit of our knowledge. Not surprisingly, different philosophers have developed different theories in response to this question. Our task is to consider which theory appears most reasonable. Roughly speaking, we can identify three major theories of knowledge: skepticism, empiricism, and rationalism. The three positions are illustrated in the following chart:

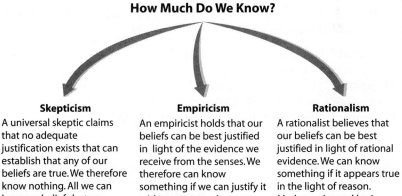

How Much Do We Know?

Skepticism
A universal skeptic claims that no adequate justification exists that can establish that any of our beliefs are true. We therefore know nothing. All we can have are beliefs but no knowledge.

Empiricism
An empiricist holds that our beliefs can be best justified in light of the evidence we receive from the senses. We therefore can know something if we can justify it with respect to what we see, hear, and feel about the world. Natural sciences such as physics, chemistry, and biology produce the most reliable knowledge.

Rationalism
A rationalist believes that our beliefs can be best justified in light of rational evidence. We can know something if it appears true in the light of reason. Mathematics and logic provide the most reliable knowledge.

The chart is, of course, an oversimplification. In addition to skepticism, empiricism, and rationalism, alternate and more refined epistemological positions exist. It is nevertheless useful to focus on these three major epistemological theories.

Skepticism

The Case for Skepticism

A skeptic is someone who denies that we have genuine knowledge. According to the skeptic, we have only beliefs about the world, and none of these beliefs can count as knowledge. We can distinguish among different forms of skepticism. On the one hand is global (universal) skepticism, which holds that no knowledge of any kind about any subject matter is possible. It is rare that someone explicitly advocates global skepticism, because it seems to undermine itself. Since global skeptics claim that there is no knowledge whatsoever, they themselves cannot know whether global skepticism is true or not. Later on, however, we will see how global skepticism can emerge in a more indirect and thus more threatening way.

Food for Thought

A skillful global skeptic is difficult to defeat in conversation. The following conversation between Jack Gladney, a college professor, and his four-teen-year-old son, Heinrich, is described in the novel *White Noise* by Don DeLillo. Although Jack and Heinrich do not use the word *knowledge*, it is clear that Jack wants to convince his son that he knows that it is raining. Heinrich, on the other hand, wants to maintain a skeptical position. Do you think you could do better than Jack and convince Heinrich that it is indeed raining?

> HEINRICH: "It is going to rain tonight."
> JACK: "It's raining now."
> HEINRICH: "The radio said tonight."
> JACK: "Look at the windshield. Is that rain or isn't it?"
> HEINRICH: "I am only telling you what they said."
> JACK: "Just because it is on the radio doesn't mean we have to suspend belief in the evidence of our senses."
> HEINRICH: "Our senses? Our senses are wrong a lot more often than they are right. This has been proved in the laboratory. Don't you know about all those theorems that say nothing is what it seems? There is no past, present, or future outside our mind. The so-called laws of motion are a big hoax. Even sound can trick the mind. Just because you don't hear a sound doesn't mean it's not out there. Dogs can hear it. Other animals. And I am sure there are sounds

even dogs can't hear. But they exist in air, in waves. Maybe they never stop. High, high, high-pitched. Coming from somewhere."

JACK: "Is it raining or isn't it?"

HEINRICH: "I wouldn't want to have to say."

JACK: "What if someone held a gun to your head?"

HEINRICH: "Who, you?"

JACK: "Someone. A man in a trench coat and smoky glasses. He holds a gun to your head and says, 'Is it raining or isn't it? All you have to do is tell the truth and I'll put away my gun and take the next flight out of here.'"

HEINRICH: "What truth does he want? Does he want the truth of someone traveling at almost the speed of light in another galaxy? Does he want the truth of someone in orbit around a neutron star? Maybe if these people could see us through a telescope we might look like we were two inches tall and it might be raining yesterday instead of today."

JACK: "He is holding the gun to your head. He wants your truth."

HEINRICH: "What good is my truth? My truth means nothing. What if this guy with the gun comes from a planet in a whole different solar system? What we call rain he calls soap. What we call apples he calls rain. So what am I supposed to tell him?"

JACK: "His name is Frank J. Smalley and he comes from St. Louis. He wants to know if it's raining now, at this very minute?"

HEINRICH: "Is there such a thing as now? 'Now' comes and goes as soon as you say it. How can I say it's raining now if your so-called 'now' becomes 'then' as soon as I say it?"[2]

A more attractive form of skepticism can be dubbed local skepticism. It is more limited in scope than global skepticism and focuses on particular fields of knowledge or particular methods of justification. A local skeptic will say that we cannot have knowledge about certain subjects (e.g., God or the existence of the external physical world) or that certain ways of acquiring beliefs (such as reading fortune cookies) can never produce knowledge. Clearly, we are all local skeptics with respect to some ways of acquiring beliefs. I am, for example, a skeptic about psychic hotlines. If you were to tell me that you broke up with your partner because a psychic informed you that your partner was seeing someone else, I would think you were extremely gullible. Your belief that your partner was unfaithful would seem completely unjustified. You certainly would be wrong to claim that you knew it on the basis of that telephone call. I am also a skeptic about astrology and alternative medicine, although a fair number of people put great faith in horoscopes and herbal treatments.

A local skeptic seeks to establish that a particular type of justification does not link our beliefs to the truth. For example, if you claim to know that you will spend a dream vacation with your partner because the moon is in Sagittarius, a skeptic about astrology would question the validity of your belief justification. How in the world, the skeptic would ask, is the position of the moon related to your vacation and your relationship? Unless there is some plausible connection, the skeptic would seem to be in a strong position to reject all astrological belief justifications. You could, of course, hold on to your belief that the position of the moon has an effect on your vacation, but the skeptic would have shown that this belief does not amount to knowledge. It seems epistemically irresponsible to modify a belief about a relationship because of a belief about the position of the moon.

Although most people agree that astrology and psychic hotlines are not reliable ways to acquire true beliefs, the question arises about whether we can trust any other methods of acquiring beliefs. I acquire, for example, a fair number of my beliefs about politics from watching Jim Lehrer on the evening news. But are the beliefs I acquire from listening to Jim Lehrer so much more reliable than the beliefs I acquire from the psychic hotline? Sure, the psychic hotline is often wrong, but isn't Jim Lehrer sometimes wrong as well? This is actually the sneaky way in which global skepticism can make its stand. If it turns out that local skepticism is plausible with respect to all subject areas and all ways of acquiring and justifying beliefs, then local skepticism has suddenly turned into global skepticism. In the remaining part of this chapter, we will investigate what form of skepticism can and should be avoided.

Food for Thought

How skeptical are you? Imagine that you meet someone who makes the claims listed here. Would you accept the claims, or would you be skeptical about them? Justify your answer.

1. I know that it is very hot at the center of the sun.
2. I know that any good person, no matter what religion he or she subscribes to, will be saved by God.
3. I know that my boyfriend is jealous.
4. I know that the picture in my television set is produced by electrons striking the back of the screen.
5. I know that people are sometimes possessed by the devil.
6. I know that miracles happen every day.
7. I know that democracy is the best form of government.
8. I know that many of my memories are false.
9. I know that tomorrow my life could change completely, and everything I like at the moment might then be something I despise.
10. I know that people who are depressed can get better without medication.

Descartes' Quest for Certainty

The French philosopher René Descartes (1596–1650) was the first modern philosopher who addressed the question of whether we can prevent skepticism from undermining every claim to knowledge. Descartes lived during confusing times, as we do now. The seventeenth century was a period of change in Europe: The Reformation had weakened the credibility of religious authorities. New scientific thinking was challenging traditional ways of thinking about physics and the universe. In short, the seventeenth century produced a hodgepodge of competing beliefs about God and the universe. But which of these beliefs were worthy of being called knowledge, Descartes asked.

To find an answer to this question, Descartes followed an original strategy. According to him, we cannot trust any of our beliefs as long as there is any chance that they might be mistaken. He wrote: "I ought no less carefully to withhold my assent from matters which are not entirely certain and indubitable than from those which appear to me manifestly to be false."[3] Through doubting and examining all of his beliefs, Descartes attempted to distill those beliefs that were certain and indubitable. He thought that only these beliefs truly deserved to be considered knowledge. This method of distinguishing mere belief from knowledge is often called **Descartes' method of doubt.**

Descartes' Method of Doubt

Let us take a look at all our beliefs and check whether we can find any reason to doubt whether they are true.

Set of beliefs:

I believe that I am very attractive.
I believe that smoking causes cancer.
I believe that I will pass this class.

Set of beliefs that cannot be doubted:

Descartes suggested that this set of beliefs is guaranteed to be true and thus can serve as a foundation for all knowledge.

Are there beliefs that we cannot doubt to be true?

Food for Thought

Descartes suggested that a belief cannot be considered an instance of knowledge if it is possible to doubt that the belief is true. In order to develop an

Continued

Continued

impression of how this method of doubt works, let us consider the following beliefs. Try to determine whether these beliefs can be doubted.

1. I will live at least until the year 2020.
2. I will pass this class.
3. My parents love me.
4. The parents who raised me are indeed my biological parents.
5. I am heterosexual.
6. I find watching movies more enjoyable than reading books.
7. 2 + 2 = 4
8. I am right now feeling a pain in my front tooth.

To respond to the threat of skepticism, let us follow this Cartesian method
of doubt. Are there beliefs that we cannot doubt are true? In day-to-day life,
most people do not doubt that what they see is true. When I walk across the
street and see a truck approaching, I have little reason to doubt that the truck
is really bearing down on me. I trust my senses and get out of the way of the
truck. But are our perceptual beliefs, that is, those beliefs that are formed on
the basis of perception, indubitable and certain? Descartes said they are not.

To show that it is possible to doubt what our senses tell us, Descartes presented a series of skeptical arguments. One of them is the famous dream argument, which can be presented in standard form as follows:

```
1. If it is possible that I am dreaming right now,
   then I have reason to doubt whether my current
   perceptual beliefs are true.
2. It is possible that I am dreaming right now.
```
Therefore: I have reason to doubt whether my cur-
rent perceptual beliefs are true (i.e., my perceptual beliefs are not indubitable and certain).

Beginning students often misunderstand Descartes' dream argument. The
point of the argument is not to show that one is dreaming or that life can be a
dream. The point of the argument is simply to show that our current perceptual beliefs (the beliefs that are based on what I see, feel, and hear right now)
are not indubitable or absolutely certain. The argument is an instance of the
argument form *modus ponens*, which we discussed in Chapter 2; it is therefore
valid. We thus need to turn our attention to the question of whether the argument is sound. Are the premises of the argument true? The first premise
appears very reasonable. For instance, at this very moment it seems to me that
I am sitting in front of a computer. I am hearing the little humming noise of the
ventilator, and I see the cursor blinking. However, if it is possible that these
experiences are part of a vivid dream, then I have reason to doubt whether I

am indeed sitting in front of a computer. If it should be the case that I am really dreaming at this very moment, then I am probably lying in bed and there is no computer in front of me. So, premise 1 seems true. If it is possible that I am dreaming, then I have reason to doubt whether my current perceptual beliefs are true. What about the second premise? Is it really possible that I am dreaming at this very moment? I feel very awake. I see my fingers moving across the keyboard. I remember waking up this morning and having breakfast. But does any of this make it certain that I am awake? Descartes said no and supported his claim with the following line of reasoning:

1. It is impossible to distinguish with certainty between dream experiences and waking experiences.
2. If it is impossible to distinguish with certainty between dream experiences and waking experiences, then I cannot know whether I am awake right now.
3. If I cannot know that I am awake right now, then it is possible that I am dreaming right now.

Therefore: It is possible that I am dreaming right now.

This argument is a combination of two valid argument forms—*modus ponens* and *hypothetical syllogism*—and is therefore valid. Premises 2 and 3 are very plausible; the key premise is premise 1. Might this premise be false? Might it be possible to distinguish with certainty between waking experiences and dream experiences? Sure, sometimes when I am dreaming, I am aware that my experiences are part of a dream. However, this is not always the case. Some dreams are so vivid that I am convinced that my dream experiences are real. How then can I tell with certainty that my current perceptual experiences are not dream experiences? Any experience that I can have right now I can, at least in principle, also experience while I am dreaming. It follows therefore that I cannot eliminate the possibility that I am right now dreaming completely. Although my belief that I am right now awake is a strong one (i.e., I would be willing to bet a good deal of money on it), I have to acknowledge that the belief is not absolutely certain to be true. There remains the genuine possibility that my current experiences are actually part of an amazingly realistic dream.

Food for Thought

Initially, most beginning students find the dream argument weak, for they are certain they can show that they are awake. Take a look at some of the following attempts to defeat the dream argument, and decide whether they are successful.

Continued

Continued

1. I always dream in black and white. I never dream in color. However, right now I am having color experiences (i.e., I see a red pen in front of me). This means that I must be awake and not dreaming.
2. Although I can experience feelings of fear, pride, and shame in my dreams, I cannot experience the sensation of sharp pains in my dreams. Right now, I am inserting a needle into my fingers, and I am experiencing a sharp pain. It follows therefore that I must be awake.
3. Whenever I dream, I can tell that I am dreaming because I actively influence what happens in my dreams. I have learned this from a dream master in China. But I do not influence and shape what is happening right now. Therefore, I am not dreaming right now.
4. I have never been bored in any of my dreams. As a matter of fact, my dreams are pretty exciting and are full of monsters and women who look like Angelina Jolie. Right now, however, I am experiencing incredible boredom while I appear to be sitting in this philosophy class. I must be awake.
5. If these experiences I am having right now are waking experiences, then later I will get tired and go to sleep. Although I do not know right now that I will later get tired and go to sleep, there will come a time when this will be the case. At the very moment just before I fall asleep, I will know that all the experiences that I am having right now were indeed waking experiences.
6. If these experiences I am having right now were dream experiences, then it would not be possible for me to remember what I had for breakfast this morning. However, I can clearly remember that I had toast with jelly for breakfast this morning. It follows therefore that I must be awake.

The essential idea behind the dream argument can be presented in a variety of ways. Descartes, for example, considered not only the possibility that we might be dreaming, but also the possibility that there might exist a devious and powerful demon that uses all its powers to deceive us. Descartes called such a being an evil genius and argued that we could not be certain that such a being does not exist. In recent times philosophers have presented Descartes' skeptical worries in a scenario suggesting that any of us might simply be a brain in a vat. Imagine a brain suspended in a liquid and wired to a computer, which feeds the brain all the current experiences you are having right now. If you were such a brain, nothing in your experience would reveal that you were actually a brain in a vat. You might believe that you were a six-foot tall, brown-haired dude from California reading a philosophy book, but that belief, together with all your other perceptual beliefs, would be false. These skeptical arguments even find their way into popular movies. The movie *The Matrix*, for example, is constructed around the idea that we only appear to be living in a normal world; in reality, we are lying in bathtubs wired to the matrix while machines harvest our energy.

Food for Thought

We have seen that there are a variety of arguments in defense of Cartesian skepticism: the dream argument, the evil-genius argument, the brain-in-a-vat argument, the matrix argument. Although all these arguments are similar to each other, some of them establish a more fundamental form of skepticism than others. Compare the dream argument with the brain-in-a-vat argument. Which of the arguments presents a stronger version of skepticism?

It is important not to lose sight of the point of these skeptical arguments. Descartes tried to find beliefs that are indubitable and certain; these skeptical arguments are designed to show that there are no such beliefs—every belief seems to be subject to doubt. How can we respond to this challenge? Three answers seem possible. First, we can simply accept global skepticism. If knowledge requires that we have to be certain that our beliefs are true, then we have to conclude in the light of these skeptical arguments that knowledge does not exist.

Second, we can follow Descartes and try to find certainty in spite of these arguments. This might seem impossible, but Descartes suggested an ingenious argument. Assume that the worst-case scenario is true and that we are brains in vats or are deceived by an evil genius. Even in this situation, we can *know* that we doubt that our beliefs are correct. But doubting is a form of thinking, and thinking requires a thinker. Thus, Descartes concluded: "After having reflected well and carefully examined all things, we must come to the definite conclusion that this proposition: I am, I exist, is necessarily true each time that I pronounce it."[4] This is Descartes' famous "I think, therefore I am" (in Latin: *Cogito, ergo sum*). It is an interesting and influential claim. Even in the light of the most fundamental skepticism, Descartes claimed that he could know—*with absolute certainty*—that he existed as long as he was thinking. It is worth noticing that Descartes' certainty was derived from thinking (reason) alone; therefore, he is classified as a rationalist. He held that reason provides the most reliable foundation for all knowledge.

Food for Thought

Descartes' *cogito* is much more complex than it appears at first glance. Descartes seemed to assert that as long as he was thinking, he could know with absolute certainty that the sentence "I think" was true, and he could conclude therefore that the sentence "I exist" had to be true as well. Bertrand Russell (1872–1970) discussed the *cogito* in his book *The Problems of Philosophy*:

> But some care is needed in using Descartes' argument. "I think, therefore I am" says rather more than is strictly certain. It might seem as though we

Continued

Continued

were quite sure of being the same person today as we were yesterday, and this is no doubt true in some sense. But the real Self is as hard to arrive at as the real table, and does not seem to have that absolute, convincing certainty that belongs to particular experiences. When I look at my table and see a certain brown color, what is quite certain at once is not "I am seeing a brown color," but rather, "a brown color is being seen." This of course involves something (or somebody) which (or who) sees the brown color, but it does not of itself involve that more or less permanent person whom we call "I." So far as immediate certainty goes, it might be that the something which sees the brown color is quite momentary, and not the same as the something which has some different experience the next moment.[5]

What do you think? Do you agree with Russell's criticism?

Even if we accept Descartes' claim that I can know that I exist as long as I think, the resulting view of what little we know is somewhat discouraging. Very few things are as certain as my belief that I exist. Ultimately, Descartes' project (although Descartes himself disagreed here[6]) seems to lead to a philosophical position called **solipsism,** which asserts that we can know only the contents of our own minds. This is a rather lonely view of the world. If solipsism is correct, it becomes very doubtful whether we can know that there is an external world or that there are other people with minds like us. But it surely seems as if we do know that there are trees, cars, and other people in the world besides us. It is therefore tempting to look for an alternative to Descartes' epistemic project.

The third, and for me most attractive, response to Cartesian skepticism is to modify our demands for epistemic justification. As we have seen, Descartes insisted that we can know something only if we can be *certain* that the belief in question is true. In short, Descartes required epistemic justification to be infallible. That is perhaps too high a standard for justification. It might be quite reasonable to say that I am justified to believe that p is the case even if there is a chance that the justification for my belief in p will later be defeated by additional evidence. For example, suppose that it is Saturday night and that you are watching *Saturday Night Live.* You hear the actors on the show utter several times that the show is broadcast live from New York. In this situation it seems plausible to say that you are justified to believe that you are watching a live broadcast. Later, however, as you watch the credits for the show, you find out that the show was actually a recording. Although your reasons for thinking that the show was a live broadcast were later defeated, you had prima facie reasons for thinking that the show was a live broadcast. The term *prima facie* is Latin for "at first sight" and refers to evidence that is immediately available.

It is tempting to construct a viable theory of epistemic justification on the basis of prima facie justification. To illustrate how such a theory might look, let us consider the *Saturday Night Live* example one more time. Suppose you are in the same situation: You are watching *Saturday Night Live* on a Saturday evening and hear the actors announce that the show is a live broadcast. Suppose further that it is indeed a live broadcast. In this scenario you had prima facie reasons for thinking that the show was a live broadcast, and these prima facie reasons were not later defeated by other evidence. It is tempting to think that prima facie justification that goes undefeated might be sufficient for knowledge. Such justification is obviously neither certain nor infallible, but it might nevertheless be the kind of justification we are looking for.

The danger we face is that such justification might permit too many weakly justified beliefs to count as knowledge. To determine whether there is room for a plausible, prima facie version of justification that is strong enough to lead to knowledge, we will have to take a closer look at two of the most attractive sources of prima facie justification for belief: experience and reason. We will start our discussion by investigating the most common theory of knowledge, empiricism.

Empiricism

Empiricism is a very plausible and intuitive theory of knowledge. It is closely associated with the British philosophers John Locke (1632–1704), George Berkeley (1685–1753), and David Hume (1711–1776). An empiricist maintains that we can know something if we can justify it with respect to what we see, hear, smell, touch, or taste. Assume, for instance, that I am right now looking at my right hand, and I see that I have five fingers on this hand. This perception triggers in me the belief that I have five fingers on my right hand. Moreover, this perception, together with my belief that my eyes are working properly, bestows such a high degree of justification on my belief that I am very confident that I *know* that I have five fingers on my right hand. Empiricists believe that examples such as these are paradigm examples of knowledge. Our beliefs about the world are most reliable when they can be justified with the help of our experiences of the world. Historically, empiricism is also associated with the idea that we are born as a *tabula rasa* (Latin for "blank slate"), which means that all of our ideas and concepts are derived from experience. Let us call beliefs that are directly derived from our experiences basic empirical beliefs. For instance, my seeing a red telephone triggers in me the belief that there is a red telephone in front of me. This belief is a basic empirical belief since it is a direct result of certain specific experiences. An empiricist maintains that basic empirical beliefs, in ordinary circumstances, are strongly justified beliefs and count as evidence.

Food for Thought

Consider the following beliefs, and decide whether they are basic empirical beliefs or not.

1. I believe that I am experiencing a throbbing pain in my head.
2. I believe that New York City has more than two million inhabitants.

Continued

Continued

    3. I believe that there are more than three people in the room in which I am standing at this very moment.

    4. I believe that my coworker is secretly in love with me.

    5. I believe that the manifold species that we see today on Earth were created by the forces of natural selection over a span of millions of years.

    6. I believe that I am reading a book right now.

    7. I believe that there are massive black holes inside the Milky Way galaxy.

    8. I believe that I had oatmeal for breakfast this morning.

The precise way in which basic empirical beliefs are justified is a matter of philosophical controversy. We will see in a later section that an empiricist faces some tough questions in this context. But setting aside possible difficulties, let us agree with the empiricist that basic empirical beliefs are justified and count as evidence and instances of knowledge. The next step for empiricists is to insist that inferential beliefs—that is, beliefs that are about what is not directly observable—must be justified with the help of basic empirical beliefs. For example, the belief that dinosaurs once roamed the earth is not a basic empirical belief. I cannot see, touch, and feel any dinosaurs in my backyard or in a zoo. It is, however, possible to justify this belief in the light of what I can see right now, namely, bones and other paleontological remains (e.g., preserved footprints). It follows, therefore, that an empiricist would consider the inferential belief that dinosaurs once roamed the earth as justified by available empirical evidence.

An empiricist insists that all such inferential claims that are to count as knowledge must be justified by empirical evidence. Empiricists are therefore skeptical about any beliefs that cannot be confirmed or falsified by empirical evidence. For example, the claim that all men are created equal is not linked in any obvious way to empirical observations. An empiricist would therefore conclude that we can believe this, but that we cannot know this to be so. Similarly, an empiricist would be skeptical about a claim like "God wrote the Bible," for it is hard to see how that belief can be justified in terms of basic empirical beliefs. In general, many empiricists are skeptical about claims of moral and religious knowledge.

Food for Thought

Suppose that you are an empiricist. Which of the following knowledge claims do you think are justified? Explain your answers.

    1. I know that there are more people in the United States than in Cuba.

    2. I know that if the United States had not used the atomic bomb, Japan would not have surrendered and many more people would have died in the subsequent fighting than died in the bombings of Hiroshima and Nagasaki.

3. I know that in the year 2020 there will be more than six billion humans on Earth.
4. I know that a baseball thrown against a cement wall will bounce off.
5. I know that Elvis Presley was addicted to drugs.
6. I know that more than forty different people have been elected president of the United States.
7. I know that the average American read fewer books in the year 2010 than in the year 1990.
8. I know that medium-sized physical objects like soccer balls and kitchen tables are ultimately only collections of molecules.
9. I know that men have brains that are different from those of women.
10. I know that another universe exists parallel to our universe.

There is something sobering and appealing about empiricism. An empiricist will not quickly jump to grand conclusions but will carefully consider the empirical evidence and see what conclusions are plausible in the light of that evidence. If the evidence is insufficient to support any final conclusions, an empiricist will withhold judgment.

The Case for Empiricism

Several arguments suggest that empiricism is the most promising epistemic theory. First, empiricists justify all knowledge in relation to basic empirical beliefs. This approach is attractive since basic empirical beliefs seem more reliable than other beliefs. I might not know whether the stock market crash of 1929 was the main cause of the Great Depression, but I surely do seem to know how the world around me feels, sounds, and looks. There are, of course, situations in which my senses are off target and misleading, but overall they seem to paint a pretty accurate picture of how the world is. We do not have to insist—as Descartes did—that justification is infallible.

Moreover, basic empirical beliefs seem directly linked to how the world around us really is. When I see a desk in front of me, something like the following seems to be happening: Light reflects off the desk into my eyes and causes cells in the retina of my eye to stimulate my optic nerves. The optic nerves, in turn, transmit information to my brain, where the visual information is processed. The details of this process are complicated, but it seems plausible to assume that we receive information through this process that produces reliable information about the desk. We do not invent what we see, feel, or hear; there is something objective about beliefs formed on the basis of empirical evidence. They are, for the most part, independent of other beliefs and directly related to how the world is.

Finally, empiricism is strongly supported by the success of the natural sciences. Physics, chemistry, and biology have made tremendous progress during the last three hundred years and seem to have increased our knowledge of the world. Because careful observations are an essential part of the scientific method, the success of natural science supports the conclusion that our knowledge ultimately rests on empirical evidence, and thus supports an empiricist perspective in epistemology.

Problems with Perception

Although empiricism is a very attractive theory of knowledge, it leads to a number of fundamental problems. We have seen that an empiricist derives knowledge from basic empirical beliefs. It follows therefore that an empiricist needs to explain how we arrive at these basic empirical beliefs and why we are justified to believe that these basic empirical beliefs are likely to be true. Thus, an empiricist has to say something about how we perceive the world. Roughly speaking, an empiricist wants to say that when we perceive a red car, we are justified to believe that there is indeed a red car out there. So an empiricist needs to establish some version of the following principle:

> Whenever we perceive an object P (e.g., a car) to have a property A (e.g., red), then object P has indeed property A.

Let us call this the principle of **perceptual realism.** Unfortunately, this principle is not obviously true. To understand why there is controversy about perceptual realism, it is helpful to distinguish among three different theories of perception: naïve realism (sometimes also called direct realism), indirect realism, and idealism.

Different Theories of Perception

Naïve Realism	Indirect Realism	Idealism
A naïve realist believes that the world is *exactly* as we perceive it to be. So, when we see a square piece of wood then there is indeed a square piece of wood out there. The naïve realist believes that all the properties we perceive an object to have, the object indeed has.	An indirect realist holds that not all the properties we perceive an object to have are indeed in the object. For example, most indirect realists do not believe that physical objects truly have colors although we perceive them to have color properties. According to indirect realism, the world is ultimately a bit different than we perceive it to be, but it is nevertheless closely related to our perceptions.	An idealist abandons the idea that there are "real" material objects "behind" our perceptions. An ordinary object like a table, for instance, is not a mind-independent thing but a collection of perceptions.

Among the three theories of perception, naïve realism provides the best support for empiricism. If we can trust that the world outside our minds is exactly as we perceive it to be, then empiricism is by far the most promising way to gain knowledge about this world. On the other hand, naïve realism is difficult to defend. First, we cannot deny that we sometimes make perceptual mistakes. It can appear to us that there is a lake in the desert, but in reality there is no lake. It may appear to us that a stick inserted into water is bent, but in reality it is straight. What can naïve realists say about these mistakes if they are absolutely committed to the principle that the world is exactly how it appears to us? Second—and more important—there are excellent reasons for thinking that certain properties like color, heat, smell, and taste are mind-dependent properties. Consider the following situation: A person stands in front of three buckets of water. The bucket to the left is full of hot water, the one to the right full of cold water, and the one in the middle full of tepid water. The person is asked to put one arm in the bucket with cold water and the other one in the bucket of hot water. The situation is depicted in the following diagram:

After several minutes the person is asked to put both hands in the bucket with tepid water. What will happen? It seems plausible that the person will report the following: "To my right hand the water in the middle feels cold, but to my left hand the water feels warm." This spells trouble for the naïve realist. If it is possible that we perceive the same body of water as being both warm and cold at the same time, then we cannot maintain any longer that the world is exactly as we perceive it to be.

Empiricists like John Locke were very much aware of this difficulty. Locke thus rejected naïve realism and suggested instead that we distinguish between two kinds of properties: primary properties and secondary properties. According to Locke, some properties that we perceive objects to possess are not really *in* the objects but rather in *us*, the observers. A good example is color perception. If you have ever looked at the ocean, you might recall that the color of the ocean changes constantly. At times the ocean looks blue, then gray, and on other days emerald green. So what color does the water in the ocean really have? According to John Locke, the ocean has no color. Color is created when we look at the ocean, so color is a secondary property—one that we perceive the ocean to have and that the ocean causes us to see, but that the ocean itself does not really have. Locke suggested that taste, smell, texture, and felt temperature are further secondary properties, "private objects" in our minds but not truly in the objects of the physical world.

Locke suggested that other properties like size, shape, molecular texture, and motion are primary properties—that is, when I perceive an object to be six feet long, it is indeed six feet long. The size of a physical object is not a property that is only in my mind; its length is something the object really has.

Food for Thought

In everyday life we probably define and identify salt in the following way: Salt is the stuff that tastes salty. This definition is problematic. For one, it seems circular; secondly, the definition attributes to salt something—namely, a certain taste—that according to Locke is not *in* the salt at all. Remember that taste is a secondary quality. Locke would prefer a definition of salt that makes reference only to the primary qualities of salt. What would such a definition look like?

The distinction between primary and secondary properties leads to the idea of **indirect realism**. According to this theory of perception, the world around us is not exactly as it appears to be. The world, independent of our perception, has neither color nor smell nor taste. It consists of extended microscopic objects that possess only primary properties—namely, size, shape, and motion. Since indirect realism can escape the objections that were raised against naïve realism, it seems to be a more plausible theory. Moreover, it is compatible with the view that the universe ultimately exists of small physical particles and collections of these particles. This metaphysical view was held by John Locke and is also referred to as *corpuscularianism*.

In defense of indirect realism one succinct line of argument, which makes use of our observations about color and other secondary properties, was suggested by Michael Huemer:[7]

```
1. If an object is composed entirely of parts that
   are colorless, that object is colorless.
2. All middle-sized physical objects are composed
   entirely of subatomic particles (protons, elec-
   trons, neutrons, and so on)
3. Subatomic particles are colorles
```

```
Therefore: All middle-sized physical objects are
colorless.
```

The argument is clearly valid, and all three premises are easy to accept. However, if you accept all three premises, you must also accept the idea that tables and chairs and all other middle-sized physical objects are in reality colorless and thus quite different from the way they appear in our perception. Indirect realism has thus become unavoidable.

Indirect realism makes it harder to explain why empiricism is the most promising theory of knowledge. For if indirect realism is true, we cannot simply know that the world is as we perceive it to be; indirect realism requires that we distinguish between how the world appears to our senses and how the world really is. The world as it appears to our senses has both primary and secondary properties, but the real world supposedly has only primary properties. This distinction leads to epistemic difficulties: An empiricist holds that we can know something if we can perceive it, but indirect realism removes the real world from our direct perceptual reach and drives a wedge between what we are aware of and the objective, external world. Since we cannot perceive a world without color, taste, and smell, we are unable to be directly aware of objects as they really are. An empiricist who accepts indirect realism must admit, therefore, that we cannot know the real world directly through our experiences. The best we can hope for is to infer that such an external, objective world exists. Unfortunately, such inferences cannot easily be justified in the light of our experiences and thereby open the possibility that pure empiricism might lead to a form of skepticism.

George Berkeley pointed to a second, more serious problem for indirect realism: The distinction between primary and secondary properties is not clear-cut. Locke had argued that color is a secondary property since the color of an object depends on how one looks at the object—that is, the same table might look blue from one perspective and gray from another. But Berkeley pointed out—correctly, it seems—that the same can be said about primary properties as well. For instance, shape is supposedly a primary property, but a round tire can look round from one perspective and elliptical from another. What then is the real shape of the tire? An analogous point can be made with motion, which is also considered a primary property of objects. Whether something is perceived to be in motion depends fundamentally on the perspective of the observer. Thus, the danger is that all properties of physical objects might turn out to be somewhat mind dependent. Berkeley concluded that we should abandon the distinction between primary and secondary qualities and instead admit that the world ultimately depends on our minds. But if we have to relinquish the distinction between primary and secondary properties, we have to abandon the theory of indirect realism as well.

Berkeley, a committed empiricist, was happy to draw this conclusion. He suggested that physical objects like cars, telephone poles, or toothbrushes are ultimately nothing but perceptions. Berkeley's famous phrase is "Esse est percipi," which is Latin for "To be is to be perceived."

Food for Thought

Most people have heard the question If a tree falls in the forest and there is nobody around to hear the fall, does it make a sound? This question strikes us as a bit silly at first. But this sort of question was raised by Berkeley, and we can now see why he thought it was important. Berkeley wanted to show that things need a perceiver to exist. Do you agree with him on this point? Suppose you put on a CD and push the Play button. If you then leave the room before the CD starts playing and nobody else is in the room, will there be music in the room?

Berkeley's position is known as **idealism**, which is compatible with empiricism. For if we say that physical objects are ultimately perceptions, then we can know those objects through perceptual experiences. However, idealism seems counterintuitive: Who would think that physical objects like tables and chairs are ultimately only perceptions? We have a strong inclination to think that physical objects are made out of matter that can exist independently of being perceived. Of course, the fact that a philosophical theory goes against the grain of common sense is not necessarily a serious flaw. However, all things being equal, it is always preferable to adopt a theory that squares well with our commonsense view of the world.

The more serious weakness in Berkeley's idealism is that it seems to make it very difficult to distinguish between true and false perceptual beliefs. In certain situations we are prone to experience perceptual illusions. For example, when we walk through a desert, we might experience a mirage and see water in the distance, although in reality there is only hot desert sand. If we believe in the existence of a mind-independent physical world, we can explain these situations as follows: Our perceptual belief that there is water in the distance is false, because our perception was not caused by water but by the hot air above the desert sand. This explanation requires us to think about the hot air above the desert sand as a mind-independent physical object, since only mind-independent physical objects can play the appropriate causal role. We have seen, however, that Berkeley's idealism denies that there are mind-independent physical objects. According to his analysis, physical objects are ultimately perceptions, so Berkeley cannot explain the mirage in the same way we just did. At this point an idealist has two options: Either decide that perceptual beliefs can never be false, or else revise the ordinary account of how perceptual beliefs can be false. The first option does not seem very attractive, and the second option suggests that idealism is philosophically rather complex. According to Ockham's razor, we have reason to prefer a simpler explanation to a more complicated one. Thus, although Berkeley's idealism is a logically possible scenario, it does not offer the simplest explanation of mistaken perceptual beliefs, and we therefore have cause to be hesitant before we embrace any form of idealism.

Let us quickly summarize the main conclusions of this discussion of perception. We have seen that empiricism needs a theory of perception that supports the principle that if we perceive an object P to have a property A, then object P has indeed property A. This principle is best supported by naïve realism, but naïve realism seems, on closer scrutiny, to give way to indirect realism about perception. And indirect realism, in turn, seems to lead to skepticism or to collapse into idealism. If we combine, as Berkley did, idealism with empiricism, we seem to be in conflict with the principle of Ockham's razor. None of this is fatal for empiricism, but it shows that an empiricist has to do serious philosophical work before being able to confidently assert that our knowledge of the world goes hand in hand with our experiences of the world.

The Problem of Induction

The second major problem for empiricism stems from the fact that our experiences of the world can confirm or disconfirm only particular facts, not general and universal claims. If we want to know, for example, whether a particular sunflower is yellow, we can simply look at that particular sunflower. However, if we want to know whether all sunflowers are yellow, we cannot directly determine that by looking at a couple of sunflowers. The empiricist needs a procedure to move from knowledge of a particular set of objects to knowledge of universal and general relationships. Such a procedure is called *induction*, a term we encountered in Chapter 2 when we discussed enumerative inductive arguments. The difficulty for the empiricist is to explain how and why we can know, on the basis of experience alone, that enumerative inductive arguments (or inferences) are justified. The philosopher David Hume was the first to draw attention to this difficulty.

At first glance you might wonder whether empiricists can simply give up on induction altogether and resign themselves to knowing only particular facts but not universal claims. The difficulty with this solution is that empiricism is supposed to underlie and explain the success of the empirical sciences, which rely on general laws like Newton's three laws of motion. These laws of nature are, of course, paradigm examples of universal claims that go beyond the limit of particular facts. If empiricism is supposed to explain how scientists can know that nature is governed by general laws, empiricists need to explain how inductive inferences can expand our knowledge.

Let us consider a relatively straightforward example. Suppose that Peter is a biologist who has spent a good deal of his time observing the habits of loggerhead turtles. He observed, for instance, that loggerhead turtles come to the same beach to lay their eggs every two years. After observing this again and again at different beaches and with a large sample of loggerhead turtles, and after finding out that other biologists had made the same observations about loggerhead turtles, Peter inferred that loggerhead turtles lay eggs every two years. The enumerative inductive argument in defense of his claim looks as follows:

```
1. All loggerhead turtles that have been observed
   in the past have laid eggs every two years.
```
Therefore: All loggerhead turtles lay eggs every two years.

This enumerative inductive argument poses an epistemic problem for the empiricist. The conclusion of the argument involves not only a judgment about what observed loggerhead turtles have done in the past, but also a prediction about what they will do in the future. Because no one has yet observed what loggerhead turtles will do in the future, an empiricist faces an epistemic problem: What reason do we have to think that unobserved loggerhead turtles will act in the future in the same way as observed loggerhead turtles have acted in the past? It is certainly logically possible that loggerhead turtles will suddenly change their egg-laying habits.

When real-life scientists are confronted with this problem, they frequently point to the **principle of the uniformity of nature**, which claims that the course of nature is not freaky. Nature is such that the laws that govern the past will also govern the future. If this principle is accepted, we can present a better version of the argument about loggerhead turtles.

```
1. All loggerhead turtles that have been observed
   in the past have laid eggs every two years.
2. Nature is uniform; that is, regularities that
   have occurred in the past will also occur in the
   future.
```
Therefore: All loggerhead turtles (past and future) lay eggs every two years.

This argument provides a much stronger justification than the earlier version; the argument now is deductively valid. However, we are facing a new challenge: We have to provide reasons in defense of premise 2. On what basis do we know that the principle of the uniformity of nature is true? Full-blown empiricists think that their experience must provide the reason that the principle of the uniformity of nature is true. Consequently, they must argue as follows:

```
1. In the past we have seen that many observed reg-
   ularities have continued to hold.
```
Therefore: All observed regularities will continue to hold in the future (i.e., nature is uniform).

The problems with this argument are easy to see. The argument itself is an inductive inference, which we can justify if the principle of the uniformity of nature is true. Alas, in order to know that that principle is true, we need to assume that a specific inductive inference works. We thus have come full circle; in order to show that inductive arguments are reliable, we had to appeal to the principle of the uniformity of nature and in order to justify the principle of the uniformity of nature we had to presuppose that inductive arguments are reliable. We thus have, as philosophers like to say, *begged the question*; we ended up presupposing what we tried to establish.

This might not be a fatal problem for empiricism, but it shows once again that committed empiricists have philosophical work to do before they can claim that scientific laws can be known solely on the basis of experiences. A potentially elegant solution to the problem of induction is to claim that we can know the uniformity of nature not on the basis of experience, but rather with the help of reason. This would show, however, that in addition to experience, human knowledge needs a second leg to stand on—namely, reason. Philosophers who claim that our knowledge depends predominantly on reason rather than experience are called **rationalists.**

Rationalism

Rationalism, the third major epistemic theory, is not as immediately plausible as empiricism, but there are some crucial similarities between these two major theories of knowledge. An empiricist believes that our knowledge is ultimately based on basic empirical beliefs; rationalism is similar in that rationalists also hold that our knowledge is based on basic beliefs. The difference is that rationalists do not justify basic beliefs with the help of experience, but rather with the help of pure reason. This might sound a bit strange: What is "pure reason" supposed to be, and how is it supposed to lead us to knowledge? An example might help to illustrate the basic thrust of rationalism.

Suppose Sarah, a skeptical friend of yours, asks: "What do you think? Is 200,763 the largest natural number?" You answer: "No, 200,763 is not the largest natural number. As a matter of fact, there is no largest natural number. For any natural number you can name, there is always a larger one." Suppose Sarah is not impressed by your answer and asks: "How in the world can you know these kinds of things? Have you looked at all natural numbers? I have a feeling that you do not really know this, but that you simply made this up." Two things seem fairly obvious at this point: First, we do indeed seem to know that there is no largest natural number, and second, we do not know this on the basis of experience. Numbers are not the kind of things we can see, feel, and touch. So if we have knowledge about them, that knowledge cannot be based on experience, but rather on our ability to think (i.e., reason).

Rationalists claim that when we think about certain propositions, we can immediately understand and grasp that the propositions must be true. For example, we can immediately grasp that the number 3 is larger than the number 2, or that any two people either know each other or they do not, or that nothing can be green and red all over at the same time. A rationalist claims that these propositions have something self-evident about them, and simple reflection suffices to show that we are justified to believe that they are likely to be true.

Food for Thought

Take a look at the following propositions, and decide whether you know that they are true or false simply by reflecting on what they assert.

1. If one multiplies any natural number by 2, the resulting number is even.
2. The income of the average worker in the United States is higher than the income of the average worker in Europe.
3. Every state must have some form of government.
4. Every event has a cause.
5. If any nation should ever use nuclear weapons again, millions of people will die.
6. Every recession in the economy is eventually followed by an economic recovery.
7. If a person freely performs an action, that person can be held responsible for the action.
8. Sugar is sweet.
9. All human beings have the same fundamental rights.
10. All cats are animals.

Some technical terminology is frequently used when philosophers discuss rationalism. The kind of justification that is crucial for rationalists is called *a priori*, a Latin phrase that literally means "from the former." The phrase is used to refer to justification that can take place prior to consulting any empirical evidence. In other words, I can know something a priori if I can know it without first seeing, touching, or hearing anything in particular. It is, for example, possible to know a priori that all red cars are colored cars, since I do not have to look at any cars to determine that the claim is true. I can also know a priori that every triangle has three sides; I do not have to see or touch any particular triangle in order to know that the claim is true.

Students are frequently confused at this point and often say, "How can you know that all triangles have three sides without having experiences? In order to know something about triangles, one surely must have seen some triangles. So it seems false to say that one can know a priori that all triangles have three sides." It is important to understand that a priori does not mean justification without reference to any experiences, but rather justification without reference to any *particular* experience. For example, in order to know that tigers are animals, I might have to see some tigers or pictures of tigers to acquire the concept of what a tiger is. However, it is not necessary to see any particular tiger, so it is correct to say that I can know a priori that tigers are animals. Any experience that allows me to acquire the concept of a tiger is sufficient to allow me to know that tigers are animals. On the other hand, I cannot know a priori whether my neighbors have a ferocious tiger in their basement. In order to know that, I need to inspect their basement (i.e., I need to have a particular experience).

A priori justification is normally contrasted with *a posteriori* justification, a Latin phrase that literally means "from the latter." A posteriori justification is the kind of justification that is typical for empiricism; it requires that we refer to specific experiences of the world. For example, I can know only a posteriori that Jody Foster's son has red hair. In order to know that, I must have had a chance to see Jody Foster's son—that is, a particular experience. Similarly, I can know only a posteriori that there are nine planets in our solar system or that the average household income in New Jersey is higher than the average household income in Tennessee.

Food for Thought

In order to test your understanding of the terms *a priori* and *a posteriori*, decide whether the following sentences are true or false.

1. I can know a priori that all bachelors are not married.
2. A fully committed empiricist holds that all our knowledge is justified a posteriori.
3. It is impossible to know a priori whether New York City has more inhabitants than Mexico City.
4. I can know a priori that there is life on other planets.
5. All of mathematics is based on a priori reasoning.
6. Nobody can know on the basis of a priori reasoning that the Empire State Building is the tallest building in the world.
7. I can know a priori that if somebody is shot to death, then somebody must have been the shooter.
8. I can know a priori that a cube must have twelve edges.
9. I can know a priori that all swans are white.

In addition to the terms *a priori* and *a posteriori*, it is useful to understand the terms **necessary truth** and **contingent truth**. A proposition is contingently true if its truth depends on how the actual world is. For example, whether the sentence "Britney Spears has sold more records than Madonna" is true depends on whether Britney Spears has indeed sold more records than Madonna. So this proposition is contingently true. Similarly, the sentences "Abraham Lincoln was shot in a theater" and "The Broncos won two successive Super Bowl titles" express contingent truths. On the other hand, the sentence

"If Britney Spears has a female sibling, then Britney Spears has a sister" is true, whether Britney Spears actually has a sister or not. Similarly, the sentences "The number 9 is larger than the number 3" and "Every rose is a flower" express necessary truths. A good way to determine whether a sentence is contingently true or necessarily true is to ask if it is logically possible that the sentence could be false. For example, it is logically possible that the sentence "Abraham Lincoln was shot in a theater" is false, for we can imagine a situation in which Abraham Lincoln was not shot at all. It follows therefore that the sentence expresses a contingent truth. On the other hand, it is not logically possible that the number 9 is smaller than the number 3 or that roses are not flowers.

Food for Thought

In order to test your understanding of the differences between necessary and contingent truths, determine whether the following sentences are necessary truths or contingent truths.

1. The moon moves around the earth.
2. All bachelors are not married.
3. The United States withdrew from Vietnam in 1975.
4. If Frank has more than two sisters, then he has at least three siblings.
5. There are infinitely many prime numbers.
6. In order to graduate from Northwestern University, one has to take at least three English classes.

A tight connection exists between necessary truths and a priori knowledge, and between contingent truths and a posteriori knowledge. If we can know something a priori (i.e., prior to looking at the world), the truth must be a necessary truth. On the other hand, if we know something a posteriori (i.e., with the help of experience), the truth must be a contingent truth. A rationalist maintains that there are important necessary truths that we can know only on the basis of a priori reasoning and that these necessary truths form the foundation of all our knowledge.

The Case for Rationalism

A fair number of thinkers do not find rationalism all that plausible. They ask, "What are these great necessary truths that we are supposed to know on the basis of reason alone?" At first glance this seems like a reasonable complaint, but if we look more carefully, we can see that rationalism is a more persuasive element in our knowledge than is initially apparent. To illustrate this, let us consider the text of the Declaration of Independence, written in 1776:

> We hold these truths to be self-evident, that all men are created equal, that they are endowed by their Creator with certain unalienable Rights, that among these

are Life, Liberty and the pursuit of Happiness. That to secure these rights, Governments are instituted among Men, deriving their just powers from the consent of the governed. That whenever any Form of Government becomes destructive of these ends, it is the Right of the People to alter or to abolish it, and to institute new Government.

What is striking here is the reference to self-evidence. The crucial claims of the Declaration of Independence are presented as self-evident truths, that is, truths that are justified in the light of reason alone. Moreover, the claims at issue— namely, that all men have equal rights and that people have the right to revolt against their government if it fails to protect them in their rights—are, if they are true, necessarily true. For it is not a contingent feature of humans to have moral rights; if humans do have fundamental moral rights, they have them necessarily. This suggests that moral knowledge is justified predominantly on the basis of a priori reasoning. The weakness with this line of reasoning is, of course, that not all people agree that moral claims are true or false—that is, there are many people who are skeptics about moral claims. We will discuss this issue more thoroughly in Chapter 8, but for now we can suggest a conditional argument in defense of rationalism, which takes the logical form of *modus ponens:*

```
1. If we have moral and political knowledge, then
   rationalism plays an important role in justify-
   ing our beliefs.
2. We have moral and political knowledge.
```
Therefore: Rationalism plays an important role in justifying our beliefs.

Food for Thought

This last argument depends on the claim that we actually have moral knowledge. What do you think—do we *know* that all humans have equal rights, or do we only *believe* that all humans have equal rights?

A second argument in defense of rationalism is based on the claim that a priori knowledge does not seem to be as vulnerable to a certain type of skepticism as empirical knowledge is. We have seen that empiricism goes hand in hand with the natural sciences, but they are in a constant process of change. Physicists used to believe that matter was made out of indivisible, small, solid particles (i.e., atoms). Then they discovered that atoms themselves consisted of parts and that atoms were not solid pieces of matter but contained a good deal of empty space. Now scientists have even detected that electrons and neutrons have parts, and no end to this process of new discoveries is in sight. Thus, empirical claims are always subject to revision, which has convinced some philosophers that the natural sciences do not produce genuine knowledge, but only beliefs. Genuine knowledge is supposed to be timeless and unchanging.

The philosopher Plato first raised this objection against empirical knowledge. Plato was a rationalist and did not think that empirical investigations of the physical world could lead to genuine knowledge, only to beliefs. Plato, like all rationalists, was much more impressed by the knowledge of mathematics. He thought that a mathematical proof, once discovered, would not later be revised. In truth, when we learn classical geometry today, we learn the same proofs that the Greek mathematician Euclid discovered more than two thousand years ago. Unlike natural science, mathematics does seem to lead to knowledge that is eternal and solidly justified in the light of reason. Thus, the gist of this argument is to increase the importance of a priori knowledge by discrediting the status of empirical knowledge. A convinced rationalist might therefore say that if there is any knowledge, it must be a priori knowledge since empirical investigation produces only beliefs.

Problems for Rationalism

Despite the support for a priori justification, rationalism faces some serious challenges. One of the more influential challenges goes back to the writings of David Hume but was most prominently advocated by a group of twentieth-century philosophers called logical positivists. Rudolph Carnap (1891–1970), Moritz Schlick (1882–1936), and Carl Gustav Hempel (1905–1997) were some of the most prominent members of this group. Logical positivists were committed empiricists who believed that a priori knowledge had only limited value. To understand their attack on rationalism and a priori reasoning, we need to understand the distinction between **analytic** and **synthetic truths.** Consider the following sentence: All electrons are subatomic particles. This sentence is obviously true, but it is true for trivial reasons. An electron is by definition a certain type of subatomic particle; thus, we can know that the sentence is true simply by analyzing the meaning of the word *electron*. No observations are necessary in order to determine whether the sentence is true. Sentences of this type express analytic truths, and analytically true sentences are true simply by virtue of the meanings of the words involved. Other examples of analytic sentences are "All bachelors are not married" or "All birches are trees."

Of course, most sentences are not analytically true. For instance, the sentence "Electrons have less mass than neutrons" cannot be determined to be true by analyzing the meaning of the word *electron*. In order to find out whether this sentence is true, we need to conduct experiments and observations. Sentences of this kind are called synthetic sentences. Further examples of synthetic sentences are "George Bush owns a Ford Focus" or "New York City has more inhabitants than Lincoln, Nebraska."

Food for Thought

In order to sharpen your understanding of the distinction between analytic truths and synthetic truths, determine whether the following sentences are analytic or synthetic.

1. All pencils and pens are writing utensils.
2. Electrons are the smallest physical particles in the universe.
3. More than twenty million people died of AIDS last year.
4. There are more heterosexual humans than there are homosexual humans.
5. Earthquakes are natural disasters.
6. Dogs and cats are both animals.
7. Texas is larger than Oklahoma.
8. The average lawyer makes more than $70,000 per year.
9. All cubes have twelve edges.

Once we have grasped the distinction between analytic and synthetic truths, it is easy to see that there is something trivial about analytic truths. If somebody tells me, "All bachelors are unmarried men," I can immediately see that what I'm hearing is true, but the truth is not very interesting. Analytic truths do not contain information about the world, but rather information about how we use the words in our language. Once we understand this feature of analytic truths, we can appreciate the attack of logical positivism on rationalism. However, that attack is devastating for a rationalist, who claims that a priori reasoning is a key element in all our knowledge.

To resist this attack, a rationalist has to show that there are important necessary truths that we can know a priori but that are not analytic. One option is to point to important moral claims like "All humans have equal rights"; if these claims are true, they are necessarily true, and the claims are synthetic, not analytic. But this move is problematic. Because logical positivists deny that we have moral knowledge, arguments that appeal to moral knowledge are not always effective.

A second defense for rationalists is to claim that there are important synthetic and necessary truths that shape our understanding of the physical universe. Traditionally, rationalists have claimed, for instance, that the sentences "Every event has a cause" or "The shortest distance between two points in space is a straight line" are synthetic and necessary truths about the universe. The problem here is that progress in science suggests that these seemingly self-evident truths are not only contingent but probably even false. Thus, the rationalist seems to have only one escape from the attack of logical positivism: the rationalist's all-time favorite field of knowledge, namely mathematical truths. However, even the status of mathematical truths is hotly debated. Many positivists, for instance, have favored the idea that mathematics ultimately reduces to analytic truths as well. Whether rationalists can escape the attack of logical positivism is an open question and is still debated among contemporary philosophers. No clear answer to the question has yet emerged.

Final Remarks on Epistemology

It is time to draw some conclusions from our introduction to epistemology. We can answer the question of whether we have knowledge in three fundamental ways. First, we can be skeptics and claim that we know very little and that most of our so-called knowledge is in fact nothing more than a bunch of beliefs. A dose of skepticism is a necessary ingredient of all philosophy; if we are too confident that we know what the world is like, we will not ask the necessary questions that initiate philosophical reflection. However, the crucial epistemological question is whether we can prevent skepticism from turning into global skepticism and thus undermining all our philosophical and scientific knowledge. Descartes' method of doubt did not produce an entirely satisfactory response to global skepticism.

Fallible versions of either empiricism or rationalism seem more promising. An empiricist argues that we can know that p if we can justify p a posteriori in the light of our experiences of the world. A rationalist, on the other hand, maintains that we can know that p if we can show a priori that p is necessarily true. Both positions have their strengths and weaknesses. In actual philosophical conversation, most people appeal to a priori justification as well as a posteriori justification. It is, however, important to determine what kind of justification plays the more fundamental role; an answer to this question will not only influence our strategy for resisting skepticism, but will also influence how we approach and evaluate arguments. An empiricist, for instance, will be skeptical toward premises that cannot be justified by our experiences. A rationalist, on the other hand, will try to solve philosophical questions predominantly with the help of a priori considerations. Equipped with these basic epistemological and logical tools, we are ready to explore some classical philosophical problems.

Study and Reflection Questions

1. Is global skepticism a self-defeating philosophical position? If yes, does this mean that skepticism is not a problem? If no, can you say what global skepticism is without undermining your own position?

2. Can you know that you are awake at this very moment? If yes, please describe precisely how you might establish this. Would Descartes be satisfied with your answer?

3. We know that the average temperature on Earth has undergone dramatic changes in the past. There have been ice ages and periods of warm weather. Suppose that we

develop a climate model that allows us to understand precisely why and how the temperature in the past has changed on Earth. Would this model allow us to predict how the temperature on Earth will develop in the future? Explain your answer as clearly as you can.

4. Is the world as it really is (i.e., independent of our experiences), identical to the world we perceive with our senses?

5. Is it possible to know that something is true simply by thinking about it? If yes, give some examples of these truths. Do you think that these kinds of truths are important in developing a satisfactory big-picture view of the world? If your answer is no, please explain your reasoning as clearly as you can.

For Further Reading

Alston, William P. *The Reliability of Sense Perception.* Ithaca, NY: Cornell University Press, 1993.

Audi, Robert. *Epistemology: A Contemporary Introduction to the Theory of Knowledge.* London: Routledge, 1998.

Bonjour, Lawrence. *Epistemology.* Lanham, MD: Rowman & Littlefield, 2002.

Chisholm, Roderick M. *Theory of Knowledge.* 3rd ed. Englewood Cliffs, NJ: Prentice Hall, 1989.

Huemer, Michael. *Skepticism and the Veil of Perception.* Lanham, MD: Rowman & Littlefield, 2001.

Lehrer, Keith. *Theory of Knowledge.* Boulder, CO: Westview Press, 1990.

Moser, Paul K. *Knowledge and Evidence.* Cambridge: Cambridge University Press, 1989.

———. *The Oxford Handbook of Epistemology.* Oxford: Oxford University Press, 2005.

Pollock, John, and Joseph, Cruz. *Contemporary Theories of Knowledge.* Lanham, MD: Rowman & Littlefield, 1999.

Plantinga, Alvin. *Warrant and Proper Function.* New York: Oxford University Press, 1993.

———. *Warrant: The Current Debate.* New York: Oxford University Press, 1993.

Sosa, Ernest. *The Blackwell Guide to Epistemology.* Malden, MA: Blackwell, 2004.

Endnotes

1. K. William Clifford, "The Ethics of Belief," in *The Ethics of Belief and Other Essays* (New York: Prometheus Books, 1999), pp. 70–96.
2. Don DeLillo, *White Noise* (New York: Penguin, 1985), pp. 12–13.
3. Rene Descartes, *Meditations on First Philosophy*, trans. Elisabeth Haldane and G. Ross (Cambridge: Cambridge University Press, 1931), p. 145.
4. Ibid., p. 146.

5. Bertrand Russell, *The Problems of Philosophy* (Oxford: Oxford University Press, 1912), p. 174.

6. After establishing that he could know with certainty that he existed as long as he was thinking, Descartes also believed that he could prove with absolute certainty-that God exists. But since God could not possibly be a deceiver and since God was the creator of Descartes and every other finite mind, it followed that ideas that appeared clearly and distinctly as true in Descartes' mind had to actually be true. Descartes concluded from this that he could know everything that he clearly and distinctly perceived to be true. Most readers of Descartes have been puzzled by his epistemic strategy since it seems to involve a vicious circle. Descartes trusted his clear and distinct ideas because he could prove that a benevolent God exists. However, in order to prove that God exists, it would seem as if one would have to trust one's clear and distinct ideas. This objection to Descartes is normally referred to as the Cartesian circle.

7. Michael Huemer, *Skepticism and the Veil of Perception* (Lanham, MD: Rowman & Littlefield, 2001), pp. 137–138.

CHAPTER FOUR

THE PROBLEM OF FREE WILL

Why Is There a Problem with Free Will?

It is natural to believe that our will is free. As we go through our lives, we often deliberate about what we are going to do in the future. Consider the example of John, who just graduated from high school and is trying to decide what to do next in life. He has the chance to go to college and also has an opportunity to work for a year in Palm Beach, Florida, together with his friends. He cannot do both, so John has to make a decision. It seems obvious that the choice he is going to make depends on his will. He seems free either to go to college or to go and work for a year, and if he cannot make up his mind, perhaps he can stay home with his parents for a year and watch TV. It is John's decision. In general, we can say that having free will means that we can make choices in our lives and that these choices are up to us. The basic idea behind having free will is illustrated in the following diagram.

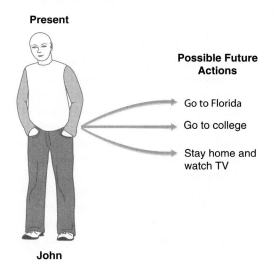

Present

Possible Future
Actions

Go to Florida

Go to college

Stay home and
watch TV

John

We all have a tendency to believe that we are like John and that we have the ability to make choices and shape our future. Why then do philosophers worry about free will? To understand why some philosophers question whether we actually have free will, let us expand that illustration and consider the past as well as the future.

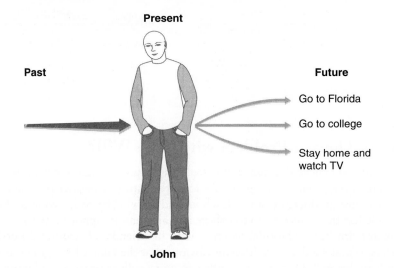

Notice that the past is quite different from the future. John's future seems open; it seems to be up to him to shape his future. The same cannot be said about John's past, which is set in stone. For example, John was born on October 17, 1992; his parents divorced when he was twelve; and he drank his first beer on his fifteenth birthday. All of these events are part of John's past and are not within John's power to change.

The question that arises is this: How much power does the past have over the future? If the link between the past and the future is strong, and if there is only one past, then the possibility arises that there is also only one future. The theory that the future is fixed by the past is called **determinism**; the illustration on the next page captures the basic idea behind this philosophical view.

It is important not to misunderstand the effects of determinism. Even if our future is determined by our past, we will not feel compelled to perform particular actions. On the contrary, in a deterministic world we still make choices, and we still deliberate about what we should do in the future. In such a world, John still contemplates what he should do with his life after high school; he will try to find the option that looks most attractive to him. It's just that John, given his particular past experiences, is determined to make one particular choice, namely to go to college. The other choices are not really open to him.

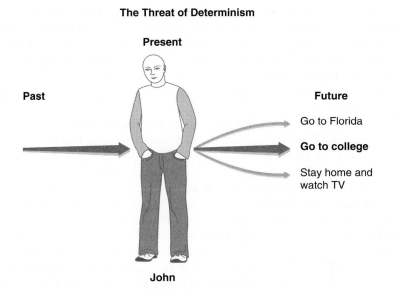

The Threat of Determinism

Present

Past

Future

Go to Florida

Go to college

Stay home and watch TV

John

Is it possible to be free if the past brings about one particular future?

The German philosopher Arthur Schopenhauer (1788–1860) illustrated the effects of determinism as follows:

> Let us imagine a man who while standing on the street, would say to himself: "It's six o'clock in the evening, the working day is over. Now I can go for a walk, or I can go to the club; I can also climb the tower to see the sun set, I can go to the theater; I can visit this friend or that one; indeed I can also run out of the gate, into the wide world, and never return. All of this is strictly up to me, in this I have complete freedom. But still I shall do none of these things now, but with just as free a will I shall go home to my wife."[1]

What Schopenhauer nicely explains here is that we do not lose our sense of freedom even if our future is already determined. The man who stands in the street and contemplates what to do after work was determined to go home to his wife. He is nevertheless quite happy to think about all the things he might do instead, even though, given his past, he is not going to do any of them.

Let us illustrate Schopenhauer's thought with an additional example. Consider the case of Stacy, who is seventeen years old and sees the U.S. women's soccer team play on TV for the first time. Stacy is excited by the great play of the U.S. team and decides that she wants to become a member of the U.S. women's soccer team as well. However, Stacy has never played soccer in her life, and given her past inexperience with soccer, it seems impossible for her to become one of the best soccer players in the United States. Thus, her past is limiting what Stacy can achieve on the soccer field in the future. This brings us back to Schopenhauer's insight: Some of the things that we think we can do in the future might actually be ruled out by events in our past. I might think that I will turn into a bank robber later in life, but this is not a real possibility in light of my past education and character development. Given the many outlandish things we think we might want to do in the future, it is easy to understand why we humans might develop an overblown sense of our own freedom. In reality, however, our past might limit our future options much more than we care to acknowledge.

We are now in a much better position to understand why free will leads to serious concerns. The main philosophical problem is to explain how the past is connected with the future and what impact this connection has on our ability to make free choices. If determinism is true, it would be a mistake to think that the future is an open field. Instead, each of us needs to acknowledge that, given our particular past, there is only one future path that is open to us. Should we fear such a conclusion? Can we still be free even if our future is already determined? You will soon discover that different philosophers have reacted in different ways to this question. On the one hand, there is **compatibilism**, which believes that freedom and determinism can coexist. On the other, there is **incompatibilism,** which believes that freedom and determinism cannot coexist. In the next section we will explore various versions of these theories. The following graphic overview should help you to develop an initial grasp of the various positions.

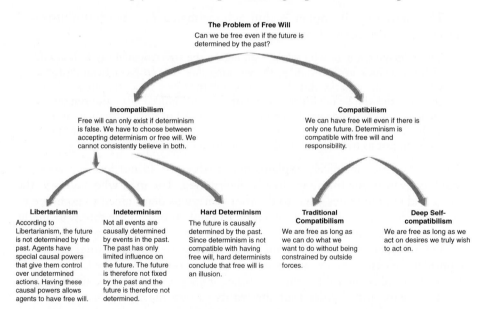

The Problem of Free Will
Can we be free even if the future is determined by the past?

Incompatibilism
Free will can only exist if determinism is false. We have to choose between accepting determinism or free will. We cannot consistently believe in both.

Compatibilism
We can have free will even if there is only one future. Determinism is compatible with free will and responsibility.

Libertarianism
According to Libertarianism, the future is not determined by the past. Agents have special causal powers that give them control over undetermined actions. Having these causal powers allows agents to have free will.

Indeterminism
Not all events are causally determined. The past has only limited influence on the future. The future is therefore not fixed by the past and the future is therefore not determined.

Hard Determinism
The future is causally determined by the past. Since determinism is not compatible with having free will, hard determinists conclude that free will is an illusion.

Traditional Compatibilism
We are free as long as we can do what we want to do without being constrained by outside forces.

Deep Self-compatibilism
We are free as long as we act on desires we truly wish to act on.

Food for Thought

The Eminem song "Lose Yourself" contains the line "You can do anything you set your mind to, man." Sentiments like these are often expressed in novels, songs, and movies. However, these unconditional proclamations of radical and unrestricted freedom promote an unrealistic conception of freedom. In fact, we can hope to achieve only what is compatible with our past. Why then do so many artists, novelists, and movie makers propagate the notion that our freedom is unlimited?

Food for Thought

In order to determine which of these various positions on free will is most compatible with your own thinking, answer the following questions with True or False. We will later see that, depending on which philosophical position we adopt, we will answer these questions differently.

1. All events are caused.
2. We are responsible for all our actions.
3. In some situations people perform actions, but they are not responsible for what they do.
4. In each and every situation in my life, I could have acted otherwise than I in fact acted.
5. To be free means that one is able to do what one wants to do.
6. If we were to roll back time to the year 1950, history would unfold in the same way as it actually did (i.e., President Kennedy would be assassinated in 1963 in Dallas, Reagan would be elected president in 1980, etc.).
7. God knows what will happen in the future. He knows especially what will happen in my life later on; that is, he knows when I will die and what I will have for dinner tomorrow evening, and so forth.
8. Nobody (not even God) can know what will happen in the future because the future has not yet happened.
9. If I had experienced a different childhood, then I would make different decisions right now.
10. Even someone who has had a terrible childhood can pull him- or herself together and make free and responsible choices about life.
11. Some features of a person's character are caused by his or her genes. For example, genes might make someone extremely afraid of heights, in which case the person is not responsible for the fear or for the actions that result from it.
12. We sometimes act on desires that are not our own but are implanted in us by advertising or peer pressure.

The Case for Hard Determinism

Hard determinists accept determinism and agree that the future is firmly fixed by the past. They also believe that a fully determined future is incompatible with free will. They argue that true freedom requires control over the future, and since we lack this control, we should accept that we are not free. According to hard determinism, our belief in free will is similar to a belief in the Easter Bunny—a childish illusion. To make this view plausible, we need to understand how past and future are related to each other. How is the past able to exercise such a powerful influence over the future? Hard determinists respond to this question by pointing to **causality.** The past causes the future, and this causal link determines what the future looks like.

Food for Thought

It is crucial not to confuse *determinism*, *hard determinism*, and *fatalism*. A determinist holds that the future is fixed by the past; determinism by itself does not say anything about free will. There are many who believe, for example, that we can be free even if the future is fixed by the past. A hard determinist, on the other hand, holds that we have no free will because determinism is true. Finally, a fatalist holds that some events in the future cannot be avoided no matter what we do. For instance, if you are a fatalist and you go to a fortune teller who predicts that you will become the emperor of China in the year 2050, then if you believe that the fortune teller speaks the truth, you will also believe that it is your fate to be the emperor of China. If this is your fate then it does not matter what you do, You cannot avoid it. You might decide to leave China and start living in the U.S. but eventually fate will catch up with you and you will become emperor. Most fatalists are not determinists, but it is possible to combine fatalism and determinism.

To assess the plausibility of this claim of hard determinists, we need to take a closer look at the idea of causality. What exactly happens when a particular event causes another event? Consider a set of domino pieces lined up in a row.

Now consider what will happen if at time t_1 the first domino piece is knocked over.

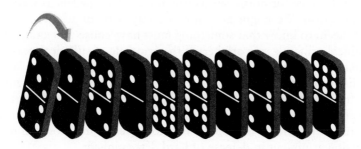

You do not have to be a physicist to predict what will happen. If the first domino falls at time t_1, at some later time t_n the last domino will fall as well. The reason for this is obvious: The fall of the first domino *causes* the second domino to fall; the fall of the second will *cause* the third to fall; and so on until the last one is knocked over. This is a good example of how causality works. It is a relationship between events; one event (called the cause) triggers a second event (called the effect), which in turn causes a new effect, and so on. It is interesting to notice two things:

1. The cause of an event happens prior to the effect.
2. Once the cause has happened, the effect has to happen as well (i.e., causes are sufficient conditions for bringing about their effects).

These two conditions explain how the past can shape the future. If the past contains the causes for a specific event E, then it is causally determined that E has to happen as well.

This insight by itself is not yet sufficient to establish determinism. We can admit that some events (e.g., the falling of the last domino) are bound to happen because they are caused by prior events (the falling of the first domino) without yet losing our sense of freedom. Who is to say that our actions are caused by prior events in the same manner as the falling of the last domino is caused by prior events? Can we be sure that all events (including our actions) are caused by past events?

Unfortunately, there are excellent reasons for thinking that all events (including our actions) have causes. Consider the following example: Suppose you are sleeping for the first time at your friend's house. Late at night you hear a strange noise; it sounds as if someone is scratching with fingernails at the door of your room. You are so frightened that you pull the blanket over your head and pray that you survive the night. In the morning you describe your experience to your friend, who answers, "Oh, this is a very old house. It is full of strange noises. But do not worry; nothing causes these noises. The noises simply happen." You would certainly not accept that as an answer. If there are noises, there must be a cause for the noises. Noises do not just happen out of the blue.

But what is true for noises seems true for all other events as well. Consider an airplane crash. We might not know exactly why an airplane has crashed, but we do seem to know that something must have caused the crash. The basic philosophical principle at work here is the **principle of sufficient reason**, which claims that anything that happens does so for a definite reason. We seem to follow this principle in all aspects of life. Think about rainstorms, earthquakes, anger tantrums, or asthma attacks. Wherever and whenever anything happens, it is caused by something. But if we accept the principle of sufficient reason, free will could be in trouble. For now, we are in a position to advance the following argument in defense of hard determinism:

```
1.All events have causes.
2.All our actions are events.
3.All caused events are determined by the past.
```
Therefore:
```
4.All our actions are determined by the past.
5.If all our actions are determined by the past,
  then we have no power to act other than we do
  indeed act.
6.If we have no power to act other than we in fact
  do act, then we have no free will.
```
Therefore:
```
7.We have no free will.
```

This argument for hard determinism has some force. The first part of the argument (premises 1, 2, and 3) is very plausible and is supported by the principle of sufficient reason, as well as by our analysis of causality. The first three premises together logically entail premise 4. Premises 5 and 6 are more problematic and can, as we will see later on, be challenged. However, most people who hear this argument for the first time do not object to any of the premises; they simply reject the conclusion! The reason can be seen in our day-to-day lives; we hold each other responsible for our actions. Suppose that I have promised to pick you up from the airport late at night. But I fail to show up, and you have to take a $60 cab ride. You are mad at me, and the next day when I call, you end our relationship. It is clear that you think I could have acted otherwise. However, if hard determinism is true and if I have no free will, then I was determined by my past to miss our appointment at the airport. In other words, there is nothing I could have done differently, so I deserve neither praise nor blame for my failure to be at the airport. But we do blame each other and find fault with our actions, and we also praise each other if we do something well or cease to engage in destructive habits like smoking or drinking. Given that we do hold each other responsible for our actions, we are in a position to advance a powerful argument against hard determinism.

```
1.If hard determinism is true, then we have no free
  will.
2.If we have no free will, then we are not respon-
  sible for our actions.
3.We are responsible for our actions.
```
Therefore: Hard determinism is false.

This argument, too, is very persuasive. The logical structure of the argument is a combination of the argument form *hypothetical syllogism* and *modus tollens* and is therefore valid. Premise 1 follows directly from the definition of hard determinism, and premises 2 and 3 are, as we have seen, intuitively plausible. We are now in a difficult situation: We have found two plausible arguments, one for hard determinism and one against it.

Food for Thought

The argument in defense of free will is based on the claim that we are responsible for our actions. Are we, however, always responsible for what we do? Take a look at the following situations, and decide whether the people in these situations are responsible for what they do.

1. A very drunk person decides that he can still drive his car home.
2. An illiterate person signs a loan with a 300% interest rate.
3. A ten-year-old child whose parents are professional thieves takes $5 from her parents without permission.
4. A student who has been told by everybody that he is bad at math fails another math exam.
5. A person who had a very serious and painful back injury is told to take strong pain medication. She takes the medication and becomes addicted to painkillers.
6. A fifteen-year-old girl who has been told all her life by her family that she is too fat becomes anorexic.
7. A fifteen-year-old boy who grows up in a violent slum neighborhood drops out of high school and starts selling drugs.
8. A person who is chronically depressed and who has no health insurance to cover medical treatment commits suicide.

Continued

Continued

9. A forty-year-old man takes his first Viagra pill, which has a very strong effect. He subsequently decides to spend $1,000 on a sex hotline.
10. A nine-year-old girl kills an eleven-year-old girl with a steak knife because the eleven-year-old had taken a ball away from the nine-year-old.

A majority of philosophers are defenders of free will and personal responsibility and are convinced that the argument against hard determinism is basically correct. However, if we want to follow their lead, we need to identify the reason that the initial argument in defense of hard determinism is mistaken. We cannot reject the argument simply because we do not like the conclusion. As we will see, various alternative theories of free will emerge as a result of denying one or more of the premises of the argument for hard determinism.

Food for Thought

Most people reject hard determinism because they believe that we humans are morally responsible for what we do. The British philosopher Galen Strawson has challenged the idea that we have full responsibility for what we do. Strawson presents the so-called basic argument: (1) We do what we do because of our character, and (2) we are not truly responsible for developing our character. Therefore: We are not fully responsible for what we do. Strawson points out that our character is formed by factors like education, parents, genes, historical events over which we cannot be said to have any control. Do you agree with Strawson that we are not fully responsible for the development of our own character, or do you think that we make ourselves into what we are?

Can Indeterminism Save Free Will?

Determinism is very attractive as long as we accept the principle of sufficient reason. But do we have to accept this principle? Is it really true that all events are caused? Is it possible that some events simply happen without being caused by the past? If we follow this line of thought, we start to embrace **indeterminism**, which holds that the future is not fixed by the past. Indeterminists challenge the idea that all events are causally necessitated by events in the past and consider the possibility that the same past can lead to different future states. Indeterminism weakens the link between the past and the future and thereby tries to create space for free will.

Indeterminism is supported by recent advances in physics. We know that small particles like neutrinos or quarks behave differently from medium-sized physical objects like chairs and tables. A table, for instance, has at each moment in time a certain set of determinate properties. It either stands in the middle of the room, or it does not. It would be silly to think that the table exists in two different positions at the same time. But the same is not true for small particles like electrons. Although these small particles obey a fixed set of rules, the world of small particles is not a deterministic world. We cannot say that a small particle is at each given moment in a clearly determinate state. All we can say is that if we measure the particle, there is a certain probability that we will find the particle in a certain position with certain properties. Take the example of an electron in a magnetic field. The electron's spin may be either aligned with the field, which is known as a spin-up state, or opposite to the field, which is known as a spin-down state. Prior to any measurements, the electron is in a so-called superposition, meaning that it is simultaneously in a spin-up and a spin-down position. Electrons and other small particles are therefore not like chairs and tables. They do not possess at each given moment a set of clearly determined properties. Thus, small particles do not live in a fully determined world.

We can take this indeterminism and apply it to what happens in our brains when we make a decision.[2] When we deliberate whether to go to a party or not, something like the following might be happening in our brains: Suppose a particular small particle is in a superposition of spin-up and spin-down. As we decide whether to go to the party, we conduct in our brains what amounts to a measurement of the particle. If we find it in a spin-up position, we will go to the party; if we find the particle in spin-down position, we will stay at home. Whether we will find the particle in one or the other position is not causally determined by prior events. Both outcomes are physically possible and can happen. In this way, indeterminism liberates us from the curse of a decision determined by past events. If our decisions are ultimately dependent on inde-terministic physical processes, we do not have to be afraid that our future is fixed and predictable on the basis of our past.

Although indeterminism can explain why the past has no power over our decisions, it runs into other serious difficulties. The contemporary philosopher Richard Taylor describes why indeterminism is as hostile to personal responsi-bility as determinism is:

> Suppose that my arm is free, according to [indeterminism]; that is that its motions are uncaused. It moves this way and that from time to time, but noth-ing causes these motions. Sometimes it moves forth vigorously, sometimes up, sometimes down, sometimes it just drifts vaguely about—these motions all being wholly free and uncaused. Manifestly I have nothing to do with them at all; they just happen, and neither I nor anyone can ever tell what this arm will be doing next. It might seize a club and lay it on the head of the nearest bystander, no less to my astonishment than his. There will never be any point in

asking why these motions occur, or in seeking any explanation of them, for under the conditions assumed there is no explanation. They just happen, from no causes at all.[3]

What Taylor shows nicely is that according to indeterminism, my actions become random events, and nobody should be held responsible for something that happens randomly.

In order to illustrate this further, consider the following example: Suppose Beth and John have been dating for several years. Beth is eager to get married, but John is undecided about whether they should tie the knot. In order to pacify Beth, John comes up with this idea: Each morning he will throw a coin twenty times, and if the coin comes up heads twenty times in a row, he'll marry Beth. Years go by and every morning John throws the coin, but heads never comes up every time. Then one day, after six years, the unlikely event finally happens—John throws heads twenty times in a row, and he marries Beth. Was John's decision to get married a genuinely free and responsible choice? It seems not; John did not have any control over when or whether he would marry Beth. It seems as if the decision wasn't his decision at all. In order to be genuinely free, we must have control over our actions. The only way we can perform responsible actions is by acting on good reasons. Indeterminism cannot explain how our actions and decisions can ever be under our control because it turns them into unpredictable and uncontrollable events.

Food for Thought

Some people try to act randomly. Take the example of Claude, who is well known for his erratic behavior. One day you see Claude at a party, where he is drinking heavily. You ask him why he drinks the tenth shot in a row, and he responds, "I have no idea, man. I simply do things. I never ask why." Everybody around Claude laughs at this answer. They say, "That is a typical Claude answer. He does crazy stuff for no reason at all." Do you think that Claude has genuine free will?

Compatibilism

Our discussion so far seems to lead to an intellectual dilemma: No matter whether we think that the future is fixed by the past (as in determinism) or whether we think that the future is not fixed by the past (as in indeterminism), free will seems to be in trouble. Determinism seems to lead to hard determinism, but indeterminism makes it impossible to explain how we can perform free and responsible actions. In order to escape from this dilemma, we need to rethink our preliminary discussions. Perhaps the hard determinists were too quick to conclude that determinism undermines free will. Let us rethink the relationship between determinism and free will and explore whether a future that is fixed by the past can make room for free will.

The philosophical position that claims that a determined future is compatible with free will is called **compatibilism**. The philosophers Thomas Hobbes (1588–1679), John Locke (1632–1704), and David Hume (1711–1776) defended early versions of compatibilism. Before we get into the details, let's look at two similar situations: First, suppose that you are walking down the street late at night and that a menacing-looking guy comes up to you and yells, "Your money or your life!" Feeling intimidated and scared, you decide to hand over your money. The second situation is different. You are again walking down the same street late at night, but this time a skinny, forlorn-looking teenager asks you whether you can help him to stay alive. Overcome by pity, you give the teenager all the money you have.

In both situations your decision to hand over your money was caused. In the first case it was caused by the threat of the menacing-looking guy; in the second case it was caused by your feeling of empathy for the teenager. A compatibilist maintains that our freedom and responsibility are not threatened by the fact that our actions are causally determined to take place. Our actions can still be free as long as they are causally determined in the right way. What's important for compatibilists is that there are no constraints that prevent people from doing what they want to do. In the first situation you wanted to keep your money, but you weren't able to. Instead, you were forced to perform an action you had no desire to do. This is not a free choice. On the other hand, you freely gave away your money in the second situation, based on your own free will. The basic tenet of compatibilism is that we are free as long as we do not encounter forces that prevent us from doing what we want to do. It doesn't matter that our actions are determined by the past.

An intuitive way to explain this feature of compatibilism is to imagine that God exists and that God knows your future. God, for example, knows that you will eat fried chicken tonight. So when dinner time comes along and you think about your dinner options, could your decision to eat fried chicken be free? A compatibilist would say yes. If you want to eat fried chicken and if you are not forced to eat it, your decision to eat fried chicken is free. It doesn't matter whether God knows about this beforehand. What matters is that you were able to act on your desires and that no constraints prevented you from doing so.

At this point you might be tempted to raise an objection: How can my decision to eat fried chicken be free if I could not have eaten sushi instead? The compatibilist responds that "could have done otherwise" should be understood hypothetically; to say that I could have eaten sushi simply means that if I had had the desire to eat sushi, I could have acted on that desire. As a matter of fact, I did *not* have a desire to eat sushi, but hypothetically I could have acted on that desire *if* it had been present. The compatibilist claims that this ability to act on different hypothetically possible desires is all that is required for freedom. It is important to realize that compatibilism introduces a new way of understanding freedom, which does not require that the future is open. All that is required for freedom is that we find no constraints on doing what we want to do. To help clarify this idea, we are going to take a look at two versions of compatibilism: traditional compatibilism and deep self-compatibilism.

Traditional Compatibilism

Traditional compatibilists suggest two conditions for freedom. An action is free if

1. The action is caused by the will of the agent.
2. The action is performed without constraints.

Both conditions are intuitively plausible; let's consider them in turn. Only an action caused by the will of the agent is a candidate for being a free action. In other words, an action can be free only if an agent's internal feelings, desires, hopes, beliefs, or wishes led him or her to take the action. Consider the case of a man who shot his neighbor by accident while cleaning his gun. In this case we do not consider the shooting to be an action the man freely performed, and we therefore do not hold the man fully responsible either. On the other hand, if I shoot somebody out of jealousy, or if I hug somebody because I love the person, these actions are truly my actions, and I am responsible for them.

In real life it is rare that we perform actions that are *not* caused by our desires and wishes. However, it does happen that we are sometimes constrained in doing what we want to do. In such situations traditional compatibilism's second condition for freedom comes into play: My actions are free only if they are performed without constraints, which can come in a variety of forms. I might be threatened at gunpoint, as in our earlier example; in this case the constraint comes from the outside. In other cases I might be constrained by a lack of resources. I may want to accept the invitation to attend Harvard, only to find out that I can't afford to go there. Similarly, I might want to play Beethoven but realize that my lack of musical ability prevents that desire from being fulfilled. In order to determine clearly whether we are constrained in a given situation, the traditional compatibilist applies the following criterion: An agent is free (not constrained) if the agent would have been able to act on a different set of desires.

Consider the case of Bernice, who is afraid of spiders. Whenever she encounters a spider, she runs away. Is Bernice's decision to run from spiders a free action? A traditional compatibilist would say that she is free; she is acting on her desire to run away from spiders and would be able to act differently if she had no fear of the hairy creatures. Nobody is holding a gun to her head and forcing Bernice to run away. Overall, traditional compatibilism leaves us with an attractive and plausible theory of freedom: We are free provided that we are acting on our will and are not constrained. The most attractive feature of this theory of free will is that it is fully compatible with the idea that our desires are determined by the past.

Food for Thought

Test your understanding of traditional compatibilism by deciding whether a traditional compatibilist would think that the following are free decisions. Explain your answers.

1. You decide to loan $400 to your roommate after he says, "You are my last hope. If you do not loan me $400, I will have to kill myself."
2. After drinking heavily, you decide to dance naked on the table.
3. After your friend drives you home, you decide to remain in the car with her and listen to her CDs. Afterward you find out that she had locked the doors to her car and would not have opened them unless you first listened to all her CDs.
4. After your best friend commits suicide, you decide to make plans to kill yourself as well.
5. After the college you attend raises tuition by 40 percent, you realize that you cannot afford to pay for it anymore and decide to quit college altogether.
6. You decide to quit your job. As you tell your boss, she tells you (truthfully) that she would have fired you today anyway.
7. While you are sleepwalking, you go to the refrigerator and make yourself a sandwich.

Deep Self-Compatibilism

Although traditional compatibilism offers a commonsensical theory of freedom, it also leads to a number of philosophical difficulties. A traditional compatibilist holds that we act with free will whenever an action is caused by our desires and we were not constrained or forced to perform it. The possibility arises, however, that some of our desires, although they prompt us to act, are not identical with our will. The following example should help to illustrate the issue: Suppose that Henry, a twenty-two-year-old college sophomore, has not yet declared his major, despite the urgings of his advisor and his parents. Henry is torn between majoring in biology and computer science. After careful reflection he realizes that he desires to study computer science only because his father thinks that it is a good degree with a bright future. Henry comes to realize that if he had no family, he would definitely study biology; deep down he has little interest in computers and dislikes writing computer programs. However, suppose that Henry's father is the most important person in Henry's life. Henry wants to please his father and is terribly afraid of letting him down. Eventually, Henry gives in and decides to major in computer science.

Was Henry's decision a free decision? A traditional compatibilist has to answer this question affirmatively: Henry had a desire to please his dad, he acted on this desire, and he was not forced to choose computer science. Neither his dad nor anybody else forced him to make this decision. The traditional compatibilist concludes, therefore, that Henry's decision was free. But did Henry *really* act on his own will? Would it not make more sense to say that Henry acted on the will of his father?

If you share this reaction, you might find deep self-compatibilism an attractive theory of free will. It is a refined version of compatibilism that was first articulated by the contemporary philosopher Harry G. Frankfurt. Deep self-compatibilism is, as the name suggests, also a form of compatibilism and thus subscribes to the idea that actions that are determined by the past can be free, but it differs from traditional compatibilism in holding that our will is genuinely free only if we act on desires that we have chosen and that we identify with. These desires are called authentic desires. For a deep self-compatibilist, free will is the ability to act on authentic desires (i.e., desires we truly want to act on). If we act on desires that are imposed upon us by other sources—parents, peer pressure, advertising—we act on inauthentic desires and do not have free will. According to deep self-compatibilism, free will is dependent on what happens deep inside us; nobody can tell from the outside whether someone is acting on authentic desires.

Food for Thought

Have you ever acted on desires that you did not identify with and that were not truly your own desires? If yes, give a description of some of the situations in which you have acted on inauthentic desires. If not, describe how you can be sure that the desires on which you act are actually your own authentic desires.

Food for Thought

Decide which of the following listed desires you have. Are these desires that you have freely chosen to have? Indicate which desires are most important to you by ranking the desires you have from most important to least important.

1. I want to have lots of money.
2. I want to find true love and live with one person for the rest of my life.

3. Every other week or so I want to get really "high" and have a good time.
4. I want to exercise every day.
5. I want to read the most famous books that have been written.
6. I want to have sex with lots of good-looking people.
7. I want to act such that my parents are proud of me.
8. I want to drive an expensive car.
9. I want to watch television every day.
10. I want to have children.
11. I want to develop my talents.
12. I want to travel to foreign countries and meet exotic people.
13. I want to help people in need.

According to deep self-compatibilism, we are full of conflicting desires, all of which urge us to act. However, as long as we are indifferent about which desires prompt us to action, we are not genuinely free. Genuine freedom emerges once we realize that not all of our desires are compatible with the interests of our deeper selves. We therefore must choose which of our desires ought to be the driving force that shapes our actions and lives. Only individuals who have identified their genuine desires and who manage to act on those authentic desires are genuinely free.

Food for Thought

Deep self-compatibilism argues that our will is free if we act on authentic desires, but it is not easy to identify our authentic desires. In the following excerpt from his essay "Schopenhauer as Educator," the philosopher Friedrich Nietzsche (1844–1900) describes a methodology that might help us to identify our authentic desires. Read through his suggestions, and determine whether you can apply Nietzsche's methodology to your own life. Does this help you to find your authentic desires?

When the great thinker despises human beings, he despises their laziness: for it is on account of their laziness that men seem like manufactured goods, unimportant, and unworthy to be associated with or instructed. Human beings who do not want to belong to the mass need only to stop being comfortable; follow their conscience, which cries out: "Be yourself! All that you are now doing, thinking, and desiring is not really yourself." But how can we find ourselves again? How can man know himself? He is a dark and veiled thing; and if the hare has seven skins, man can shed seventy times seven and still not be able to say: "This is really you, this is no longer slough." In addition, it is a painful and dangerous mission to tunnel into oneself and make a forced descent into the shaft of one's being by the

Continued

Continued

nearest path. Doing so can easily cause damage that no physician can heal. And besides: what need should there be for it, when given all the evidence of our nature, our friendships and enmities, our glance and the clasp of our hand, our memory and that which we forget, our books and our handwriting. This, however, is the means to plan the most important inquiry. Let the youthful soul look back on life with the question: What have you truly loved up to now, what has elevated your soul, what has mastered it and at the same time delighted it? Place these venerated objects before you in a row, and perhaps they will yield for you, through their nature and their sequence, a law, the fundamental law of your true self. Compare these objects, see how one complements, expands, surpasses, transfigures another, how they form a stepladder upon which you have climbed up to yourself as you are now; for your true nature lies, not hidden deep within you, but immeasurably high above you, or at least above that which you normally take to be yourself.[4]

A good way to illustrate the difference between traditional compatibilism and deep self-compatibilism is to consider the case of animals. Do animals have free will? According to traditional compatibilism, a dog that barks at night performs a free action; the action is caused by its desire to bark, and the dog is not forced to bark. But a deep self-compatibilist would disagree with this analysis. Although the barking is indeed caused by the dog's desire to bark, that desire is not something the dog has actually chosen to have. According to deep self-compatibilism, animals should not be considered to have genuine free will, for they lack the ability to choose and identify with their desires. Human beings, on the other hand, have this capacity. Deep self-compatibilism maintains, therefore, that we act freely only if we act on those desires that we have chosen and with which we identify.

Food for Thought

In order to determine whether you find traditional compatibilism more plausible than deep self-compatibilism, it should be helpful to consider the following situations. Determine first whether a traditional compatibilist or a deep self-compatibilist would say that each individual has free will. Decide then whether you agree with one or the other position.

1. Helmut sits in a high-security prison for killing a policeman. Helmut has come to the realization that he is a danger to society and needs to be locked up. He thus decides that he wants to stay in prison and that he would not leave even if the authorities would let him go. Does Helmut have free will?

2. Andrea has a strong desire to undergo plastic surgery. She thinks that her breasts are too small, so she spends her savings on a breast enlargement operation. A year later she breaks up with her boyfriend, and she suddenly realizes that her desire to have larger breasts was caused by her boyfriend; she herself prefers to have smaller breasts. Did Andrea have free will when she decided to undergo her breast operation?

3. Nick decides to go to medical school. His father and his grandfather have both been physicians, and he is expected to be one as well. However, what he really wants to do is play professional baseball. Does Nick have free will?

4. Rose decides to break up with her boyfriend, Chris. Although Rose herself is very happy with Chris, she can enjoy his company only when the two are alone with each other. In the presence of others, Rose feels embarrassed because Chris is greatly overweight. Rose is tired of feeling that embarrassment and decides to end the relationship. Is Rose's decision free?

5. Antonio has a drinking problem. For two years he has been trying to stop drinking alcohol but has not been able to do it. Finally, Antonio undergoes hypnosis. The hypnotist tells Antonio that he can implant in him an unconscious response that will make him vomit whenever he smells or drinks alcohol. The hypnosis works, and Antonio quits drinking. Was Antonio's decision to quit a free choice?

6. Nadia has promised her husband, Chad, who hates traveling more than anything else, that she will stay with him forever. After ten years of marriage, Nadia develops a strong desire to leave Chad and to travel the world. This desire becomes stronger and stronger, but Nadia feels that it would not be proper to act on it. So she suppresses her desires and remains married to Chad for the rest of her life. Was Nadia's decision free?

A Fundamental Problem for Compatibilism

Although traditional compatibilism and deep self-compatibilism differ in important respects, they share the central assumption that our actions can be free even if they are caused and determined. However, this insistence that determinism and freedom are compatible with each other leads to a central objection. Many philosophers have questioned whether our actions can be free if they are indeed determined by the past. For this reason, William James labeled compatibilism a "quagmire of evasion,"[5] and Immanuel Kant classified compatibilism as a "wretched subterfuge."[6] If we take compatibilism seriously, it seems to follow that we are morally responsible for a future that we cannot change. Is this a realistic idea? Many people think not.

In order to understand the objection to compatibilism, it is useful to consider the **consequence argument**, most recently presented by contemporary philosopher Peter van Inwagen (1952–). The consequence argument is an argument for incompatibilism that claims that determinism is not compatible with moral responsibility. This is a fairly sophisticated argument, but a basic formulation of it can provide an initial impression:

```
1.No one has power over the past and the laws of
  nature.
2.Our future actions are the necessary conse-
  quences of the past and the laws of nature.
3.If we have no power over X, then we also have no
  power over the future necessary consequences
  of X.
```
```
Therefore:
4.We have no power over our future actions.
5.In order to be responsible for our future actions,
  we must have power over our future actions.
```
```
Therefore:
6.We are not responsible for our future actions.
```

Premises 1 and 2 are very plausible: We have indeed no power to change the past, and as long as we accept determinism, we also have to accept premise 2. Premise 3, which is sometimes called the transfer of powerlessness principle, requires some explanation.

Consider the example of Jamela, who was born without arms. It is clear that Jamela had no control over this condition. Moreover, the fact that she never learned how to play the piano is a direct consequence of her disability. Given that Jamela had no control over the fact that she was born without arms, and given that her inability to learn piano was a necessary consequence of her having been born without arms, it seems to follow that Jamela also had no control over the fact that she didn't learn how to play the piano. The story about Jamela illustrates why the transfer of powerlessness principle is attractive. If one has no control over a given situation S and if S necessarily leads to P, then it seems to follow that one also has no power over P. If we accept this principle, then premise 3 of the consequence argument has to be accepted as well, and the argument seems to hold. What the consequence argument shows is that compatibilism seems to lead to a dead end. It might be true that determinism permits us to formulate a theory of free will, but a compatibilist account of free will cannot make room for moral responsibility. This may lead people to ask, "What good is free will if it does not entail moral responsibility?" And this is the main reason that people have rejected a compatibilist conception of freedom.

Food for Thought

Daniel Dennett, a staunch defender of a compatibilist account of free will, urges us to consider the case of Martin Luther, the founder of the Reformation. Although it is historically suspect, Luther has been reported as saying at the diet of Worms in 1521: "Here I stand, I can do no other. God help me. Amen." With these words Luther rejected the request to recant his theological writings in public. Dennett thinks that the case of Luther provides a good defense of compatibilism. If we take Luther's words seriously, he seems to have, in this situation, no power to act in any other way than he does act. However, according to Dennett, this does not mean that Luther is not responsible for what he did. The consequence argument is therefore mistaken: Moral responsibility is fully compatible with a future that is not open. What do you think? Is Dennett justified in claiming that the case of Luther supports a compatibilist account of freedom?

Many philosophers think that it is a necessary condition for freedom and responsibility to have the power to act other than we in fact have acted. This principle is often called the principle of alternative possibilities (PAP). If we agree that PAP is necessary for moral responsibility, then we embrace the philosophical position of **incompatibilism,** which holds that a world in which the future is fixed by the past is incompatible with freedom. If we accept incompatibilism, we either have to give up on free will, as the hard determinists do, or else we need to explain how an indeterminist world can lead to freedom and responsibility. In our initial discussion of indeterminism, we encountered difficulties in explaining how one could have control over undetermined events. Let us explore whether a more refined discussion of indeterminism can solve this problem.

Libertarianism

The Case for Libertarianism

We have seen in our initial discussion of indeterminism that it leads to a fundamental problem—if we think that our actions happen by chance, it seems difficult to explain how we can control them. Here libertarianism comes into play. **Libertarianism** is a branch of indeterminism that holds the future is open and that we have the power to shape it. If we imagine two agents with the exact same past, libertarians believe that the two agents nevertheless can make different decisions in the present. In addition, libertarians try to avoid the standard problem of indeterminism by developing additional ideas about how we can have control over undetermined actions.

Since there are different explanations, there are consequently different versions of libertarianism. We will focus exclusively on an agent causation account of libertarianism since this version is most accessible. According to libertarianism, there is something special about human beings that makes them different from rocks, trees, or planets. If we translate the libertarian position into religious language, we might say that humans are made to have free will. But what exactly is this extra element that gives humans a status different from that of everything else in the physical universe? The libertarian points to a special form of causal power.

In order to understand this more clearly, we need to distinguish between event causation and agent causation. Think back to our discussion of hard determinism and the domino effect; the action of dominoes falling in succession is a classic example of event causation. **Event causation** is the process of one event causing another: The first falling domino (the first event) causes the second domino to fall (the second event), which causes the third domino to fall (the third event), and so on. What is true for dominoes is also true for other physical events; all physical events are necessitated by other physical events. Physical events are, therefore, determined to take place. However, when it comes to humans (or agents), libertarians see things differently. When an agent acts, the action does not have to be the result of prior events. This means that when you act, there is the possibility that your action is not determined by your past. In fact, agents have the power to cause something without being subject to causal determination; this is known as **agent causation**. It means that an agent can act without prior events necessitating the agent's action—the agent can act spontaneously to cause something to happen.

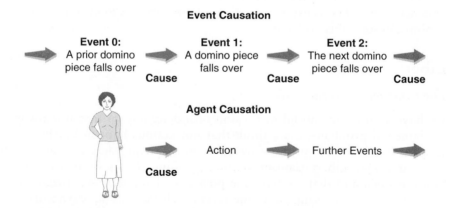

Libertarianism distinguishes between two forms of causation. Agent causation, in contrast to event causation, originates in agents and cannot be traced back in time.

One way to make agent causation clear is to think about a godlike being prior to the creation of the physical universe. Suppose that this being—let us call it Fred the World Maker—decides to create the physical universe. Two things are clear in this situation: First, the creation of the physical universe is caused by Fred's action. Second, Fred's action is not causally determined to take place by prior physical events. There is, after all, no physical universe prior to this action. The deed of Fred the World Maker is therefore a self-caused action that originates completely from within Fred. According to libertarianism, all of us are a bit like Fred when it comes to performing actions. Although we are the cause of our actions, we are not causally determined by prior events to perform the action. We therefore have genuine free will. American philosopher Roderick Chisholm (1916–1999) wrote in this context:

> If we are responsible . . . [and if libertarianism is true] then we have a prerogative which some would attribute only to God: each of us, when we act, is a prime mover unmoved. In doing what we do, we cause certain events to happen, and nothing—or no one—causes us to cause those events to happen.[7]

Problems for Libertarianism

If libertarianism is true, we all have the power to act contrary to the influences of our past, our families, and our genetic heritage. What we do is strictly up to us, since we—as substances—are the causal originators of our actions. The question arises, however, whether this might not lead to a distorted view of moral responsibility. According to libertarianism, insofar as we act as agents, we are—as a matter of metaphysical necessity—fully responsible for what we do. But this might be difficult to reconcile with how we assign moral responsibility in day-to-day life. In ordinary circumstances we frequently attribute limited responsibility to agents. Such attribution requires that events play a role in bringing about our actions, and this runs counter to the strict distinction between event and agent causation that is advocated by libertarianism.

In order to illustrate this point, let's consider the example of Alexa, who suffers from depression. On many days she lies in bed and finds no energy or motivation to get up. Sometimes she spends the entire day in bed sleeping, much to the chagrin of her mother, who is a staunch libertarian. She firmly believes that Alexa has free will and that no matter how her brain might affect her, she has the power to decide to get up. She likes to say to her, "Come on, Alexa, my free agent, make use of your free will and get yourself out of bed." Doesn't it seem as if Alexa's mother is misunderstanding the position Alexa is in? And isn't it clear that events in Alexa's brain are causing her not to be able to get out of bed? Libertarians are bound to deny this idea. Anything that happens in Alexa's brain is just an event, and according to libertarianism, event causation cannot undermine the freedom to choose. But in this case, as in many others, the libertarian view seems unscientific and dogmatic because medical research suggests that biochemical events in our brains can make it impossible to perform certain acts. In order to respond to this difficulty, the libertarian would need a clear account of how and when events can undermine freedom, but any such account might also undermine the necessary clear distinction between event and agent causation.

A second group of objections charges libertarianism with introducing too much metaphysical baggage. We have seen that philosophers tend to be careful when it comes to introducing new fundamental entities into our worldview. If it is possible to explain the world without referring to ghosts, vampires, witches, or black magic, the principle of Ockham's razor suggests that we should do so. Simplicity is an intellectual virtue. Libertarianism, however, is quite a loaded philosophical theory: It introduces two fundamentally new entities into our understanding of the world—agents and agent causation. The question is whether it might not be better to avoid commitment to these entities.

Third, libertarians believe that something very special happens when agents cause actions. Agents can cause actions to take place without there being prior causes that prompt the agents to perform the actions. But if there are no prior causes, how can there be any explanation of why the agents did what they did? The philosopher Harry Frankfurt, for instance, observed that according to a libertarian account of freedom, any free action has the status of a miracle since it interrupts the natural order of causes.[8] But to give free actions that status is basically equivalent to admitting that there are no explanations of how free actions are possible. Miracles are, after all, events that do not fit within our standard explanatory frameworks. Free will turns, therefore, into something mysterious and inexplicable—not a very satisfactory result.

Food for Thought

In Asian intellectual traditions, the free will debate takes a very different form than people are used to reading about in the Western philosophical tradition. Many strands in Buddhism, for example, reject as naïve the idea that human beings have absolute freedom. According to Buddhism, we have to acknowledge that we are creatures with a particular past and with particular needs and desires. These and other factors clearly influence how we act. Many Buddhists also acknowledge that past lives can influence our behavior as well. However, Buddhists do not conclude from this that our lives are predetermined; we have the freedom to develop compassion and to achieve higher forms of being. Buddhism, therefore, cannot be characterized as a form of determinism nor as a form of libertarianism or compatibilism. Buddhism and other strands of Eastern thought go beyond the conceptual framework found in the traditional Western debate.

Final Remarks on the Problem of Free Will

Among all philosophical problems, the problem of free will is perhaps furthest from any comprehensive solution. Peter van Inwagen (1952–) has written: "I conclude that there is no position that one can take on the matter of free will that does not confront its adherents with mystery."[9] Although there are good arguments in defense of compatibilism or incompatibilism, each specific account of free will seems to run into serious difficulties. This situation raises an interesting question: Why should we discuss free will if we cannot settle the question once and for all? I think there are several benefits that come from discussing free will even if the discussion remains inconclusive. First, by being aware that all positions about free will face serious challenges, we become more tolerant towards other positions that differ from our own assessment. Second, our discussion of free will has revealed that there are different respectable ways to think about freedom. Freedom is often said to be the central value of our country, but it is rare that people realize how many different ways there are to think about freedom. Because of this, I think it's useful to summarize the various conceptions of freedom that are contained within the various theories.

One way to think about freedom is to think that people are free if they have the power to do what they want to do without any constraints. We might call this view freedom of action, which is supported by the traditional compatibilist account of freedom. An alternative way to think about freedom is to say that individuals are free if they are able to act on the desires they have determined to be their authentic desires. Let us call this perspective freedom as self-control. Finally, there is freedom as the power to be fully and ultimately responsible for all our actions, a view most closely associated with libertarianism.

Our discussion shows that our own selves present one of the most mysterious and puzzling elements in the universe. Are we free agents with special causal powers? Or are we natural entities that are fully integrated within the causal network of the physical world? Both positions are plausible, but only one can be true. This is mysterious. Although we encounter our selves every day, the nature of our own selves stands in need of clarification. Thinking about the problem of free will has alerted us to the need to look at our own being more closely than we normally do in our day-to-day life. If we avoid this reflection, we run the risk, as the poet Rainer Maria Rilke observed, of treating our lives like an envelope that we never open. Let us try to open this envelope and continue our exploration of the self in the next chapter.

Study and Reflection Questions

1. Imagine a situation in which you perform an action for which you are not fully responsible. Describe the situation, and then decide which theory of free will is best supported by this scenario.

2. Are we fully responsible for everything we do in our lives? Think about this question in light of the various theories of free will discussed in this chapter. How do these theories answer this question? What answer is most compatible with your own thinking about free will and moral responsibility?

3. If deep self-compatibilism is right, then we need to distinguish between authentic and inauthentic desires. Is there a clear method available through which we can identify whether a desire is authentic? If yes, please describe the method. If no, does this undermine the plausibility of deep self-compatibilism?

4. The French philosopher Jean Paul Sartre once wrote that we humans "are condemned to be free." Could Sartre be right that freedom might be a burden and a punishment rather than a gift? What do you think? Has freedom ever been a burden in your life?

5. The contemporary British philosopher Ted Honderich has argued that our lives become better if we admit that we are not the ultimate originators of our successes and failures in life. He thinks that even if our character and actions are not within our control, we cannot know how things will turn out for us, and so we must go on trying to do the best we can. If Honderich is right, hard determinism gives no reason for despair; life can still be good even if we admit that we are not in control and have no free will. To what degree do you agree with Honderich's thinking about the effects of hard determinism?

For Further Reading

Fischer, John Martin. *The Metaphysics of Free Will*. Cambridge, MA: Blackwell, 1994.

———. *My Way: Essays on Moral Responsibility*. Oxford: Oxford University Press, 2007.

Honderich, Ted. *How Free Are You? The Determinism Problem*. New York: Oxford University Press, 2003.

Kane, Robert. *A Contemporary Introduction to Free Will*. New York: Oxford University Press, 2005.

———. *The Oxford Handbook of Free Will*. New York: Oxford University Press, 2002.

Pereboom, Derek, ed. *Free Will*. Indianapolis, IN: Hackett, 1997.

Taylor, Richard. *Metaphysics*. Englewood Cliffs, NJ: Prentice Hall, 1992.

Van Inwagen, Peter. *An Essay on Free Will*. Oxford: Clarendon Press, 1983.

Endnotes

1. Arthur Schopenhauer, *On the Freedom of the Will* (Oxford: Blackwell, 1985), p. 47.
2. It should be pointed out that this description of how quantum phenomena could make mental decisions indeterministic is probably only a conceptual possibility and not a real physical possibility. Although quantum indeterminacy is significant for

elementary particles, its indeterministic effects are probably not significant for larger physical systems such as the human brain.

3. Richard Taylor, *Metaphysics* (Englewood Cliff, NJ: Prentice Hall, 1974), pp. 51–52.
4. Friedrich Nietzsche, *Untimely Meditations*, trans. R. J. Hollingdale (Cambridge: Cambridge University Press, 1983), p. 73.
5. William James, *The Will to Believe: And Other Essays in Popular Philosophy* (Cambridge, MA: Harvard University Press, 1979), p. 149.
6. Immanuel Kant, *The Critique of Practical Reason*, trans. Lewis White Beck (New York: Macmillan, 1985), p. 76.
7. Roderick Chisholm, "Human Freedom and the Self," in *Free Will*, ed. Derk Pereboom (Indianapolis, IN: Hackett, 1997), pp. 143–155.
8. Harry Frankfurt, "Freedom of the Will and the Concept of a Person," in *Free Will*, ed. Derk Pereboom (Indianapolis, IN: Hackett, 1997), pp. 167–183.
9. Peter van Inwagen, *Metaphysics* (Boulder, CO: Westview Press, 1993), p. 197.

CHAPTER FIVE

THE PROBLEM OF PERSONAL IDENTITY

What Is the Problem?

Our discussion of free will has made us aware that it is far from clear what kind of beings we truly are. Are we simply advanced animals, complicated

Cassius Marcellus Clay converted to Islam and adopted the name Muhammad Ali. Does this mean that one person was annihilated and a new person born?

machines, or godlike agents who shape the future? In this chapter we will continue our exploration of the nature of the self by turning our attention to the problem of personal identity. In day-to-day conversation we sometimes say that someone is not "the same" anymore. For example, we can imagine a married woman who files for divorce because she thinks that her husband is no longer the same person she married ten years ago. In religious contexts people are said to be "reborn." The boxer Cassius Clay changed his name to Muhammad Ali when he converted to Islam. Middle-aged individuals sometimes report that none of their accomplishments have any meaning for the persons they have become. What are we to think about these transformations? Is it possible that we change who we are or that we lose our sense of self?

We do change constantly. As time goes by, we grow from being a baby into an adult, and we subsequently turn into an older person. Not only do our bodies change, but our ideas, desires, and values undergo even more radical transformations. This permanent change leads to obvious questions: Do we always remain one and the same person, no matter how much we change? What kind of change can bring our existence to an end? Is our physical death necessarily the end of us? What happens to our self if we have Alzheimer's and we lose our memories? Are we still around, or have we gone out of existence with the last passing memory? These questions lead us to a central philosophical problem—the problem of personal identity.

The problem of personal identity is not a single problem but rather a set of loosely connected questions that need to be distinguished from one another. One question in this set concerns the values that are most important to us. Consider the case of Marcel, who during his twenties was interested only in making money. However, later in life, Marcel changed his life radically. He lost all interest in making money and now spends all his time helping disabled children. In this case it makes sense to ask whether Marcel is still the same person. If we answer no, we mean that Marcel's values have radically changed; he now cares about different kinds of things than he used to. But we do not mean that the young Marcel has ceased to exist; Marcel the person has changed, but Marcel the person did not go out of existence.

A different type of question about personal identity focuses on how unified our selves really are. Are we each one singular being, or is it possible that there is more than one person in me? Taking this question seriously does not have to mean that we have a personality disorder; even in normal circumstances it might be possible to detect different distinct elements in us that cannot be unified within one coherent personality. A third question about personal identity relates to persistence through time. What accounts for the fact that I—the person who exists right now—am identical to a person in the past or in the future? The main questions surrounding the problem of personal identity are illustrated in the following graphic.

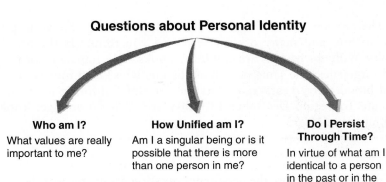

Questions about Personal Identity

Who am I?
What values are really important to me?

How Unified am I?
Am I a singular being or is it possible that there is more than one person in me?

Do I Persist Through Time?
In virtue of what am I identical to a person in the past or in the future?

In our discussion of personal identity, we will focus on the persistence question: What is required for the same person to persist from one time to another? Questions about persistence have attracted the most fruitful philosophical discussions in recent times. Moreover, the question about persistence is closely intertwined with our thoughts about death. What we think about death is shaped by our response to the persistence question, and clarifying our thoughts about death is an important element in any introduction to philosophy. Given that the problem of personal identity is broad and involves several different questions, our exploration of the persistence question cannot possibly answer everything we want to know about personal identity. However, our discussion will provide us with a good introduction to the philosophical puzzles that surround personal identity.

Food for Thought

Stanley "Tookie" Williams grew up in a tough neighborhood in Los Angeles. In 1971, together with his friend Raymond Lee, he founded a gang that became known as the Crips. Tookie was a ferocious street fighter and a ruthless gang leader. In 1981 he was convicted of killing four people in cold blood and was placed on death row. However, while on death row, Tookie underwent a transformation. He wrote several books for elementary-school-aged children in the series *Tookie Speaks Out Against Gang Violence*. He also wrote the following:

> So today I apologize to you all—the children of America and South Africa—who must cope every day with dangerous street gangs. I no longer participate in the so-called gangster lifestyle, and I deeply regret that I ever did. . . . My goal is to reach as many young minds as possible to warn you about the perils of a gang lifestyle. I am no longer part of the problem. Thanks to the Almighty, I am no longer sleepwalking through life. I pray that one day my apology will be accepted.

The rap star Snoop Dogg has said that Tookie became an inspiration to him and many others. What do you think? Is the Stanley Tookie Williams who writes children's books and campaigns for peace and forgiveness the same person as the one who killed four people in cold blood thirty years ago? Was the state of California justified to execute Tookie on December 13, 2005, for crimes a younger Tookie committed in 1979?

As we begin to explore the persistence question, let us consider the pictures shown here:

Do we persist through time even if undergo radical changes?

The pictures seem to represent different stages in the life of one person, but can we be sure that we are dealing with just one person here? How can we eliminate the possibility that these pictures show us different persons? The persistence question asks under what circumstances a person who exists at one time (e.g., the African American-looking child that sang with the Jackson 5) is identical to a person who exists at another time (e.g., the Caucasian-looking adult who underwent extreme facial surgery). Can we specify what kind of changes a person can survive while remaining one numerical person? An alternative approach to the persistence question is to look at the beginning of life. When exactly did the person who I am right now begin to exist? Did I come into being when I was born, or did I start to exist when I started to develop higher cognitive abilities as a toddler? Perhaps I started to exist at the time of conception? Different theories answer these questions in different ways.

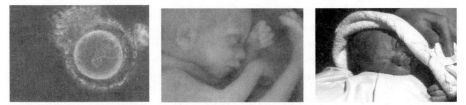

When did we start to exist—as a fertilized egg? a fetus? a baby?

However, before we explore the various responses to the persistence question, we need to draw an important philosophical distinction. The use of the word *same* is ambiguous. When we speak of identical twins, we often say that they are the *same*, meaning that they look alike and exhibit no visual differences. In similar fashion we might say that my neighbor has the *same* car that I have, meaning that my neighbor and I own two versions of the same type of vehicle. When we use the word *same* in this way, we refer to **qualitative identity**; two things are qualitatively identical if they look the same, i.e., if they have the same properties.

At times we use the word *same* with a different meaning. For instance, when I say that the kid across the street was seen riding the *same* bicycle that was stolen from my garage last week, I mean the *very same* bicycle that was stolen from my garage. This sense of the word *same* is called **numerical identity.** Something is numerically identical with something else only if both are one and the same thing. For example, the person who wrote *The Critique of Pure Reason* is numerically identical to the person who wrote *The Critique of Practical Reason*; one and the same man, Immanuel Kant, wrote both books.

Food for Thought

Practice your sensitivity toward the ambiguity in the word *same* by determining whether the word is used in the following sentences to refer to qualitative identity or numerical identity.

1. Jane is the same age as Roberto.
2. Anakin Skywalker is the same as Darth Vader.
3. The Evening Star and the Morning Star are the same.
4. The person who was secretary of defense in 1990 is the same man who was vice president in 2005.
5. I think this is the same policeman who pulled over my sister yesterday.
6. Why do I always get the same grade in all my classes?
7. You have the same haircut as Christina Aguilera.
8. Peter is not the same any more.

The persistence question deals exclusively with numerical identity. When we wonder whether we persist through time, we are not interested in knowing whether we look the same at different times. We want to know instead whether we are numerically the same throughout different life stages. Suppose, for instance, that you have an accident and lose consciousness permanently but your body is still alive. Are you still around, or have you gone out of existence? Questions like these we will address when we explore the persistence question of personal identity.

Food for Thought

To clarify your initial reactions to the problem of personal identity, answer the following questions with True or False:

1. If, after a serious accident, a person suffers from complete amnesia, he has lost his sense of self and effectively starts a new life.
2. Even if we can't remember doing something, we are still responsible for what we have done.
3. If someone undergoes a successful sex-change operation, he or she does not remain the same person.

4. It is logically possible to survive one's death and continue life in a new spiritual body in heaven.
5. We change from moment to moment and become a new person every day.
6. It is logically possible that conversion to a new religion turns someone into a new person.
7. If a person has a severe case of Alzheimer's disease, she is not the same person as she used to be.
8. What really makes someone a person is not the body but rather the soul.
9. If, after a serious car accident that destroyed my body, a surgeon transplanted my brain (and hence my consciousness) into a new body, I would have survived the accident although my body would not have.

The following chart should provide a useful introduction to the various responses that have been developed to the persistence question.

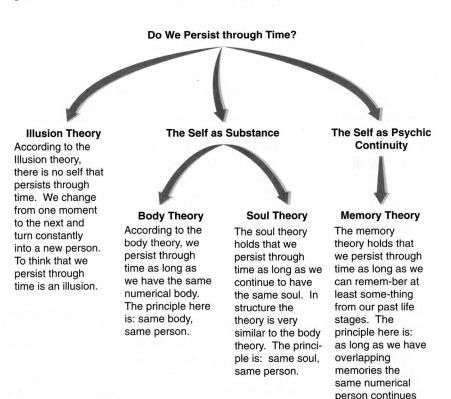

Do We Persist through Time?

Illusion Theory
According to the Illusion theory, there is no self that persists through time. We change from one moment to the next and turn constantly into a new person. To think that we persist through time is an illusion.

The Self as Substance

The Self as Psychic Continuity

Body Theory
According to the body theory, we persist through time as long as we have the same numerical body. The principle here is: same body, same person.

Soul Theory
The soul theory holds that we persist through time as long as we continue to have the same soul. In structure the theory is very similar to the body theory. The principle is: same soul, same person.

Memory Theory
The memory theory holds that we persist through time as long as we can remem-ber at least some-thing from our past life stages. The principle here is: as long as we have overlapping memories the same numerical person continues to exist.

The Illusion Theory

The Case for the Illusion Theory

The illusion theory of personal identity takes its starting point from the observation that we all undergo continuous qualitative change. From minute to minute, our bodies are constantly gaining and losing physical material. According to recent biological studies, a human organism changes its entire physical makeup every seven years, which means that seven years from now, all of the current molecules and atoms in your body will have been replaced by new ones. We have already seen that many thinkers want to insist that there is something permanent behind this process, but why do we have to make this assumption? If we are good empiricists and trust our senses, we can observe only change, but not a permanent self. Thus, the empirical evidence points to the possibility that there is no permanent and unchanging self. If we adopt this position, we embrace the illusion theory of personal identity, which claims that a permanent self is merely an illusion.

Food for Thought

The philosopher David Hume was the first empiricist to draw attention to the fact that we cannot observe any permanent self. He wrote in his *Treatise on Human Nature*:

> For my part, when I enter most intimately into what I call myself, I always stumble on some particular perception or other, of heat or cold, light or shade, love or hatred, pain or pleasure. I can never catch myself at any time without perception, and can never observe anything but the perception. . . . The mind is a kind of theatre, where several perceptions successively make their appearance; pass, re-pass, glide away, and mingle in an infinite variety of postures and situations. There is properly no simplicity in it at any one time, nor identity in different; whatever natural propensity we may have to imagine that simplicity and identity.[1]

Do you agree with Hume's observations that it is not possible to discover a permanent self when we analyze and reflect on what is happening in our minds?

The idea that everything in the universe (including ourselves) undergoes permanent change has been around for a long time. The ancient Greek philosopher Heraclitus (ca. 535–475 BCE) was the first to embrace it unconditionally. He wrote in a well-known fragment: "It is not possible to step twice into the same river . . . it scatters and again comes together, and approaches and recedes." If Heraclitus is right and everything changes, then it is indeed tempting to think about our selves in terms of a river. Although we call one river at different points by the same name, it is not possible to point to anything permanent that actually is the river. The water in the river changes constantly, and even the riverbanks undergo a constant transformation. If the illusion theory is correct, we should think about our selves as something that undergoes constant change as well. The American philosopher William James agreed with the view that we experience our personal selves as a constantly changing river:

> Thoughts connected as we feel them to be connected are what we mean by personal selves. . . . [Our] consciousness is in constant change. I do not mean by this to say that no one state of mind has any duration—even if true, that would be hard to establish. What I wish to lay stress on is this, that no state once gone can recur and be identical with what it was before. . . . Often we are ourselves struck at the strange differences in our successive view of the same thing. We wonder how we ever could have opined as we did last month about a certain matter. We have outgrown the possibility of that state of mind, we know not how. From one year to another we see things in new lights. What was unreal has grown real, and what was exciting is insipid. The friends we used to care the world for are shrunken to shadows; the women once so divine, the stars, the woods, and the waters, how now so dull and common! . . . Consciousness . . . flows. A "river" or stream is the metaphor by which it is most naturally described.[2]

James's observation that our consciousness undergoes permanent change appears credible. It follows then that not only our bodies undergo continuous change, but our minds as well. In light of this, it seems plausible to conclude that the idea of a permanent self that persists through time is indeed only a convenient illusion.

Asian religions also support the view that there is no permanent self. Like Heraclitus, the Chinese Daoist thinker Zhuangzi (ca. 4th century BCE) believed there are no permanent conditions of any kind. Zhuangzi compared time and change to a horse that runs on and on. Daoists believe that, owing to this situation, it is futile to make plans. Instead, we should live instinctually according to the principle of *wu-wei*, having no deliberate actions. Likewise, Buddhists argue that the main source of suffering is our perpetual dissatisfaction with our condition; in hopes of finding happiness, we desire to gain what we do not have and form aversions toward the things we do have. However, according to the Buddha, these attempts to satisfy the individual self only perpetuate suffering. If we believe that we exist in the present as well as in the future, then it is easy to be afraid that things will turn out badly for us. We consequently make preparations for the future and direct our attention away from the present. In doing this, we spend all our energy planning and plotting for future success, and we forget that we need to pay attention to what is happening right now. This pattern quickly leads to greed, regret, and ultimately suffering. For Buddhists there is no self; they call the belief in a permanently abiding self "ignorance."

Food for Thought

In the *Diamond Sutra*, one of the best-known Buddhist scriptures, the Buddha explains to his disciple Subhuti that individuals who are becoming enlightened (Bodhisattvas) do not believe in a self. They also do not believe that the phenomenal world is ultimately real. The Buddha says this:

> O Subhuti, there does not exist in those noble-minded Bodhisattvas the idea of self, there does not exist the idea of a being, the idea of a living being, the idea of a person. Nor does there exist, O Subhuti, for these noble-minded Bodhisattvas the idea of quality (dharma), nor of no-quality. Neither does there exist, O Subhuti, an idea or no-idea. And why? Because, O Subhuti, if there existed for these noble-minded Bodhisattvas the idea of quality, then they would believe in a self, they would believe in a being, they would believe in a living being, they would believe in a person. And if there existed for them the idea of no-quality, even then they would believe in a self, they would believe in a being, they would believe in a living being, they would believe in a person. And why? Because, O Subhuti, neither quality nor no-quality is to be accepted by a noble-minded Bodhisattva. Therefore this hidden saying has been preached by the Tathagata (i.e., the Buddha): "By those who know the teaching of the Law, as like unto a raft, all qualities indeed must be abandoned; much more no qualities."[3]

Do you agree with this perspective on personal identity? Explain why or why not.

Problems for the Illusion Theory

Even as there are a number of reasons that make the illusion theory of personal identity attractive, there are also some obvious difficulties. If we agree that there is no permanent self, then strictly speaking, we will not be around tomorrow or ten years from now. From a pragmatic point of view, this is clearly significant. There are many things that I do today only because of my belief that I will enjoy the benefits of these actions later. For example, a good portion of my monthly paycheck flows into a retirement account. If the illusion theory of personal identity is correct, I should seriously rethink the wisdom of that practice. If there is no permanent self, the person who will live comfortably on my retirement savings is not identical to the person I am today! So the illusion theory of personal identity makes it look rational to spend most, if not all, of my money in the present. However, this does not fit well with my natural inclinations; I do care about what happens in the future, and I strongly believe (and hope) that the person who will live on my retirement savings is identical to the person I am today.

Of course, you may not be bothered by the idea that your self does not persist through time. We have seen that Buddhists think that a life focused on the moment rather than on the future is a good life. Nonetheless, things become a bit more complicated once we think not only about our own selves but also about our relationships with other people. Our lives become meaningful as we love and care for others. For example, I have a strong relationship with my parents. When I think about the love I feel for my mother, I do think that the person who reared me is the same person who now (forty years later) calls me and takes an interest in my life. I take comfort in the fact that my mother is the same person now as the person who walked with me on my first day of school. If the illusion theory is true, I would have to understand my love for other people in a different way. I would have to conclude that my mother today is closely related to the person who brought me up but, strictly speaking, that person is not around anymore. This conclusion seems problematic. My attachment to and love for others seems to presuppose that these other people persist through time, and this provides a good reason to look for an alternative to the illusion theory.

The illusion theory also has a hard time explaining why we punish people for crimes they have committed in the distant past. Suppose that Karl robbed a bank ten years ago and managed to elude the authorities until last Monday, when he was finally captured. It seems fair and just to punish Karl for what he did ten years ago, and few people would object to this practice. However, inflicting a punishment on Karl now is incompatible with the illusion theory of personal identity. If that theory is correct, we should conclude that we would be punishing an innocent person, for the Karl who robbed the bank ten years ago is not around anymore and is certainly not identical to the Karl who was captured last Monday.

These objections to the identity theory rest on pragmatic concerns: They show that we live our lives in the firm belief that we are going to be around in the future and also that it is just to punish people for what they did in the past. The objections do not show that the illusion theory is inconsistent. Thus, if we believe in the illusion theory strongly enough, we might start to change our lives accordingly and eliminate the pragmatic concerns. We might start living more in the moment and stop worrying about the future. We might also stop blaming people for what they did in the past and thereby eliminate a good deal of resentment and hate. However, if you are like me and have a strong attachment to the belief that we persist through time, then it seems desirable to look for alternatives to the illusion theory of personal identity.

The Body Theory, or Animalism

The Case for the Body Theory

Suppose that twenty years ago Charlita, your very best friend, vanished on an ocean cruise in the South Pacific. The ship she was on sank in a storm, and nobody has since heard from Charlita or anybody else who was aboard that ship. Suppose further that a person now rings your doorbell and claims to be Charlita, alleging that she managed to swim to a hidden island and lived there all these years. You are not sure whether to believe this story. After all, the person looks nothing like the Charlita you remember. What would you do to find out whether the person at your door is identical to your best friend? Doesn't it seem tempting to do a DNA test or to take fingerprints? If this person has the same fingerprints as your lost friend, then it seems to follow that she is indeed Charlita.

If you agree with this process, you are in effect embracing the principle of same body–same person, and you are thus subscribing to the body theory of personal identity. According to this theory, we are identical to our biological bodies, and we persist through time as long as our bodies retain functional organization. That is, we are identical to our living bodies. If I should be run over by a truck, then I am not around anymore although something that resembles my living body still is—namely, my corpse. For this reason the body theory is often referred to as **animalism**; the identity conditions for humans are in principle the same as for all other animals—that is, we are around as long as our biological living bodies are around. It is important not to misunderstand the principle of same body–same self. By sameness here we do not mean qualitative sameness, but numerical sameness. Our living bodies change considerably throughout our lives; it is even possible that we might lose a hand or a foot in an accident. However, such change does not mean that we would have become a different person since we are numerically still dealing with the same physical body.

Food for Thought

Imagine the following scenario: Jennifer—a thirty-year-old, blond, Caucasian mother of a son named Jacob—has been in a serious car accident. Her body is seriously injured, and the doctors in the hospital are unable to keep her alive for more than a few hours. However, when Jennifer dies, the doctors are able to remove her uninjured brain from her skull and transplant the brain into the healthy body of a twenty-two-year-old African American woman who has died from a brain tumor. The operation is a success. What would you tell Jacob in this situation? Would you tell him that his mother has survived the accident and is still alive?

One of the strongest supports for the body theory is connected with situations in which people fall into a persistent vegetative state. Suppose, for example, that you visit your Uncle Steve in the hospital. The night before your visit he had temporary heart failure, which deprived his brain of oxygen for an extended period of time and severely damaged it. He is still able to breathe, and his heart is still pumping, but your Uncle Steve will never regain consciousness; he has lost all higher brain function forever. Has your Uncle Steve gone out of existence? It seems wrong to say that he is dead. After all, he is still breathing, and his heart is still pumping. If you think that your uncle is still around, even though he has fallen into a permanent vegetative state, then you have reason to subscribe to the body theory of personal identity. According to that theory, Uncle Steve is around as long as his body is alive; it doesn't matter that his brain has been damaged.

Food for Thought

Although the principle that our personal identity is preserved as long as we inhabit the numerically same body is plausible and well established, it seems questionable at times. Consider the situation of Robert, who used to be a very athletic person, spending all of his free time playing basketball and riding motorcycles. In August 2002 Robert crashed his motorcycle and is now paraplegic. Although he still has the same (numerical) body as before, he feels that he is not the same person since he cannot do the things he loves most. Do you agree with him? If yes, what consequences does this have for the body theory of personal identity?

Problems for the Body Theory

The story about Uncle Steve can also be used as a reason to criticize the body theory. When some people hear the story about him, they think that the body theory comes to the wrong conclusion. Although Uncle Steve's body is alive, it is wrong to think that Uncle Steve—the person—has survived the brain damage. Because they think that a person must be able to think and reason, they reject the body theory.

Another reason to object to this theory relates to the prospect of life after death. Even if someone does not believe that life after death is plausible, it seems logically possible that we continue to exist after our physical bodies stop functioning. It is possible, after all, to make a movie about a continued existence after physical death. However, the body theory runs into fundamental difficulties when it comes to explaining this possibility. First, according to most religions that speak of life after death, people will not have the same kind of body in the afterlife that they have had on Earth. Many religions introduce the idea of a spiritual body, but according to the body theory, a person would not persist through the change from a physical body to a spiritual body. In other words, if I exist only as long as I have the numerically same body as I have on Earth, and if my new spiritual body is numerically distinct from my physical body, then I do not remain the same person.

Theorists can avoid this difficulty by insisting that God will recreate the same physical body that existed on Earth, but it is not clear whether that body will be in the same state as it was right before death. If it is, life in heaven might not be very pleasurable, since old bodies are often the source of major discomfort. On the other hand, if God recreates physical bodies in the state in which they were at a younger age, then the question arises as to whether the bodies will start to age again. If my resurrected body is physically identical to my body on Earth, it is a matter of causal necessity that it will age again. But that conclusion is incompatible with the idea that eternal life in heaven would be enjoyable. Thus, no matter how we twist the story, it seems as if the body theory of personal identity is not compatible with the idea that life after death is logically possible. Some people might take this as a reason to claim that life after death is logically incoherent, but most people will probably want to search for a different theory of personal identity.

In addition to the issue of life after death, there is another closely related problem for the body theory. The philosopher John Locke pointed out that it seems logically possible for two different persons to switch their bodies. Such body switches have been the subject of stories and fairy tales and have also provided the theme for Hollywood movies. The movie *Freaky Friday*, for instance, deals with the complications that arise when a daughter switches bodies with her mother. Given that we can make movies about this situation; it seems plausible to conclude that body switches are logically possible. However, according to the body theory of personal identity, body switches should be logically impossible—not a very convincing conclusion.

A final weakness of the body theory has to do with cases of total amnesia. It seems reasonable to say that individuals who suffer from complete amnesia have lost their sense of self and are no longer the same persons. This conclusion indicates that our sense of personal identity is dependent on psychological continuity. However, according to the body theory, a person who suffers from complete amnesia is still the same person as long as he or she has the numerically same body. This might strike many people as rather unorthodox thinking.

The Soul Theory

The Case for the Soul Theory

The soul theory of personal identity follows a similar philosophical strategy to that of the body theory. Both theories attempt to tie our personal identity to an enduring entity. The body theory focuses on the physical living body; the soul theory is centered on the idea of a nonphysical soul. The key principle of the soul theory is same soul–same person. The great advantage of the soul theory over the body theory is that it can easily explain how life after death is logically possible. According to the soul theory, our personal identity is not affected by the death of our physical bodies. When the heart stops beating and the brain stops functioning, the nonphysical soul simply continues to exist and allows us to continue on.

The soul theory is firmly grounded in popular culture. Singers and song-writers frequently talk about the soul as the center of the self. Religious texts support these sentiments as well by using the concepts "soul" and "self" inter-changeably. It is therefore no surprise that many people feel very comfortable embracing the soul theory of personal identity. Unfortunately, this theory also leads to some serious philosophical difficulties.

Food for Thought

The soul theory has been around for a long time. The philosopher Plato was one of the first thinkers to develop the soul theory in greater detail. According to Plato, the soul has no gender—that is, it is possible that one and the same soul could have a male body in one life and a female body in another reincarnation. Do you agree on this point with Plato? Do you think that you could be the same person even if you changed your gender?

Problems for the Soul Theory

Good philosophical theories should not only appear plausible, but they also need to help us explain the world. The soul theory of personal identity seems plausible to many people, but it runs into difficulties when it comes to offering explanations for our beliefs and our judgments about personal identity. Consider an example from college life: Suppose you are enrolled in a Monday-Wednesday-Friday philosophy class. Your teacher is a brown-haired, fairly tall woman with a British accent. It is the second class meeting of the semester, and the student who sits next to you and who missed the first class session asks, "Is she the same person who taught this class on Monday?" You answer, "Yes, she is." Now suppose the student does not quite trust you and continues, "Do you know this for sure?" You answer, "Yes, she has the same accent, the same brown hair, and the same height. She is the same person." Notice that in justi-fying your knowledge, you made reference to the person's body. If you were a firm believer in the soul theory, you would have responded to the second ques-tion of your classmate with something like this: "Well, I am not entirely sure whether that is the same person who taught the class on Monday. I am not able to check whether she has the same soul as the person on Monday."

That second answer seems peculiar. Most of us would feel very confident in asserting that we do indeed *know* that the teacher was the same as on Monday. But it is hard to see how a supporter of the soul theory could ever justify such a judgment. Thus, the soul theory of personal identity leads to a form of skep-ticism; we can never be sure whether we are dealing with the same person because we have no means of checking whether the person continues to have the same soul. Souls are, after all, invisible, nonphysical substances that cannot be seen, heard, or tasted. The skepticism would even extend to judgments about our own selves. By what means can I verify that I have the same soul as yesterday? Perhaps my soul has disintegrated, or it has multiplied. There seems to be no way of making sure that such change has not occurred. If we want to avoid such pervasive skepticism about personal identity, we need to look for an alternative to the soul theory.

Food for Thought

The soul theory also leads to certain theological difficulties. If the soul theory is correct and our self consists of an immaterial, nonphysical substance, then we actually never die. What happens at death is simply the separation of the soul from the body. Thus, we never really vanish but continue to exist. The theological difficulty with this view is its effect on the concept of resurrection. If we never die, we do not need to be resurrected. However, many religions adhere to the idea of resurrection. Can you think of a way in which we can make the soul theory of personal identity compatible with the idea of resurrection?

In addition to these skeptical worries, the soul theory is confronted with some serious metaphysical challenges, which are normally discussed in the context of the mind/body problem. We will discuss these questions in the next chapter.

The Memory Theory

The Case for the Memory Theory

The body theory and the soul theory attempt to provide an account of personal identity that assumes that our personal selves are substances. The body theory claims that we are physical substances, and the soul theory claims that we are immaterial substances. Since both theories run into problems, it is tempting to look for alternative accounts of personal identity. A promising alternative is to explain personal identity in terms of a psychological connection between different life stages. The best-known version of such a psychological connection theory of personal identity is the memory theory. The English philosopher John Locke was the first to discuss the memory theory in some detail:

> For since consciousness always accompanies thinking, and 'tis that, that makes every one to be, what he calls *self*; and thereby distinguishes himself from all other thinking things, in this alone consists *personal Identity, i.e.* the sameness of a rational Being: And as far as this consciousness can be extended backwards to any past Action or Thought, so far reaches the Identity of that *Person*.[4]

The basic idea behind the memory theory of personal identity is the following: I am identical to a person who existed in the past as long as I can remember at least some events that were experienced by that person. Right now, for example, I can remember what it felt like to receive a failing grade on a Latin examination in eighth grade. If I can remember this experience, it is clear that I am the person who received the failing grade in eighth grade. Nobody else can possibly remember what it felt like to fail that Latin exam. My self, therefore, extends back as far as I can remember past experiences. Thus, we are connected with the past as long as the past is somehow present within us, and we will be connected with our present in the future, as long as we are able to remember this present.

The memory theory can solve the problems that undermined the body and the soul theories of personal identity. First, according to the memory theory, it is logically possible to survive one's death. For example, if after my death a person in heaven can remember what I did on this Earth, it seems plausible to conclude that this person is identical to the person I am today. It is of no consequence whether that person has a spiritual body or is simply a nonphysical soul that exists in a different sphere. As long as my memories are around, I myself am around.

Moreover, unlike the soul theory, the memory theory can explain how we can know that the person we see today is the same person we knew in the past. If we are in doubt, we can simply ask the person about various past life experiences. Consider the example of a twenty-year class reunion: Suppose you see a person who looks somewhat like your old buddy Marissa. However, you are not quite sure whether she is indeed your old buddy. According to the memory theory, all you need to do is start a conversation and ask that person a couple of questions about the past. If the person can remember some of the adventures you and Marissa survived together, you have good reason to think that the person is indeed the same Marissa, no matter what she looks like.

There are also other reasons that support the memory theory. The German philosopher Gottfried Wilhelm Leibniz (1646–1716) suggested the following thought experiment: Suppose that you are offered the chance to become the king or queen of China (i.e., a person with unlimited wealth and every opportunity to fulfill all desires) on the condition that you undergo a brainwashing that will destroy every memory you currently have. Would you accept that offer? Most of us, I suppose, would decline. What good is it to become rich and powerful if we have to sacrifice our memories? Our sense of self seems essentially connected with our ability to remember our past. A person who does not know any of my past experiences does not seem to be me, even if the person has the same body I currently have.

Problems for the Memory Theory

Although the memory theory is compatible with common sense and is able to solve many of the difficulties that plagued the body theory and the soul theory, it leads to some difficulties as well. The Scottish philosopher Thomas Reid

(1710–1796) pointed out that the memory theory leads to potential inconsistencies. Reid imagined the following scenario: Suppose that an old retired general (G) still has vivid memories of his experiences as a middle-aged officer (M) but has completely forgotten everything about his childhood (Y). Suppose further that when he was a middle-aged officer (M), the general still had a very detailed recollection of his childhood (Y). The logical problem that arises in this situation is the following: Since M can remember his life as a young boy Y, we have to conclude that M is identical to Y. And since G can remember his life as a middle-aged officer M, we also need to conclude that G is identical to M. However, since the old general G has absolutely no recollection of his life as a young boy, we need to hold that G is not identical to Y. Thus, the memory theory seems to lead to a set of inconsistent propositions:

1. M = Y
2. G = M
3. G ≠ Y

Any philosophical theory that leads to inconsistencies is in serious trouble. We can take this as a reason to abandon the memory theory completely, or we can try to modify the theory such that the inconsistency can be avoided. In reality, a small modification of the theory will correct the problem; all we need to do is to distinguish between direct and indirect memories. A **direct memory** is one that can be recalled consciously right at this very moment. For example, I have a direct memory of what I ate for breakfast this morning. However, I have no direct memory of what shirt I was wearing ten days ago; when I try to think about it, I simply draw a blank. **Indirect memories** are those that I cannot recall directly but that a former version of my self was able to recall directly. For instance, I cannot directly remember the name of my first English teacher in high school, but there was a time in my life when I was able to recall this easily, and I am linked to that time by direct memories that I can recall right now.

Food for Thought

Decide whether you have direct or indirect memories of the following events in your life:

1. Your sixteenth birthday
2. The name of your best friend in fourth grade
3. The name of the lead singer in your first favorite music group
4. Your tenth birthday
5. The title of the first book you ever read
6. The name of your favorite elementary school teacher

This distinction between direct and indirect memories puts us in a position to solve the difficulty that was raised by Thomas Reid. Although the old general cannot directly recall his experiences as a boy, he has an indirect memory of these events, since a former version of him (the middle-aged officer) was able to recall these experiences directly. Thus, if we modify the memory theory so that being the same self requires only that we have an indirect memory link to the past, we can successfully avoid the prior inconsistency

This modification of the memory theory also helps us to deal with cases of Alzheimer's disease. Consider the following situation: Suppose that one of your close relatives has an advanced case of Alzheimer's. You visit her in the nursing home at the beginning of the week and have a great conversation. A couple of days later, during your next visit, the condition of your relative has deteriorated; when you enter her room, she greets you with the words, "Who in the world are you?" In this situation it would be odd to say that your relative is no longer the same self as she was several days earlier, although the original memory theory would have led to this conclusion. Stating the memory theory in terms of indirect memories resolves this problem. In this case we can argue that your relative probably has some direct memories that link her to the person you visited several days ago, when she could still directly remember who you were. We are therefore able to conclude that your relative is still identical to the person who remembered you several days ago.

A more serious challenge to the memory theory is raised by the problem of false memories. It is well known that memories can be deceiving. I seem to remember, for instance, that as a three-year-old child I got lost in a crowded shopping mall for several hours. However, I am not quite sure whether this is really a genuine memory or simply something I seem to remember because my mother told me about the incident later in my life. Let us call memories that are not caused by actual experiences "false" memories. It is obvious that false memories can lead to a false sense of self. Suppose that I seem to remember the experiences of Napoleon. I am clearly not justified to claim on the basis of these memories that I am identical to Napoleon unless I can be sure that these memories are genuine and true.

Food for Thought

The problem of false memories is especially pressing when people seem to remember experiences from past lives. Take a look at the following experience that was anonymously described on a Web page with the title "Practical Guide to Past-Life Memories":

> My husband and I went on a camping trip last summer. We had never done anything like it before, and I found it hard to fall asleep outdoors under the stars. It was beautiful lying there in my husband's arms, but once he fell asleep I'd lie there for hours, half expecting an attack at any moment.

Continued

Continued

> Three days into the vacation I managed to fall asleep in the middle of the night and dreamt that I was a young American Indian boy lost in the same area we were camping in. I could feel the young boy's nervousness and fear as he struggled to find food and make his way home. He lay on the ground at night, just as I was doing, and he wasn't able to sleep either as he was aware of every sound and movement. He seemed to think he was being followed or pursued, and all day long he kept looking behind him. He did this day after day. Eventually, it all got to be too much for him and he began to run. He caught his foot in the root of a tree and fell, breaking a leg. He couldn't move, and he lay on the ground waiting for death. When I woke up, I was sweating and my heart was racing. I'm convinced that I was that boy. It was far too vivid and real to be a dream.

Would this person be justified to believe that she is the same person as the young American Indian boy?

Similar problems appear when people seem to remember (often under hypnosis) certain dramatic events from their early childhood. Thus, in order to provide an accurate account of personal identity on the basis of memories, we need to distinguish between false and genuine memories. We might draw this distinction by defining a genuine memory as a memory of an experience that in fact happened to *me*. Although this definition seems natural, it creates a serious logical problem. The memory theory explains personal identity in terms of genuine memories. If we now define genuine memories as memories of experiences that in fact happened to me, we are involved in a vicious circle. For we define who we are in terms of genuine memories and then define genuine memories in terms of who we are. This is logically unacceptable.

Food for Thought

Scott Abraham wrote in *M.E.N.* magazine:

> Twenty-eight years after I was raped . . . though I retained memories of some of the less damning incidents, I repressed most of the horror: the scenes, feelings, and actions were far too agonizing for a little child to bear. I had no witnesses to corroborate my story, no pictures, no medical records. My mother had terrified me with literal torture in the privacy of my family home. . . . In a brilliant adaptation to unbearable pain, I disassociated myself from the memory, and for all that time, I could not consciously hold the whole of the reality in my mind. . . . For years, I was a drug addict and alcoholic, a sexually-compulsive womanizer, and a violent misanthrope. Like hundreds of thousands of others like me, it was not until I found sobriety that the barriers to memory began to crumble. . . . I joined abuse recovery

groups, and found a healing community of peers who supported my healing and believed my memories.

Scott Abraham's story is not rare. Every year, hundreds of adults seem to recall repressed memories of childhood abuse. Some of these recovered memories are true, but many have been proven to be bogus. How do we tell the difference?

To avoid the circularity objection, the Australian philosopher Sydney Shoemaker introduced the concept of a **quasi-memory**, which is an experience

1. That we seem to remember
2. That somebody actually had
3. That is caused by an actual experience

It is not important to understand this rather technical concept precisely. What is important is to understand that this concept of a quasi-memory allows us to state the memory theory of personal identity without presupposing that we already understand the concept of self. We can say now that a person at time t_1 is identical to a person at time t_2 only if the person at time t_2 quasi-remembers the experiences of the person at time t_1.

The concept of a quasi-memory has some drawbacks, however. Take a look at the third condition of the definition. We quasi-remember something only if it is caused by actual experiences. This condition makes sure that mere illusions and false memories do not count as quasi-memories. However, the condition raises an epistemic problem: How can we know that condition 3 applies to our memories? We obviously cannot know this directly. The philosopher John Perry has concluded that causal memory theories can successfully avoid the charge that they offer a circular account of personal identity, but they do so "at the cost of making 'the self' an inferred entity."[5] This is not an entirely satisfactory result.

Food for Thought

The philosopher Bernard Williams suggested the following thought experiment as an objection to the memory theory: Suppose someone informs you that at a future time t, you will be tortured. Upon hearing this, you are scared and fearful. But then you are told that prior to t, all your memories will be erased as well. Will this alleviate your fears? Williams argues that this additional information will do nothing to quell your fears of torture. Do you agree with Williams? If yes, what theory of personal identity is supported by this answer?

A final and more pressing difficulty for the memory theories concerns so-called reduplication or branching cases. Imagine for a moment that a machine can create a molecule-by-molecule copy of you. Although such a machine is not yet causally possible, the machine is certainly logically possible, and in the near future such a machine might even be causally possible. In such a situation your molecule-by-molecule copy has the same memory connection with your past as you do; it remembers playing with your siblings and being raised by your parents. If we want to maintain that the copy is only a copy and is not identical to you, we would have to appeal to the body. The memory theory alone is not in a good position to deal with reduplication problems.

The British philosopher Derek Parfit (1942–) has taken reduplication problems as a reason to question the importance of identity. Parfit points out that in reduplication cases it does not seem to matter with whom we are identical. Imagine, for example, that right after you are copied by the reduplication machine, an explosion kills your original body but leaves your copy intact. In this case it would be wrong to say that you have been killed since somebody who has your body and all your memories is still around. You would have survived even if the survivor is not, strictly speaking, identical to you. Parfit argues that what we should care about is survival and not identity. Needless to say, not everybody has been convinced by Parfit's arguments.

Final Remarks on Personal Identity

The deeper we think about the persistence question, the more it becomes clear that none of the theories we have discussed can put all our worries to rest. At the end of the day, reflections on personal identity lead to more questions than answers. However, this result can be very useful. We have seen that the persistence question is connected to a number of important cases in applied ethics. When we have to decide whether to pull the plug on a machine keeping a loved one alive, the question of whether this loved one is identical to a living body is obviously crucial. The inconclusive result of our discussion indicates that we should approach these decisions with some care; nobody can claim that end-of-life issues, or for that matter beginning-of-life issues, are clear-cut and trivial. If our discussion makes us more thoughtful when we approach these decisions, it has been useful. Moreover, our discussion has shown that the nature of our own self is mysterious; it is far from clear when the person who I am right now came into this world or when the person I am will cease to exist. This mystery is intellectually stimulating and entices us to explore the true nature or our selves more fully.

Study and Reflection Questions

1. The problem of personal identity consists of a set of different questions. What question of personal identity do you find most interesting? Explain why.

2. Suppose that sometime in the future a crazy scientist creates a perfect clone of you. The clone has a qualitatively identical body to yours and has the same memories as you have as well as the same voice, character, and so on. How would you convince a court of law that the clone is not really you? What theory of personal identity would help you to make your case?

3. The person you are right now grew and developed out of a fetus in your mother's womb. Should we say that you are identical to that fetus? Explain why different theories of personal identity answer this question in different ways. Explain what answer you find most compelling.

4. Suppose you are in a serious accident and end up in a vegetative state. Would you want your family to pull the plug? Defend your answer with the help of theories of personal identity.

5. Christianity is essentially linked to the notion of resurrection. Is it possible to make sense of resurrection, or is any account of resurrection flawed?

For Further Reading

Barresi, John, and Raymond Martin, eds. *Personal Identity*. Malden, MA: Blackwell, 2003.

Olsen, Eric T. *The Human Animal: Personal Identity Without Psychology*. Oxford: Oxford University Press, 1999.

———. *What Are We? A Study in Personal Ontology*. Oxford: Oxford University Press, 2007.

Parfit, Derek. *Reasons and Persons*. Oxford: Clarendon Press, 1984.

Perry, John. *A Dialogue on Personal Identity and Immortality*. Indianapolis, IN: Hackett, 1978.

———. *Personal Identity*. Berkeley: University of California Press, 2008.

Rorty, Amelie, ed. *The Identities of Persons*. Berkeley: University of California Press, 1976.

Shoemaker, Sydney, and Richard Swinburne, eds. *Personal Identity*. Oxford: Blackwell, 1984.

Endnotes

1. David Hume *A Treatise of Human Nature,* edited by L. A. Selby-Bigge, 2nd ed. revised by P.H. Nidditch, (Oxford: Clarendon Press, 1975), p. 252.
2. William James, "The Stream of Consciousness," in *Psychology* (New York: Henry Holt, 1910), pp. 151–175.
3. "The Vagrakkhedika, or Diamond-Cutter," trans. F. Max Müller, in *Buddhist Mahayana Texts*, ed. E. B. Cowell (New York: Dover, 1969).
4. John Locke, *An Essay Concerning Human Understanding* (Oxford: Clarendon Press, 1975), p. 332.
5. John Perry, "The Importance of Being Identical," in *The Identities of Persons,* ed. Amelie Rorty (Berkeley: University of California Press, 1976), p. 69.

CHAPTER SIX

THE MIND/BODY PROBLEM

What Is the Problem?

The problem of personal identity has introduced us to the idea that our selves have a physical as well as a psychic component. In this chapter we will explore the relationship between our bodies and our minds in more detail. Initially, you might be surprised to hear that philosophers find the relationship between body and mind problematic. Humans like you and me have a body, and we also have a mind. What is so mysterious about this? At first glance very little, but certain questions begin to emerge as soon as we describe the features of bodies and minds in more detail.

Let us start by describing some characteristics of human bodies, using my own body as an example. My body is 5'7" tall and weighs 160 pounds. It has brown hair and blue eyes. My body's nose is rather crooked since I broke it several times in my youth, and my feet are rather small. It is not particularly challenging to describe bodies, which have **physical properties** just like any other physical object. Bodies have color, shape, size, and texture; we can see them with our eyes, measure their weight, and take pictures of them. Moreover, human bodies are subject to the laws of physics. If you take my body and throw it through a second-floor window, it will crash to the ground like a rock. A physicist would be able to calculate the impact velocity without any difficulty, and we would be able to predict that my body would not survive such a fall without damage. Human bodies are similar to complex machines. If we treat them without proper care, they fall apart, and sooner or later (even with proper care) they will stop functioning.

Let us now turn to a description of minds. Initially, it might seem as if human minds are more difficult to describe than human bodies. We cannot take pictures of them or measure their size or weight. Notice that if I say, "My brain is a gray organic mass that weighs four pounds," I have not told you anything about my mind, but rather something about the internal structure of my body. My brain is part of my body, and the fact that my brain is perhaps smaller than yours would not entitle you to conclude that you have a bigger or sharper mind than I have. When we want to describe our minds, we cannot simply give a description of our brains.

Although minds cannot be described in the same way that we describe our bodies, there are things we can easily say about our minds. After all, we are aware of the thoughts and sensations that happen within them. Right now, for example, I am thinking that later today I have to buy a present for my mother's birthday. This thought is something that happens in my mind. Having thoughts and beliefs is part of my mental life. But there is more to the mind than that. Another key ingredient of the mind is sensations or feelings. If somebody told me that I am an incompetent teacher of philosophy, I would feel sad and disappointed. These feelings are also part of my mental life. If I merely had a body without a mind, my life would certainly be less cumbersome. There would be no feelings of fear or regret, and I would never be depressed, but life would also be rather dull. Without a mind there would be no joy or happiness, no dreams or hopes. A steak would have no flavor, and a kiss would have no passion.

Food for Thought

In order to come to terms with the role that minds play in this universe, it may be useful to engage in this thought experiment: Imagine, as clearly as you can, a universe that consists only of physical objects and physical properties but that lacks minds and mental properties. Would this universe contain colors and sounds? Would there be space and time? Would pineapples still taste sweet and the sea salty? Would roses still be beautiful? Make a list of those features of the world that would vanish if all minds were suddenly wiped out.

A good way to approach the mind is to understand it as something that allows us to engage in a wide range of activities, which are shown in the following illustration:

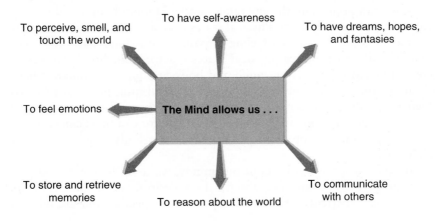

We have seen that bodies have physical properties; minds, on the other hand, can be described in terms of **mental states**. Memories, sensations, beliefs, and dreams are all examples of mental states. Using one general term to refer to all mental phenomena might suggest that all mental states share common characteristics. However, it is notoriously difficult to find a universal feature that is essential to all mental states. Mental states are diverse and varied, as the following exercise illustrates.

Food for Thought

Take a look at the following examples of mental states, and try to determine whether they can be grouped into a number of larger categories.

1. Feeling a sharp pain
2. Being convinced that the Red Sox are going to win the World Series this year
3. Knowing that 2 + 2 = 4
4. Smelling freshly brewed coffee
5. Seeing a lunar eclipse
6. Dreaming of winning the lottery
7. Remembering to buy some milk at the grocery store
8. Imagining a perfect vacation
9. Fearing that the war on terrorism will never be over
10. Knowing that there are nine planets in the solar system
11. Perceiving a yellow sunflower
12. Thinking that the Earth is round
13. Experiencing great frustration

Now that we have developed a rough description of human bodies and minds, we can appreciate the emerging puzzle: Human bodies and minds are intimately tied to each other. Physical states (like a cut on my finger) can produce mental states (such as a feeling of pain), and mental states (like feeling embarrassed) can produce physical states (such as blushing). However, in spite of this close interaction, mind and body are quite dissimilar. When we talk about our bodies, we describe them as exhibiting physical properties, which are **public** in the sense that others can observe and measure what kind of physical state my body is in. A medical doctor, for example, can easily measure a wide range of physical properties of my body (e.g., temperature, weight, size).

However, when we talk about our minds, we describe mental states and mental properties and thus talk about beliefs, desires, and wishes. These mental states are experienced from a **first-person perspective** and are inherently

private. Others cannot tell from the outside what it feels like to have my desires or sensations. A medical doctor can tell me that my body is running a fever but cannot tell me what it feels like to have this fever. The experience of having this fever happens in my mind and seems inaccessible to anybody but me. This realization leads us to the central question of the mind/body problem: How exactly are the physical states of human bodies related to the mental states of human minds?

Food for Thought

Before we discuss several solutions to the mind/body problem in more detail, it may be interesting for you to record your own initial beliefs and ideas about the relationship between mind and body. Answer the following questions with True or False:

1. It is possible for my mind to survive the death of my body.
2. Someday in the future it will be possible to build machines that have a mind just like mine.
3. The best way to treat depression is to change the chemical reactions inside the brain.
4. Sometime in the future it might be possible for a crazy scientist to create false memories in my mind by simply injecting certain chemicals into my brain.
5. Although scientists can understand the composition and nature of clouds, planets, black holes, and other physical objects, they will never understand the true nature of emotions like anger, love, or hate.
6. Dogs and cats have beliefs and hopes just like humans do.
7. Sometime in the future computers might have consciousness and self-awareness.
8. My thoughts and ideas are the product of my environment and my upbringing.
9. Conscious beings who do have beliefs and self-awareness but who do not have brains like ours might exist on other planets.
10. Because it is impossible for machines to be creative or funny, even the most advanced robots could never be stand-up comedians.

Possible Solutions to the Mind/Body Problem

Theories about the relationship between physical states and mental states fall into three broad categories: physicalism, dualism, and idealism. The basic ideas behind these theories are explained in the following chart.

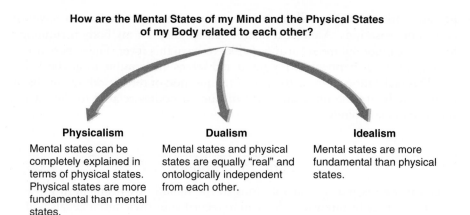

How are the Mental States of my Mind and the Physical States of my Body related to each other?

Physicalism	Dualism	Idealism
Mental states can be completely explained in terms of physical states. Physical states are more fundamental than mental states.	Mental states and physical states are equally "real" and ontologically independent from each other.	Mental states are more fundamental than physical states.

Let us take a closer look at each of these theories. Supporters of **physicalism** believe that the physical states of the body are more fundamental than the mental states of the mind. But what exactly does that mean? Let us clarify this idea with the help of an analogy: Consider the relationship between Huckleberry Finn and Mark Twain, each of whom has various properties. Huckleberry Finn is a young boy who runs away from home and travels on the Mississippi River. Mark Twain is a well-known American author who was born in Florida, Missouri. It is easy to see that Mark Twain is a more fundamental entity than Huckleberry Finn. If we want to explain why Huckleberry Finn has certain features, we need to appeal to the ideas of Mark Twain. It would be silly to reverse this explanatory relationship. Huckleberry Finn is, after all, a fictional character that would not exist if Mark Twain had never been born. Philosophers use the term **ontological dependence** to describe the relationship between Huckleberry Finn and Mark Twain. In general, we can say that one entity depends ontologically on another entity if the first cannot exist without the second.

Food for Thought

In order to understand the term *ontological dependence* better, answer the following claims with True or False:

1. Tigers are ontologically dependent on lions.
2. Rainbows are ontologically dependent on water and light.
3. Wood is ontologically dependent on trees.
4. Oranges are ontologically dependent on apples.
5. Children are ontologically dependent on their parents.
6. Birds are ontologically dependent on dinosaurs.
7. Heat is ontologically dependent on the velocity of molecules.

Physicalists believe that the relationship between body and mind is similar to the relationship between Mark Twain and Huckleberry Finn. They believe that we can explain the nature of mental states in terms of the physical states of our bodies. Although there is some controversy among physicalists about exactly how mental states depend on physical states, they all agree that physical states are more fundamental entities than mental states are.

Dualism rejects the idea that our minds and mental states are less fundamental than our bodies and physical states. According to dualism, the universe contains two different and equally real substances: mind and body. The relationship between these two substances is in some ways similar to the relationship between apples and oranges. Just as oranges can exist without apples and apples without oranges, so minds can exist independently of the body. Although many dualists accept the idea that minds and bodies can interact with each other, they maintain that minds are **ontologically independent** of bodies, and they reject the idea that minds can be explained in terms of the body. Critics of dualism sometimes have dubbed it the doctrine of the "ghost within the machine" because dualists believe that there is something irreducibly nonphysical within conscious beings.

Idealism is a third theory that explains how minds and bodies relate to each other. We have already encountered a version of idealism in George Berkeley's defense of an empiricist theory of knowledge. Idealism is the reverse of physicalism; idealism holds that minds are more fundamental than physical bodies. At first encounter idealism seems outlandish: How can anybody think that the existence of my leg, for example, is ontologically dependent on the thought that I have a leg? We normally think that legs, tables, cars, and other physical objects exist regardless of whether there are minds or not. In the Food for Thought exercise on page 127, I asked you to imagine what the universe would be like if we were to eliminate all minds from it. An idealist believes that such a universe would be empty, since minds rather than matter are the fundamental building blocks of the universe. This is a fascinating idea, but since idealism plays no significant role in the contemporary philosophical debate about the mind/body problem, I will omit a fuller discussion and focus on the debate between dualism and physicalism.

Substance Dualism

The classical version of dualism is **substance dualism (1596–1650)**. Its most famous proponent was the French philosopher René Descartes, who argued that minds and bodies are different kinds of entities. Bodies are physical substances that are located in space and time and are subject to the laws of physics. Minds, on the other hand, are nonextended thinking substances. Mind substance is much more difficult to describe since it lacks physical properties. However, we can at least describe it negatively as a substance that is not subject to the laws of physics.

Arguments for Substance Dualism

Near-Death Experiences   Consider this popular, though often neglected, argument in support of substance dualism:

```
1.If substance dualism is false, then my mind can-
   not exist independently from my body.
2.My mind can exist independently from my body.
```
Therefore: Substance dualism is true.

This argument is an instance of the deductive argument form *modus tollens* and is therefore valid. Let us try to determine whether it is also sound. Premise 1 seems to be true, but how plausible is premise 2? Many religions support the idea that our minds will survive our bodily deaths and that our minds (on their own or with new spiritual bodies) have the chance to enter heaven. Although this religious conviction can help us to see why the idea of life after death is attractive, it alone cannot determine whether it is rational to believe that minds can exist separately from bodies. Since philosophers are committed to adopting the most rational beliefs about the universe, we need to go beyond religion to determine whether this belief that our minds can exist without our bodies is reasonable. The best evidence in support of this idea is so-called near-death experiences. Consider what Gloria G. experienced during brain surgery:

> As I was lying on the table I heard the doctors pronounce the operation a failure and pronounce me dead. I then remember them frantically trying to resuscitate me. While they were trying to bring me back to life, I was just floating up near the ceiling. It was a weird feeling because I was up there and this body was below. . . . Then I seemed to wander up through the floors of the hospital. I saw plainly, for instance, a young man who had been injured in an automobile accident. . . . Then everything began to get dark: I passed through a spiraling tunnel until I seemed to come to a place illuminated by an immensely bright light. . . . A tremendous peace overcame me. My grandmother, who had died nine years before, was there. I couldn't see her—for she seemed behind me—but I could feel her presence and hear her voice. . . . Suddenly, I was thrust back into my body. I don't know how or why. My next recollection is of the nurse standing near me in the recovery room.[1]

Gloria's experience is rare, but not unique. Other people have reported very similar near-death experiences. In the book *Life After Life*, Raymond Moody summarizes the experiences of over fifty people who went through extraordinary experiences when they were close to death.[2] Many of these experiences corroborate the basic details of what Gloria G. experienced.[3] These reports suggest the following argument:

```
1.Some people report that they had experiences
   while being outside their bodies.
```

> 2.The best explanation for these reports is that
>   minds can indeed exist without bodies.

Therefore: Minds probably can exist independently
from bodies.

This is an inductive argument and therefore cannot establish its conclusion with absolute certainty. However, we need to determine how strongly this best-explanation argument supports its conclusion. Remember what we learned in Chapter 2: In order to find out whether a given explanation is indeed the best, we need to compare the explanation to other available explanations of the same fact. How else can we explain the many accounts of near-death experiences? One possibility is that these experiences are caused by oxygen deprivation. We know that people whose brains have been deprived of oxygen frequently report having visions and unusual experiences. Another possibility is that these experiences are caused by anesthetic drugs like ketamine. Moreover, neurologists who recently studied the brain of a patient who had reported out-of-body experiences found that a part of the patient's brain known as the angular gyrus was very active during these experiences. This suggests that out-of-body experiences might be caused by neurological processes in the brain. It is therefore possible to explain near-death experiences without accepting the claim that minds have the ability to leave their physical bodies.

These alternative neurological explanations have the advantage of being relatively simple since they refer only to physical entities (e.g., brains, neurological processes, angular gyrus) and avoid any reference to nonmaterial minds. In addition, they appear to be more conservative, since many people find the idea that the world consists only of physical entities to be in agreement with their overall picture of the world. For this reason, most contemporary philosophers and scientists do not think that near-death experiences provide very good support for substance dualism. However, it should be pointed out that there is an ongoing debate about their status. Some philosophers go so far as to claim that near-death experiences and other paranormal psychological phenomena like telepathy and clairvoyance provide good reasons for accepting a dualistic solution to the mind/body problem.[4] The fact that there is so much debate and disagreement suggests, however, that we cannot settle the mind/body problem with arguments that appeal to near-death experiences and other paranormal phenomena. It is prudent to look for alternative arguments for and against dualism.

Food for Thought

A good example to illustrate the ambiguity most philosophers feel about near-death experiences is given by the British philosopher A. J. Ayer (1910–1989). One year before his death, Ayer, who had been an atheist

Continued

and a physicalist all his life, was in intensive care, and his heart stopped beating for four minutes. Upon awakening, he reported: "I was confronted by a red light, exceedingly bright, and also very painful, even when I was turned away from it. I was aware that this light was responsible for the government of the universe." After several days Ayer drew the following conclusion from his experiences: "My recent experiences have slightly weakened my conviction that my death will be the end of me, though I continue to hope that it will be." What conclusion would you draw if you had undergone a similar near-death experience as A. J. Ayer?

The Conceivability Argument   There are several alternative arguments in support of dualism, but we will focus on one very prominent one—the **conceivability argument**. To understand this argument clearly, we need to know more about what philosophers say about the relation "x is identical to y." Let us look at a hypothetical story: Suppose you have a conversation with Paul, who is a big fan of conspiracy theories. Among other things, Paul believes that George W. Bush is not really who he claims he is. Paul is convinced that George W. is actually the same person as Dan Quayle. According to Paul, Dan Quayle realized that he could never win the presidency as long as people recognized him as Dan Quayle, so he proceeded to pass himself off as the oldest son of his mentor, George Bush. According to Paul, the rest is history, for Dan Quayle (disguised as George W. Bush) reached his ultimate goal and became President of the United States.

Paul's theory that George W. Bush and Dan Quayle are the same person is, of course, rather silly. But how can you refute him? The answer is pretty straightforward: A and B are identical to each other only if they have all properties in common. This principle is known as **Leibniz's law,** and it plays an important role in many areas of philosophy. If you apply Leibniz's law to Paul's theory, George W. and Dan Quayle can be identical to each other only if they have all properties in common. Suppose you find out that Dan Quayle is 5'9" tall, whereas George W. is 6'1". This is sufficient evidence to refute Paul's theory, for you have now shown that Dan Quayle has at least one property that George W. lacks. This fact, together with Leibniz's law, establishes that Dan Quayle and George W. Bush cannot be the same person and that Paul's conspiracy theory is false.

The Quayle/Bush story illustrates a general argumentative strategy in support of substance dualism. If we can find at least one property of minds that bodies do not have, we are entitled to draw the conclusion that minds and bodies cannot be one and the same thing. This is the basic strategy of the conceivability argument, which was first introduced by René Descartes. In standard form this argument appears as follows:

```
1.I can conceive that I exist without a body.
2.I cannot conceive that I exist without a mind.
```
Therefore:

3. My mind is more intimately connected to me than my body is, and thus my mind has a property (the property of being essentially connected to me) that my body lacks.
4. If my mind has at least one different property than my body has, then my mind cannot be identical to my body.

Therefore: My mind is not identical to my body.

At first glance all premises of the conceivability argument appear to be true, and the argument therefore seems to make an impressive case for substance dualism. However, many philosophers have expressed reservations about it. First, consider premise 1: Can I really conceive that I exist without a body? If I have no body whatsoever, then I also have no eyes, and no ears, and no tongue. But how can I be myself without being able to smell, see, or hear? It is easy to imagine that I exist with a different body from the one I have right now; I could be seven feet tall and weigh four hundred pounds. But this is not enough for the argument to succeed, for I can equally well imagine that I exist with a different mind. So in order to draw the necessary distinction between body and mind, I need to make sense of the idea that I can exist without any body at all. Some thinkers have doubted that it is logically possible for a person to be identical to a disembodied being.

Food for Thought

According to many religions, we can exist in heaven with a spiritual body. But this raises the question of what spiritual bodies would be like. Would all spiritual bodies look alike? Would there be a male spiritual body and a female spiritual body? Would my spiritual body be similar to the body I used to have when I was eighteen, or would it be more like the body I will have when I am seventy-five? How would you answer these questions?

The second problem with the conceivability argument is that the concept of conceivability is not sufficient to justify the conclusion that entities are not identical to one another. Consider the following, obviously flawed, argument:

1. I can conceive that Clark Kent is an ordinary human being.
2. I cannot conceive that Superman is an ordinary human being.

It follows therefore that Clark Kent has a property that Superman lacks, and that entails by Leibniz's law that Clark Kent is not the same person as Superman.

This argument demonstrates that we need to be very careful when we apply Leibniz's law to properties that are a result of our beliefs. There is a crucial difference between the sentences "The car in the yard is red" and "I believe the car in the yard is red." The latter sentence can be true even if the car in the yard is orange. Thus, *conceiving* of objects A and B as different does not warrant the conclusion that A and B are in fact different. Conceived differences might be caused by the fact that we describe A and B differently and that these different descriptions cause us to have different beliefs about A and B. In other words, one and the same object—for example, the planet Venus—might be described in two different ways (as Evening Star or Morning Star), and we therefore might have different beliefs about the same object if we encounter it under different descriptions. For instance, I might believe that the Morning Star is a planet, whereas I might believe that the Evening Star is an actual star. This reality suggests that our inability to conceive that we exist without our minds might reflect only that we describe minds and bodies differently. Therefore, the observation that we conceive of the relationship between our selves and our bodies and minds differently is not strong enough to establish that minds and bodies are ontologically independent entities.

Intentionality Even though the conceivability argument fails, the general strategy of the argument is promising. The best arguments in defense of dualism rest on the attempt to find properties that distinguish minds from bodies. In the contemporary discussion many philosophers focus their attention on **intentionality,** which is a technical philosophical term that refers to a property of mental states. Some mental states—for example, the thought that I should buy a present for my mother—are *about* something else. In this case the mental state is about my mother and the present I want to buy. To say that mental states have intentionality is to say that mental states represent something else.

Notice, however, that it is not clear how ordinary physical objects like trees, cars, or brain states can be *about* other things in the same way that mental states are. A tree and any other physical object are what they are, and it is hard to see that they could represent something else. It would be strange to say that a tree is about my mother. This has prompted some philosophers to resurrect the general strategy of the conceivability argument in a different form. They argue that it is in principle impossible for physical states of the body to have intentionality. But since mental states do have this property, it seems to follow that bodies and minds are different kinds of entities. The debate about intentionality is still ongoing, with no clear resolution in sight.

Arguments Against Substance Dualism

We have seen that the arguments in defense of dualism are open to objections. When one fails to establish a philosophical position, it is always advisable to determine whether it would not be easier to disprove the theory instead of proving it. Let us turn our attention, therefore, to some of the more serious objections to dualism.

The Problem of Interaction   Substance dualists like Descartes believe not only that minds and bodies are independent substances, but also that minds and bodies interact with each other. When you raise your arm up into the air, the physical movement of your body was probably preceded by a mental event: the decision to raise your arm. In situations like this, it seems natural to say that the mind caused the body to move. On the other hand, there are instances when your body seems to influence your mind. Suppose, for example, that you expose your body to eight hours of intense sunlight. The chances are great that the resulting state of your body will lead to a considerable amount of pain sensation. In this case a physical state (burned skin) has caused a mental state (sensation of pain). Once we realize that mind and body interact so closely with each other, we can also see that substance dualism faces a serious problem. Given that minds and bodies are different substances, how is it possible for them to influence each other?

The following hypothetical situation might help you to understand this impasse more clearly: Suppose you are playing a game of pool with Joe Shark. Joe is more skilled than you, and he is already working on the eight ball while you still have most of your balls on the table. Suddenly, Joe stops and puts down his cue. He closes his eyes and stands very still. At first you think that Joe is simply concentrating before he attempts to sink the eight ball, but after several minutes you become irritated and ask, "Hey, Joe, what are you doing? You're supposed to take your shot." Joe responds, "I'm in the process of taking my shot. I have decided to sink this last ball with my mind. Just give me a couple of minutes to focus all of my mental energies on the ball." What would you say to Joe in this situation? Maybe, "Joe, you can stand there and think about sinking the eight ball until you're blue in the face, but I can tell you one thing for sure—it's not going to go anywhere. In order to move the eight ball, you need another physical object like a stick or a hand. Minds alone can't move matter." And if Joe does not accept your explanation, wouldn't you conclude that he has a rather bizarre sense of reality?

This hypothetical story illustrates that substance dualism cannot explain how material bodies can causally interact with immaterial minds. The basic structure of the problem can be illustrated with the following *reductio ad absurdum*-style argument:

```
1.Assume that substance dualism is true.
2.If substance dualism is true, then the mind is an
  immaterial, nonextended thinking substance, and
  the body is an extended physical substance.
3.Immaterial, nonextended substances cannot inter-
  act with extended physical substances.
4.Mind and body interact with each other.
```

Therefore: Substance dualism is false.

This argument is valid, and all of its premises seem to be true. You might wonder on what grounds people accept premise 3. Can we be sure that immaterial and nonextended substances cannot causally interact with extended physical substances? In defense of this premise, we can point to a fundamental physical principle that physical energy is neither created nor destroyed—a principle known as the *conservation of energy*. If we were to believe that nonphysical events could cause physical entities to move, the total amount of energy in the universe would increase, and the principle of the conservation of energy would be violated. As long as we subscribe to the principle of the conservation of energy, premise 3 is well established.

Food for Thought

We have seen that substance dualism is in conflict with a fundamental principle of physical science—the conservation of energy. However, not everybody would agree that this is a devastating objection to dualism. Some people believe that phenomena exist that are not explainable by the common physical laws of matter and energy. One such possible phenomenon is **telekinesis**, the ability to move objects from a distance with one's mind. What do you think about telekinesis? Do you think we should take seriously reports from people who claim that they can move physical objects from a distance? Recall the movie *Star Wars*, when Luke Skywalker uses the "force" to pull a spaceship out of the swamp. Do we have any reasons to think that this might be causally possible in our universe?

Some dualists, those who embrace a position known as **parallelism**, have tried to save their theory from this argument by denying premise 4. They claim that minds and bodies exist in parallel worlds and thus never interact with each other. But parallelism faces the difficult task of explaining why mental events and physical events, although disconnected, are so well coordinated with each other. Some thinkers have tried to explain this harmony by arguing that God intervenes and assures that mind and body are appropriately linked—a solution known as **occasionalism**. But it is easy to see that occasionalism is a rather convoluted theory that is in conflict with Ockham's razor. Overall, there seems to exist no easy way for a dualist to escape the problem of interaction.

A Category Mistake   The Oxford philosopher Gilbert Ryle (1900–1976) developed a further objection to dualism. Ryle claimed that dualists put the term *mind* into the wrong logical category and thus commit a category mistake. To explain the logical framework of category mistakes, Ryle presented the following hypothetical situation: Suppose your parents come to visit you for the first time on campus. They are eager to see the university, so you take them on a little tour of the campus. You show them the library, the dorms, the lecture halls, and the auditorium. After the tour you can see that your parents are disappointed, so you ask them why they are not enjoying themselves. They say, "We came here to see the university, but all you have shown us are the lecture halls, the dorms, and the library. That's great! But would you now please show us the university itself?" Your parents have committed a semantic mistake. They think that the university is a specific building like the library or the dormitory; they do not realize that the term *university* refers to a whole group of buildings. Thus, they have put the term into the wrong logical category—a good example of a category mistake.

Food for Thought

Category mistakes occur not only in the context of the mind/body problem, but also in many other fields. Take a look at the following claims, and explain why they, too, might entail a category mistake:

1. The world spirit helped Napoleon to conquer Europe.
2. Nothingness stared into his eyes and made him jump from the bridge.
3. The American Revolution was caused by the Enlightenment.
4. The average American lives next door.
5. Love is my best friend.

According to Ryle, substance dualists are guilty of committing a category mistake. Dualists classify minds as substances. They say, for instance, that minds can leave the body and that minds can cause the body to move. Dualists therefore attribute properties to minds that we normally attribute only to separately existing physical things. According to Ryle, dualists fail to realize that the term *mind* does not refer to a specific entity like the body, but rather refers to certain aspects of our bodies. Defenders of dualism can accuse Ryle of simply begging the question: By insisting that minds should not be classified as substances, Ryle seems to assume what he is trying to prove. However, Ryle's criticism of dualism shows that it might be fruitful to think about the mind as something other than a nonphysical substance.

Varieties of Physicalism

The basic tenet of physicalist theories about the mind is the idea that we can explain mental states in terms of physical states of the body. This idea is especially attractive in light of recent advances in neuroscience. We know, for example, that injuries to the frontal lobe of the cerebral cortex affect language capabilities in most people. We further know that chemicals like cocaine, alcohol, or anesthetics can affect our emotions and thoughts. Moreover, we have learned that memory loss can be caused by the degeneration of nerve tissues in the brain. All of these findings suggest that our mental life is dependent on physical processes within our bodies (especially in the brain). To develop a satisfactory physicalistic theory of the mind, however, we need to do more than simply state the fact that our minds are dependent on our bodies. In addition, we need to say precisely what kind of physical states constitute mental states like pain or the feeling of love. At this point thinkers who are attracted to physicalism begin to disagree and develop different kinds of physicalistic theories about the mind. The following chart provides an overview of some basic physicalistic theories.

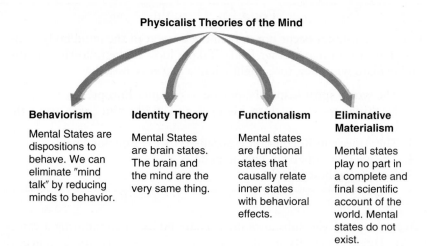

Physicalist Theories of the Mind

Behaviorism

Mental States are dispositions to behave. We can eliminate "mind talk" by reducing minds to behavior.

Identity Theory

Mental States are brain states. The brain and the mind are the very same thing.

Functionalism

Mental states are functional states that causally relate inner states with behavioral effects.

Eliminative Materialism

Mental states play no part in a complete and final scientific account of the world. Mental states do not exist.

In order to determine whether physicalism is a plausible solution to the mind/body problem, we need to see whether any of these theories provide a satisfactory account of the relationship between body and mind.

Behaviorism

Behaviorism is closely tied to the development of psychology, which is not a very old scientific discipline. It was only at the start of the twentieth century that psychology gradually established itself as an independent scientific field of study. The main challenge for psychology was to develop a satisfactory scientific methodology with which to study the human mind.

Every science relies heavily on observations and measurements. However, it is far from easy to observe and measure what happens in the minds of human beings. At first, psychologists tried to solve this problem by asking subjects to report on their sensations, feelings, or thoughts in experimental situations. But the results of this approach were disappointing; psychologists found out that many people have a hard time reporting reliably what happens in their minds. For example, suppose Susan is a psychologist who wants to study pain. Among other things, she wants to develop a classification of different types of pain. To this end, she creates experimental settings that should help her to determine whether experiences of type X are more painful than experiences of type Y. She starts her investigation with a relatively ordinary experiment: She wants to investigate whether it is more painful to pierce one's nose or one's navel. Now suppose that you participate in Susan's study and that, under her supervision, you pierce your nose as well as your navel. After the procedures Susan asks you to compare your pain experiences. It certainly would be challenging for you to report with a high degree of confidence that one pain sensation was more intense than the other—it is not easy to compare sensations. But even if you were sure that piercing your navel was more painful than piercing your nose, it would not follow that this would be true for other subjects as well. Introspective reports about sensations and mental content are idiosyncratic and cannot generate or support general laws about the human mind.

After realizing that introspective reports did not lead to a secure scientific foundation for psychology, psychologists started to look for other ways to study the mind. The solution was to study human behavior. How can human behavior tell us anything about human minds? Consider the following examples: Suppose I want to find out whether your belief in God is stronger today than it was last year. To find the answer to this question, I could simply ask you. However, we have already seen that this approach leads to certain methodological difficulties, and you yourself might not know whether the degree of your belief has increased or decreased. A better way to find an answer to this question might be to simply study how you behave. If you used to go to church weekly and read the Bible every evening but now you go to church only occasionally and have stopped reading the Bible, it is quite reasonable to conclude that your belief in God has decreased. Studying your behavior (going to church, reading the Bible, talking about God) is an excellent way to gain knowledge about your mind (the degree to which you believe in God).

Food for Thought

Consider one more time the research project of Susan, the psychologist. Would she be able to find an answer to the question of whether piercing one's navel is more painful than piercing one's nose if she were to study behavior rather than rely on introspective reports? What do you think?

Logical Behaviorism

Observing behavior as a way of studying the mind is known as **methodological behaviorism,** the cornerstone of a scientific study of the mind. Methodological behaviorism proved to be pretty successful and thus caused several philosophers to push the behavioristic approach to the mind even further. They developed so-called **logical behaviorism**, which was most prominently defended by B. F. Skinner (1904–1990). The key idea is that we can eliminate all mental terms like *pain*, *belief*, or *hope* from our scientific discourse by translating these terms into claims about human behavior.

Consider the sentence "John loves Lucy." According to Skinner and other logical behaviorists, this sentence should not be part of good scientific language since we cannot determine clearly under what conditions this sentence is true or false. In order to make progress, we first need to translate the sentence into a statement about John's behavior. We should say something like "John has a tendency to bring flowers to Lucy, to hug her repeatedly, and to tell her 'I love you.'" This sentence about John's behavior can be verified as true or false and thus can be an acceptable part of scientific discourse. In general, logical behaviorists suggest that all mental phenomena like beliefs or sensations can be understood as dispositions to behave in certain ways. Logical behaviorism is therefore an eliminative theory about mental terms because it holds that all terms like *pain* or *belief* can be replaced by descriptions that refer only to behavior.

Food for Thought

How would a logical behaviorist transform the following sentences, so that they become a legitimate part of scientific discourse?

1. Henry is angry with Maud.
2. Torsten believes that he is ugly.
3. Nikisha wants to become rich.
4. Tonya is in severe pain.
5. Avrindam has learned Spanish well.

Logical behaviorism is a rather economical theory of the mind. It solves the mind/body problem by explaining minds in terms of behavior. Consequently, it does not face the problem of interaction, which creates such severe problems for dualistic thinkers. For logical behaviorists our talk about minds is just a convoluted way to talk about our behavior. Because minds are *not* fundamental entities in the world, the question of how minds can interact with bodies is thus eliminated. Logical behaviorism also provides a theoretical framework for psychological research. Since human behavior can be understood in terms of **stimuli**, **conditioning**, and **responses**, behaviorism allows us to learn about the mind by constructing theories centered upon these observable terms. According to behaviorism, our "mental life" is simply a set of learned behavioral responses to various stimuli and reinforcements from our environment.

Arguments Against Logical Behaviorism

In spite of its elegance and simplicity, logical behaviorism is open to some serious objections. One fundamental problem can be illustrated with a hypothetical story: Suppose Julie's best friend Sara arranges a blind date for Julie with Sara's old love, Bill. Sara is convinced that Julie and Bill will be a perfect fit. However, when Julie meets Bill for the first time in person, she can see right away that Bill is the date from hell. He is boring, ill-mannered, and simply ugly. But since she does not want to hurt Sara's feelings, Julie pretends to have a good time with Bill. She laughs at his dull jokes and pretends to take an interest in his life stories, even as she is dreading every minute of this first— and last—date with Bill. Now suppose that Bill is a behaviorist. What would Bill say about Julie's feelings for him? He feels entitled to say that Julie likes him because she displayed all the necessary "liking behavior." However, Bill has been fundamentally wrong about Julie's mental state; her real feelings did not correspond to her behavior at all.

This is not a knockdown argument against behaviorism, since a behaviorist can claim that Julie would have acted differently if the circumstances had been different (i.e., if she had not wanted to pretend to like Bill for the sake of her friend Sara). A behaviorist might still maintain that Julie had a disposition to display "nonliking" behavior toward Bill; she simply chose not to act on this disposition. The story nevertheless illustrates two weaknesses of logical behaviorism. First, to explain why Julie chose not to display her nonliking behavior toward Bill, one must refer to the fact that she believed this behavior would hurt the feelings of her friend Sara. A behaviorist, however, cannot refer to mental states and must therefore offer an inadequate and incomplete explanation of why she displayed liking behavior toward Bill. Second, the story illustrates that displaying a certain type of behavior is neither a necessary nor a sufficient condition for being in a certain mental state. Mental states seem to be the cause of behavior, but they are not the same things as behavior or dispositions to behave.

Food for Thought

If you understand logical behaviorism clearly, you should be able to understand why the following joke is funny: After having sex, one logical behaviorist says to the other: "It was good for you, how was it for me?"

The linguist Noam Chomsky developed a further objection to logical behaviorism. According to logical behaviorism, it is possible to explain our future behavior (and thus our minds) in terms of past conditioning and responses. Behaviorists believe that there are lawful connections between our past behavioral experiences and our dispositions to behave in certain ways in the future.

However, this explanatory model makes it impossible to explain why we sometimes display completely novel verbal behavior. When we speak or write, we sometimes express propositions that nobody (to our knowledge) has uttered before. Right now, for example, I am writing a sentence that I have probably never written or read before. The most natural explanation for my behavior is that I have certain ideas in my mind that I want to express. But a behaviorist cannot make use of this explanation, because mental states are not supposed to play any role in explaining our behavior. Thus, logical behaviorism cannot explain how people manage to display novel (linguistic) behavior.

Although there are further objections to logical behaviorism, we can already see that an exclusively behavioristic theory of the mind is too restrictive. Logical behaviorism draws attention to the fact that our behavior is closely linked to what happens in our minds and that the study of behavior can help us to develop a scientific theory of the mind; however, it is problematic to reduce all mental states to dispositions to behave in certain ways. If we want to develop a satisfactory physicalist theory of the mind, a complete account of our mental life will involve more than talk about our behavior.

The Identity Theory

Behaviorism is not a very natural theory about the mind and mental phenomena; few people would think that their mental life can be reduced to talk about behavior. The **identity theory**, on the other hand, is a very intuitive theory that seems immediately plausible. The basic thrust of this theory can be illustrated by a historical example: In 1848 in a small town in Vermont, the railroad worker Phineas Gage was seriously injured while setting a charge of dynamite. The explosion was set off early and sent a steel bar right through his head. Surprisingly, Phineas Gage survived the accident and recovered from his head injuries. However, the accident caused serious repercussions. After Phineas Gage had recovered from his injuries, his behavior changed dramatically. Whereas he used to be easygoing and polite, he became obnoxious and ill-mannered. Friends who knew Phineas Gage before the accident claimed that the accident had turned him into a different person. How can we explain what happened to Phineas Gage?

According to the identity theory, the answer is simple and straightforward: Although Phineas Gage's body survived the accident, his brain was significantly altered by the steel bar. If we assume that mind and brain are the same thing, we can explain Phineas Gage's change in behavior without problems; we can claim that the steel bar injured not only Phineas Gage's brain, but his mind as well. The general claim that mental states are ultimately brain states is the central thesis of the identity theory.

This theory is well supported by recent advances in neuroscience, which has discovered that much of our mental functioning can be associated with specific parts of the brain. For example, identity theorists have no problem explaining that damage to the posterior sectors of the left-brain hemisphere is associated with impaired reading, writing, and speaking abilities. They also have no problem explaining why persons who suffer strokes in the right cortex experience difficulty with three-dimensional thinking or pattern recognition. If mind and brain are identical to each other, we should expect damage to particular parts of the brain to correspond to damage of specific mental functions. Moreover, the identity theory provides a fruitful framework for neuroscientific research. If mind and brain are the same thing, we can understand all mental phenomena as a physical, chemical reaction of neurons. My thought that my grandmother is a sweet old lady is perhaps nothing else but the firing of neuron #27883 to neuron #30152. Feelings of depression or schizophrenia might be nothing else but chemical imbalances in the brain. The task of neuroscience is to identify which type of physical chemical reaction corresponds to which type of mental state.

Food for Thought

A good way to test whether you understand competing philosophical theories is to apply the theories to the same situation and try to determine why they lead to different explanations or predictions. Let us try this with behaviorism and the identity theory. Consider the following situation: Suppose that you are going through a difficult time in your life. Each evening after you go to bed, you start thinking that your life is simply meaningless and empty. You are tired of having these thoughts and decide that you want to change your mind. You want to get rid of these depressing late-night thoughts.

1. Suppose behaviorism is true. How would a behaviorist try to change his mind in this situation?
2. Suppose the identity theory is true. How would an identity theorist go about changing her mind?

Arguments Against the Identity Theory

In spite of its attractiveness, the identity theory is open to objections. One crucial objection is well illustrated by the philosopher John Searle:

> Imagine that your brain starts to deteriorate in such a way that you are slowly going blind. Imagine that the desperate doctors, anxious to alleviate your condition, try any method to restore your vision. As a last resort, they try plugging silicon chips into your visual cortex. Imagine that to your amazement and theirs, it turns out that the silicon chips restore your vision to its normal state. Now, imagine further that your brain, depressingly, continues to deteriorate and the doctors continue to implant more silicon chips. You can see where the thought experiment is going already: in the end, we imagine that your brain is entirely replaced by silicon chips; that as you shake your head, you can hear the chips rattling around

inside your skull. In such a situation there would be various possibilities. One logical possibility, not to be excluded on any a priori grounds alone, is surely this: you continue to have all of the sorts of thoughts, experiences, memories, etc., that you had previously; the sequence of your mental life remains unaffected.[5]

Searle's thought experiment points to a crucial weakness of the identity theory; it identifies mental states with brain states and thus is committed to the general claim that *wherever there is no brain, there is no mind.* But is this claim really plausible? The thought experiment shows that it is logically possible that a being whose brain has been replaced by silicon chips has a mind. Thus, a strong version of the identity theory (sometimes called type-type identity theory), according to which mental states and brain states are necessarily identical, would be false. The identity theory leads to a certain kind of chauvinism by insisting that beings without the appropriate "hardware" (i.e., brain states) cannot have a mental life. This seems problematic in light of the fact that lower animals, for example an octopus, seem perfectly capable of experiencing mental states like pain without having a brain similar to ours. It also appears problematic in light of the possibilities that advanced machines or space aliens might have minds. Suppose, for example, that we encounter an alien space creature that is made entirely of previously unknown materials. We certainly would not be entitled to conclude that it does not have a mind simply because it does not have a brain like ours. Although our own mental life seems intimately tied to our brains, the general claim that mental states are brain states appears suspect. This conclusion does not mean that we have to abandon the identity theory completely, but it does mean that we have to modify the theory to make room for the fact that other creatures besides humans could have minds.

Functionalism

Functionalism developed as a response to the central weakness of the identity theory; functionalists take seriously the idea that minds can be realized in different physical materials. They thus reject the idea that minds are necessarily tied to brains. According to functionalism, mental states are functional states. But what exactly does this mean?

Functional Concepts and "Stuff" Concepts

If someone were to ask you to explain the nature of water, you would probably say that water is a certain kind of substance. More precisely, you might want to say that water is H_2O. Water is a "stuff" concept, that is, it can be defined as a particular kind of material stuff. Gold and wood are further examples of stuff concepts. Now, consider the term *money.* To clarify what money is, it is not very helpful to say something about silver or printed paper. Money can come in a wide variety of different material manifestations. A credit card, for example, is a form of money. To clarify what money is, we need to make reference to the functional role that money plays in our lives. We might say that everything that allows us to purchase goods is money. This functional definition of money would apply to silver coins as well as to credit cards or paper money. The term *money* therefore does not refer to a stuff concept but rather to a functional concept.

Food for Thought

Determine whether the following concepts are stuff concepts or functional concepts:

1. Food
2. Lion
3. Pen
4. Uranium
5. Shoes

Functionalism: Mind as Software

The basic idea of functionalism is to treat *mind* as a functional concept. We can roughly say that according to functionalism, something is a mind if it functions appropriately. This explains why space aliens or advanced machines might have a mind although they do not have a brain. As long as an entity possesses a physical mechanism that can play the same functional role as our neurons play in our brain, that entity has a mind. It does not matter whether the entity consists of organic tissue, silicon chips, or glass fibers. Functionalism is therefore well positioned to deal with the chauvinism that created so many problems for the identity theory. An analogy might be useful to illustrate the basic tenet of functionalism: According to functionalism, the mind is similar to a software program, which can run on very different computers as long as the hardware of the computers is complex enough to run the program. Similarly, a functionalist believes that any physical system that is complex enough to recreate the functional interactions among neurons in our brain can have a mind.

Functionalism and Artificial Intelligence: The Turing Test

Functionalism clearly supports the idea that it should be possible to create artificial intelligence (AI). If we succeed in building machines that can play the same functional role as our brains, these machines must, according to functionalism, have a mind. Alan Turing (1912–1953), one of the founders of modern computer science, suggested a method to determine whether advanced machines indeed have minds. The basic idea of the **Turing test** is to put a human being, whom we will call the tester, in front of a computer terminal.

The tester can type questions about any subject matter into the computer terminal, and the questions are answered by somebody in another room. What the tester does not know is whether the questions are answered by another human being or by an advanced machine. It is the job of the tester to determine whether he is interacting with a machine or with a real human being. Alan Turing suggested that if we could create a machine that could answer the questions of the tester such that the tester is convinced that he is dealing with a human being, then we could conclude that the machine has a mind. In this case we would say that the machine has passed the Turing test.

Supporters of functionalism should accept the Turing test. Being able to conduct a conversation is, after all, one of the crucial functions of minds. Since functionalists agree that anything that plays the appropriate functional role is a mind, they must also accept the idea that a machine that passes the Turing test has a mind. Functionalism therefore supports the idea that artificial intelligence is possible.

Food for Thought

The question of whether advanced computers can have minds is a hot philosophical issue. One cannot deny that computers have come a long way and that they are capable of astounding things. But is it also possible that computers might someday develop consciousness and a sense of self-identity? Many people are convinced that this could never happen; they believe that no machine could ever have a mind. However, not all of their supporting arguments are very convincing. Take a look at the following arguments, and decide whether or not they are compelling:

1. Computers are not alive. Only living things can have a mind. Therefore: Computers cannot have minds.
2. Computers only follow programs and thus do not act creatively or in unpredictable ways. In order to have a mind, one needs to be able to act creatively and unpredictably. Therefore: Computers cannot have minds.
3. Computers cannot have feelings and emotions. A thing without emotions and feelings cannot have a mind. Therefore: Computers cannot have minds.

Arguments Against Functionalism

The Chinese Room Argument   A number of thinkers have objected to the idea that machines could have minds simply by virtue of enacting the appropriate functional program. John Searle is perhaps the best-known philosopher who has attacked functionalism on this point. To refute functionalism and the related idea of artificial intelligence, Searle presented the Chinese room argument:

> Consider a language you don't understand. In my case, I do not understand Chinese. To me Chinese writing looks like so many meaningless squiggles. Now suppose I am placed in a room containing baskets full of Chinese symbols. Suppose also that I am given a rule book in English for matching Chinese symbols with other Chinese symbols. The rules identify the symbols entirely by their shapes and do not require that I understand any of them. The rules might say such things as, "Take a squiggle-squiggle sign from basket number one and put it next to a squoggle-squoggle sign from basket number two."
>
> Imagine that people outside the room who understand Chinese hand in small bunches of symbols and that in response I manipulate the symbols according to the rule book and hand back more small bunches of symbols. Now, the rule book is the "computer program." The people who wrote it are "programmers" and I am the "computer." The baskets full of symbols are the "data base," the small bunches that are handed in to me are "questions" and the bunches I then hand out are "answers."
>
> Now suppose that the rule book is written in such a way that my "answers" to the "questions" are indistinguishable from those of a native Chinese speaker. For example, the people outside might hand me some symbols that unknown to me mean, "What's your favorite color?" and I might after going through the rules give back symbols that, also unknown to me, mean "My favorite is blue, but I also like green a lot." I satisfy the Turing Test for understanding Chinese. All the same, I am totally ignorant of Chinese. And there is no way I could come to understand Chinese in the system as described, since there is no way that I can learn the meanings of any of the symbols. Like a computer, I manipulate symbols, but I attach no meaning to the symbols.[6]

Searle's Chinese room argument is intended to show that computers are, in principle, not capable of understanding the meanings (semantics) of words and symbols; computers are limited to processing symbols on the basis of their shapes (syntax). Genuine minds, on the other hand, are capable of understanding the meanings of words. Searle concludes therefore that computers only appear as if they have minds; in reality they do not. Passing the Turing test is not a sufficient condition for having mental states.

Defenders of functionalism and artificial intelligence are normally not impressed by the Chinese room argument and point to several weaknesses. First, Searle's argument is built around an analogy between the Chinese room and the inner workings of computers. This analogy might not be as close as Searle makes it out to be. Currently, computers process information in a sequential, step-by-step manner that is roughly analogous to what happens in the Chinese room. But current computers also cannot pass the Turing test; perhaps computers that actually pass the Turing test might function differently from the manner that Searle describes. Computers that pass the Turing test might, for example, be based on parallel distributive processing rather than sequential processors. Thus, the central analogy between computers and the Chinese room might be misleading.

The second objection to the Chinese room argument is called the **systems reply**. The Chinese room argument shows that the person in the room does not understand Chinese. The person, however, is only one part of the system. What would happen if we were to consider the system as a whole? Could the system as a whole understand Chinese? Consider the workings of my brain for a moment: It is quite plausible to think that no one part of my brain understands the meaning of English sentences. Instead, understanding and consciousness might be a result of my whole brain working together. Perhaps Searle is overlooking the possibility that the whole Chinese room together is capable of understanding Chinese.

Searle himself has responded to these objections at considerable length. At this point, it would be too much to explore the debate about the Chinese room argument in full. For our purposes it is sufficient to note that the Chinese room argument is by no means a knockdown argument against functionalism. However, if you agree with John Searle and believe that even the most advanced computers cannot have minds, it might be interesting to explore how the Chinese room argument can be strengthened.

Problems with Qualia   A more serious objection to functionalism is raised by so-called inverted spectrum cases. Consider two twin brothers, Alf and Tony, who experience the same colors differently. Tony sees red and green as normal people experience these colors. Alf, on the other hand, experiences red as Tony experiences green, and green as Tony experiences red. However, neither Tony nor Alf (nor anybody else, for that matter) will ever discover that they have different sensations with respect to the same colors. When Tony sees a ripe tomato, he will say, "Look at that great red tomato!" And Alf, who has learned to associate his experience of green with the word *red*, will say the same thing. Alf is perfectly capable of picking out red things. It is just that what people call red causes a green sensation in him, and what people call green causes a red sensation in him. This thought experiment raises a fundamental problem for functionalism; from a functional perspective. Alf and Tony appear to be equivalent. They can do the same things (e.g., recognize green and red), and they display the same verbal behavior in similar circumstances. So according to functionalism, both are in the same mental state when they see and experience red things.[7] This, however, is clearly not the case, for Alf and Tony experience the same color differently and thus have different color sensations.

Inverted spectrum cases show that functionalism has a difficult time making room for what philosophers have called **qualia**, which refers to the phenomenal aspect of mental states. The philosopher Frank Jackson gives the following examples of qualia: "the itchiness of itches, pangs of jealousy, . . . the characteristic experience of tasting a lemon, smelling a rose. . . ."[8] It is hard to deny that some of our mental states, especially sensations, have a characteristic phenomenal feeling (i.e., qualia) when we experience them. When I smell freshly brewed coffee, run my fingers over sandpaper, or see bright red, I am the subject of mental states with distinctive phenomenal characteristics. But it is problematic to explain qualia in functional terms, because it seems possible that functionally equivalent mental states are associated with completely different subjective qualia. The philosopher David Chalmers puts it this way:

> Nobody knows why physical brain processes are accompanied by conscious experiences at all. Why is it that when our brains process light of a certain wave-length, we have an experience of deep purple? Why do we have any experiences at all? Could not an unconscious automation have performed the same task just as well?[9]

Chalmers argues that it is logically possible that there are beings who act like us in every respect and who process information as we do but who lack any kind of subjective consciousness (and hence any qualia). Chalmers calls these beings *zombies* (not to be confused with Hollywood zombies). Since Chalmers's zombies are functionally equivalent to us (i.e., they do and say the same things that we do) but lack subjective phenomenal qualia, they seem to illustrate that functional accounts of the mind are incomplete. Philosophers have called this quandary the problem of the explanatory gap. Frank Jackson wrote in this context:

> Tell me everything physical there is to tell about what is going on in a living brain, the kind of states, their functional role, their relation to what goes on at other times and in other brains, and so on and so forth, and be I as clever as can be in fitting it all together, you won't have told me about the hurtfulness of pains, the itchiness of itches, pangs of jealousy, or about the characteristic experience of tasting a lemon, smelling a rose, hearing a loud noise or seeing the sky.[10]

It seems as if functionalism—and perhaps any purely physicalistic theory of the mind—does not provide a complete account of what minds really are.

Food for Thought

Are Chalmers's zombies really logically possible? Some philosophers have doubted the coherence of the idea that there could be beings that do all the things we do without having any feelings at all. Consider specific activities in your life, and decide whether a zombie could participate in these activities without any subjective feelings.

Eliminative Materialism

Since functionalism is facing some serious difficulties, it is tempting to look for alternatives. One alternative physicalist theory is **eliminative materialism,** which has been advocated by, among others, contemporary American philosophers Patricia and Paul Churchland. Eliminative materialists suggest that we abandon the attempt to incorporate mental states into our picture of the world; they hold that mental states are not part of a scientific and accurate view of the world. Eliminative materialists claim that mental states do not really exist—they are nothing but convenient illusions. At first glance this sounds outrageous, but much can be said in defense of this position.

In order to get a better understanding of eliminative materialism, consider the following scenarios: Suppose that early one morning you walk on the beach and watch the sun rise. You mumble to yourself, "Oh, my God, the sun is rising spectacularly. I had forgotten how beautiful that is." These sentences make perfect sense, even though the first sentence is literally false. The sun does not actually rise at all; it only looks to us as if the sun is rising. In reality there is no rising sun but only the Earth in motion.

Consider another example: Suppose it is April 15, and you are in the process of filling out your tax return. In order to make things easier, you have bought a computer income tax program. Unfortunately, your computer has difficulty with the new program and is crashing frequently. Shortly before midnight, you cry out in desperation, "I think my computer is mad at me. It doesn't want me to fill out my tax forms on time." Again, this sentence makes perfect sense, although it is not literally true. It might seem as if your computer has desires and intentions, but it does not really care about the fact that you are having problems. Nonetheless, we find it quite natural to talk as if computers have intentions and desires.

Consider one further example: Suppose you observe an octopus emitting a black inky substance. In this situation it is natural to say, "The octopus believes that a predator is close by and therefore emits the inky substance in order to become harder for the predator to spot." Although it is natural for us to speak as if octopuses have beliefs and desires, we would not be surprised to find out that in reality octopuses do not have beliefs and desires at all. There is a biological, chemical process in the octopus that can be fully explained and understood without any reference to beliefs and desires.

Once we understand that we talk naturally as if other creatures and entities have minds even though they do not really have any mental states, the possibility arises that the same might be true for us as well. It certainly seems to us as if we have a rich array of mental states, and we certainly talk as if we have these mental states, but eliminative materialists maintain that this is an illusion caused by our habits of speech. In reality, they say, there are no beliefs, desires, or wishes, but only neurons, synapses, and neurotransmitters. Thus, eliminative materialism rids us of all the traditional puzzles of the mind/body problem.

If we accept eliminative materialism, there is no difficulty in explaining how the mind is related to the body; if the mind does not exist, all we have are the neurological processes in the brain, which will eventually, as science progresses, be understood in greater and greater detail. Nothing more is required to bury the mind/body problem once and for all.

This is an elegant and radical solution to the mind/body problem. However, it is easy to see challenges to eliminative materialism. First, some might find it impossible to accept the idea that minds and mental states are illusions. We might follow Descartes and argue that—given our own thinking experiences— our own minds must necessarily exist and we can know that this is so. Of course, an advocate of eliminative materialism will not be impressed by this line of reasoning and will dismiss these Cartesian thoughts as powerful illusions. However, it does not seem clear to me that if eliminative materialism and Cartesian intuitions clash with each other, then reason requires us to abandon Descartes. It is just as, if not more, tempting to abandon eliminative materialism. Second, we might point out that eliminative materialism seems to be self-refuting. If it is true that nobody believes anything (since minds do not really exist), then how are we to believe that eliminative materialism is true? Does not any philosophical argument presuppose that we have beliefs and a mental life?

Final Remarks on the Mind/Body Problem

The relationship between body and mind is today as mysterious as it was in the past. From a commonsense perspective, Descartes' substance dualism seems very attractive. It is supported by religious beliefs and near-death experiences, but it leads to a number of prominent difficulties: the problem of interaction and Ryle's charge of a category mistake.

Physicalist theories about the mind are attractive in light of recent advances in neuroscience. We have seen, however, that a purely behaviorist approach to the mind cannot produce a satisfactory theory. The identity theory is more promising, but it too leads to a central problem: the possibility that mental states can be realized in multiple physical systems. Functionalism is well suited to deal with this difficulty, but it has a hard time accounting for the subjective, qualitative character (qualia) of mental states. It is not quite clear yet how serious the qualia problem really is. Some contemporary philosophers simply deny that inverted spectrum cases or Chalmers's zombies raise fundamental problems for physicalistic theories of the mind. They argue that these cases do not present genuine logical possibilities.

Others have taken the qualia problem as a reason to reintroduce eliminative materialism or a version of dualism—**property dualism**, which is a mixture of physicalism and dualism. Property dualists reject substance dualism and agree with the physicalists that our minds have a purely physical foundation. However, property dualists deny that every mental property can be reduced to physical processes. This puts property dualists in a position to accept qualia as irreducible mental properties. Whether property dualism is a fruitful theory is not yet quite clear.

Philosophy of mind is one of the most active fields in contemporary philosophy. Our present discussion is only a preliminary introduction to the main positions and questions. However, the discussion should have given you a chance to think about the relationship between body and mind on your own. In the course of reading this chapter, you may have revised some of your own ideas about how bodies and minds are related to each other. It might be interesting now for you to go back to the Food for Thought exercise on page 129 and see whether you would answer the questions there differently.

Study and Reflection Questions

1. It seems pretty clear that higher developed animals like dolphins or elephants also have some sort of mind. However, it is much less clear whether chickens have minds. What do you think? Do chickens have minds? Which mind/body theory would you use to defend your answer?

2. Are you more attracted to physicalism or dualism? Develop reasons in defense of your choice.

3. Will computers be able to develop self-consciousness? Defend your answer in light of various theories about the mind/body relationship.

4. Many people report near-death experiences. What significance, if any, do these experiences have for our understanding of the mind/body relationship?

5. We speak of Santa Claus and the Easter Bunny, which we know do not exist. Is it also possible, as eliminative materialism claims, that there are no beliefs, hopes, or desires—in short, that there are no real mental states? What do you think?

For Further Reading

Block, N., O. Flanagan, and G. Guzeldere, eds. *The Nature of Consciousness: Philosophical Debates*. Cambridge, MA: MIT Press, 1997.

Chalmers, David. *The Conscious Mind: In Search of a Fundamental Theory*. New York: Oxford University Press, 1996.

Churchland, Paul. *Matter and Consciousness*. Cambridge, MA: MIT Press, 1988.

Dennett, Daniel. *Kinds of Minds: Toward an Understanding of Consciousness*. New York: Basic Books, 1996.

Graham, George. *Philosophy of Mind: An Introduction*. Oxford: Blackwell, 1998.

Guttenplan, Samuel. ed. *A Companion to the Philosophy of Mind*. Oxford: Blackwell, 1994.

Heil, John. *Philosophy of Mind: A Contemporary Introduction*. New York: Routledge, 2003.

Ravenscroft, Ian. *Philosophy of Mind: A Beginner's Guide.* Oxford: Oxford University Press, 2005.

Ryle, Gilbert. *The Concept of Mind.* London: Hutchinson, 1949.

Searle, John R. *Mind: A Brief Introduction.* Oxford: Oxford University Press, 2004.

Endnotes

1. This near-death experience is described in George Graham, *Philosophy of Mind: An Introduction* (Oxford: Blackwell, 1998), pp. 22–23.
2. Raymond Moody, *Life After Life: The Investigation of a Phenomenon—Survival of Bodily Death*, 2nd ed. (San Francisco, CA: HarperSanFrancisco, 2001).
3. For a more complete discussion of the significance of near-death experiences, see Susan Blackmore, *Dying to Live* (London: HarperCollins, 1993).
4. See Betty L. Stafford, "Mind, Paranormal Experience, and the Inadequacy of Materialism," *International Philosophical Quarterly* 44, no. 3 (September 2004): 373–392.
5. John Searle, *The Rediscovery of the Mind* (Cambridge, MA: MIT Press, 1992), p. 65.
6. John Searle, "Is the Brain's Mind a Computer Program?" *Scientific American* 262 (January 1990): 26.
7. A convinced functionalist will probably deny that Alf and Tony are in functionally equivalent states. Since Alf and Tony represent the color red differently, one might argue that there also must be a functional difference between Alf and Tony. This points to the best response a functionalist can muster in response to inverted spectrum cases, which is simply to deny that these cases are logically possible. In order to establish this, a functionalist would have to show that inverted spectrum cases contain hidden contradictions.
8. Frank Jackson, "Epiphenomenal Qualia," *Philosophical Quarterly* 32 (1982): 127–136.
9. David Chalmers, "The Puzzle of Conscious Experience," *Scientific American* 237 (December 1995): 53.
10. Frank Jackson, "Epiphenomenal Qualia," *Philosophical Quarterly* 32 (1982): 127–136.

CHAPTER SEVEN

DOES GOD EXIST?

God, Faith, and Reason

Some philosophical problems seem far removed from the way we live our day-to-day lives. However, this is not true when we deal with questions about God. If God exists, we must understand ourselves and the universe in terms of a relationship with a perfect and necessary being. Part of our lives should then be devoted to building this relationship through prayer, observance of religious rituals, or the reading of holy books like the Bible or the Koran. If, on the other hand, God does not exist, we are faced with a different situation. While we would be free to dismiss most religious activities as nonsense, we would have to accept the idea that we are finite beings who live in a universe without ultimate meaning or purpose.[1] The question of whether God exists is therefore of obvious interest, and the answer we give to the question has an immediate impact upon our lives and our understanding of the world.

It is nevertheless frequently difficult to engage people in a thorough discussion about God's existence. Many people hold that religious beliefs are a matter of faith only and should not be scrutinized with the help of reason. For them, religious beliefs are a matter of the heart (faith) and not a matter of the head (reason). There is something to be said for this position—some well-known philosophers such as Kierkegaard (1813–1855) have defended it—but extreme versions of this so-called **fideistic** approach to religious beliefs are difficult to justify. To illustrate this difficulty, consider the following example: Suppose you find out that a friend of yours has joined a radical religious group that considers higher education a work of the devil and consequently advocates the destruction of all college campuses. The next time you meet your friend, he is on his way to class with dynamite strapped to his body. You feel a strong moral obligation to stop him, but how? If you are stronger than he is, you might try to wrestle him to the ground, or you might try to get the help of a nearby police officer. But suppose that there is no police officer and that your friend is much stronger than you. At this point your only option is to try to convince your friend—with the help of arguments—that he is mistaken to think that God wants all college campuses to be destroyed. Of course, this is an extreme example, but it suggests that all of us—whether we are Christians, atheists, Jews, Muslims, Hindus, Buddhists, or advocates of some other religious perspective—have an obligation to test and analyze our religious beliefs by means of reason. Reason might not be able to answer all religious questions,[2] but it can provide a framework that prevents people from misusing religious sentiments for dangerous ends. It is, therefore, a vital task to determine to what degree we can justify religious beliefs with the help of rational evidence. In this chapter we will limit ourselves to exploring one of the most fundamental religious questions: Does God exist?

Food for Thought

On May 11, 2003, Deanne Laney, a thirty-nine-year-old mother and housewife, stoned two of her children to death and seriously injured a third. When asked for an explanation, she said, "I felt like I obeyed God, and I believe there will be good out of this. I feel like he will reveal his power, and they will be raised up. They will become alive again." This story illustrates one of the inherent difficulties in radical fideism. If we accept our religious beliefs without checking whether they are reasonable or not, we have no way of excluding extreme and fanatical religious beliefs. Can you think of other examples in which accepting religious beliefs on the basis of blind faith alone might lead to harmful consequences?

What Do We Mean by the Word *God*?

At first glance it might seem as if we can respond to the question of whether God exists in only two ways: Either we answer with a yes and embrace a **theistic** position, or we answer with a no and support a version of **atheism.** However, there are more than two options here. For one, we may decide to subscribe to an **agnostic** position, which holds that it is possible for God to exist but that we humans can never know whether that possibility is actually true. A further complication is raised by the inherent ambiguity of the term *God.* Although most people (approximately 88 percent of the American population) agree that God exists;[3] many people have conflicting ideas about what kind of being God is supposed to be. Some understand God as universal energy, whereas others see and experience God as a personal friend. Unless we can clarify what we mean by the term *God*, we can hardly determine whether there are any good reasons to believe that such a being exists.

Food for Thought

What properties are essential to God? Decide whether you believe that the following assertions about God are true or false.

1. God is eternal.
2. God is male.
3. God has a physical body.
4. God is all-powerful (omnipotent).
5. God knows everything (omniscient).
6. God reveals himself differently in different cultures.
7. God is all-good (omnibenevolent).
8. God is the greatest being that we can think of.
9. God and Jesus are one and the same person.
10. God is everywhere in nature.
11. God helps those who deserve help.
12. God causes miracles.
13. God is sometimes really mad at human beings.
14. God loves all humans equally.
15. God is so different from us that we have no idea what God is like.
16. When I talk to God, I know that he listens.
17. God likes some countries (e.g., the U.S.) more than other countries.

As you can see from this exercise, there can be much disagreement about which properties are essential to God. To gain some point of reference, we can divide the various conceptions of God into three broad categories—classical theism, pantheism, and new age conception—as illustrated in the following diagram:

Different Conceptions of God

Classical Theism

Classical theism is embraced by three monotheistic world religions: Judaism, Christianity, and Islam. According to this conception, God is separate from the universe (i.e., is the creator of the universe). God is a person and performs acts (miracles). Moreover, God is seen as omniscient, omnipotent, and omnibenevolent.

Pantheism

According to this conception, God is everywhere. Nature and God are one. God is not separate from the universe. This conception is especially popular among the romantics and some Asian religions.

New-Age Conception

A broad category that refers most prominently to those who think that God is a spiritual, personal guide. Writers in this group tend to draw a distinction between religion and spirituality. More recent, more personal writings play a more prominent role than traditional religious texts.

This classification is somewhat simplistic, but it nevertheless helps us to see that classical theism, the view of God supported by the three major theistic religions of the world, is not the only conception of God. Notably, Asian religions embrace a quite different perspective. In the Western philosophical tradition, however, most thinkers have embraced a classical theistic conception of God, and we will focus our discussion on that viewpoint. However, this does not mean that we will disregard nonclassical conceptions of God completely. Later in this chapter, we will see that certain philosophical puzzles might be approached differently if we revise the classical conception of God.

Let us begin by clarifying classical theism in more detail. According to classical theism, God has several key features: God is the creator of the universe, and he is omnipotent, omniscient, and perfectly good (worthy of worship). He is infinite, everlasting, and not dependent on anything other than himself (i.e., he is self-existent and necessary). Most importantly, the classical theistic God of the Torah, the New Testament, and the Koran is a person. That means that God is the kind of being who can act, who is capable of love and creativity, and who can enter into relationships with humans. It is by virtue of God's personhood that God can be our friend or helper. The philosopher Richard Swinburne defines the god of classical theism as follows: "A person without a body (i.e., a spirit), present everywhere, the creator and sustainer of the universe, a free agent, able to do anything (i.e., omnipotent), knowing all things, perfectly good, a source of moral obligation, immutable, eternal, a necessary being, holy and worthy of worship."[4]

Classical theism does not yield a completely unified conception of God; there are many questions that are hotly debated within this broad tradition. For example, is God capable of having emotions, or is he impassible? To what degree does God know the future? What is the relationship between God, the Holy Spirit, and Jesus? Which—if any—is the true word of God: the Koran, the Torah, or the Bible? In spite of these difficulties, it is nevertheless possible to extract a fairly coherent conception of God from these three theistic religions. From here on, we will understand the question of whether God exists as the question of whether an omnipotent, omniscient, omnibenevolent, and personal creator of the universe exists.

So far, our discussion has helped us clarify what we mean by the term *God*, but this does not yet help us to understand what reason tells us about God. Does reason tell us that classical theism is true? Or does reason tell us the opposite? Is reason perhaps unable to settle the question, and should we therefore adopt an agnostic position? In order to answer this question, we need to take a closer look at the various arguments for and against classical theism. The chart that follows illustrates the most popular philosophical responses to the question of whether there are any good reasons for thinking that God exists.

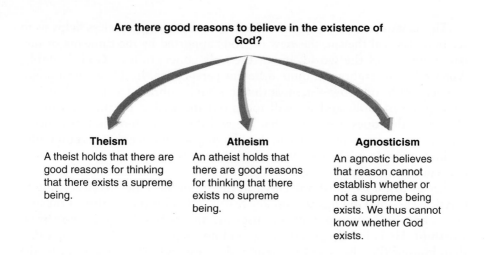

Are there good reasons to believe in the existence of God?

Theism
A theist holds that there are good reasons for thinking that there exists a supreme being.

Atheism
An atheist holds that there are good reasons for thinking that there exists no supreme being.

Agnosticism
An agnostic believes that reason cannot establish whether or not a supreme being exists. We thus cannot know whether God exists.

In the following pages we will explore a multitude of arguments for and against classical theism. Since the discussion involves so many different points of view, it is possible to get lost. To keep track of the big-picture view of our discussion, this graphic overview should be helpful.

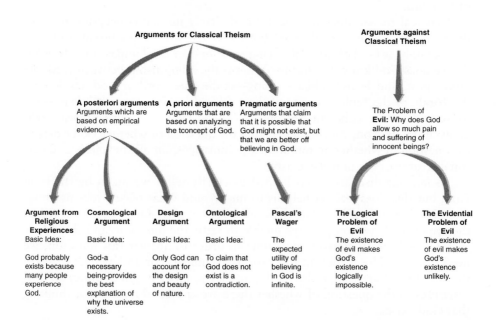

Arguments for Classical Theism

Arguments against Classical Theism

A posteriori arguments
Arguments which are based on empirical evidence.

A priori arguments
Arguments that are based on analyzing the tconcept of God.

Pragmatic arguments
Arguments that claim that it is possible that God might not exist, but that we are better off believing in God.

The Problem of **Evil:** Why does God allow so much pain and suffering of innocent beings?

Argument from Religious Experiences
Basic Idea:

God probably exists because many people experience God.

Cosmological Argument
Basic Idea:

God–a necessary being–provides the best explanation of why the universe exists.

Design Argument
Basic Idea:

Only God can account for the design and beauty of nature.

Ontological Argument
Basic Idea:

To claim that God does not exist is a contradiction.

Pascal's Wager

The expected utility of believing in God is infinite.

The Logical Problem of Evil
The existence of evil makes God's existence logically impossible.

The Evidential Problem of Evil
The existence of evil makes God's existence unlikely.

Arguments in Defense of Classical Theism

Arguments from Religious Experiences

Some of the most persuasive arguments in defense of the existence of God are based on religious experiences. Consider the following description of a religious experience:

> Now Moses was keeping the flock of his father-in-law . . . and the angel of the Lord appeared to him in a flame of fire out of the midst of a bush; and he looks, and lo, the bush was burning, yet it was not consumed. . . . God called to him out of the bush, "Moses, Moses!" (Exod. 3:1–4)

Suppose for a moment that you have a chance to speak with Moses after he had the experience just described. Suppose you ask, "Moses, do you have any reason to believe that God exists?" Wouldn't Moses be amused by that question? What better reason can one have for thinking that God exists than hearing God's voice in a burning bush? Let us become clear on the nature of the argument that stands behind Moses's reasoning. In standard form the argument can be represented as follows:

```
1.I have experiences that seem to be caused by God.
2.The best explanation for these experiences is
  that God indeed has caused them.
```
Therefore: God probably exists.

This is an inductive argument; it aims to establish its conclusion with a high degree of probability. Even if we have experiences that seem to have been caused by God, it is of course possible that we are mistaken and that these experiences have been caused by something else (e.g., hallucinations, wishful thinking, sleep deprivation). The argument does not overlook this possibility, but it tries to establish that it is much more likely that the religious experiences were caused by God rather than by hallucinations or some other cause. In order to understand the thrust of the argument better, it is useful to compare this argument with a related argument that tries to establish the existence of mind-independent physical objects. In standard form the argument can be presented as follows:

```
1.I have experiences that seem to be caused by
  mind-independent physical objects (e.g., chairs
  or tables).
2.The best explanation for these experiences is
  that mind-independent physical objects indeed
  caused my experiences.
```
Therefore: Mind-independent physical objects (e.g., chairs or tables) probably exist.

This argument strikes me as a perfectly plausible argument in defense of my belief that mind-independent physical objects exist in the world. It is natural to think that the best explanation for my visual experiences of physical objects is that there are indeed physical objects out there. Of course, the possibility exists that I am mistaken about this and that I am really just a brain in a vat or a person trapped in the matrix, but these scenarios seem far-fetched and not very likely to be true. My argument, therefore, establishes its conclusion with a high degree of probability, and that is all that matters for a good inductive argument. Once we realize that the argument in support of the existence of mind-independent physical objects is cogent, we can take advantage of the similarity between the two arguments and advance the following argument by analogy:

1. The inductive argument that tries to establish the existence of mind-independent physical objects on the basis of our experiences of these objects provides us with a good reason for thinking that there are mind-independent physical objects.
2. The argument that tries to establish the existence of God on the basis of experiences of God is similar to the argument that tries to establish the existence of mind-independent physical objects on the basis of our experiences of these objects.

Therefore: The argument that tries to establish the existence of God on the basis of experiences of God provides us with a good reason for thinking that God exists.

This argument by analogy is attractive. However, in order to assess whether we ought to accept this argument, we need to compare the two arguments in more detail. The crucial question is whether the two arguments are sufficiently similar: Does the argument that infers the existence of God from religious experiences resemble the argument that infers the existence of external physical objects from my experiences of these objects, or are there significant and relevant differences that undermine the argument by analogy? Let us explore this question in more detail. First, it is clear that experiences of physical objects are widespread. Nearly everyone has had visual experiences of tables or chairs. Religious experiences, on the other hand, are much rarer. Moses might have heard God's voice in a burning bush, and Joseph Smith might have seen the angel Maroni in the forest, but most of us have never had these kinds of experiences. This weakens the argument, but it does not pose a decisive objection. We can respond to this concern by limiting the scope of the argument; although the argument does not work for everyone, it might work for those who have had the relevant religious experiences. In addition, we can point out that even somebody who has never had a religious experience in the past could have such an experience in the future. This would assure that the argument is at least of some interest to those who lack the relevant experiences.

A second, more serious problem with the argument is raised by concerns about the trustworthiness (reliability) of the religious experiences. It cannot be denied that some religious experiences are the product of wishful thinking, lively imaginations, and hallucinations. Does this indicate that all religious experiences can never be trusted and should not be counted as evidence? In order to clarify this issue, the contemporary American philosopher Richard Swinburne introduced the so-called **Principle of Credulity,** which says that if a person has experiences that seem to be of X, then the person has reason to believe that X exists unless the person has further reason to indicate that the experiences should not be trusted.

Let us see how the principle of credulity works in the case of visual experiences. Suppose, for instance, that it is late at night and I am walking through a forest. Suddenly, it seems to me that I see a vampire behind a tree. In this situation the principle of credulity says that my experience of seeing a vampire does not give me a reason to think that vampires exist because I know that my visual experiences are not reliable when walking through a dark forest. However, the principle of credulity would say that my visual experience of seeing a yellow frog in front of me in broad daylight when I am not intoxicated provides a very good reason for thinking that yellow frogs exist.

What then should we say about religious experiences? Suppose that it seems to me that I experience God's presence. Suppose further that I am aware that I am very tired when I am having this religious experience. Does my being tired give me reason to think that my religious experience is unreliable? It is impossible to know for sure, because nobody knows under what conditions religious experiences are reliable perceptions of a higher reality. We simply do not know how religious experiences work. Different philosophers draw different conclusions from this; Richard Swinburne, for instance, thinks that the fact that we do not know whether religious experiences are unreliable gives us a reason to take them as evidence. Many other philosophers, however, think that our ignorance about when religious experiences are reliable and our inability to corroborate religious experiences with others make it impossible to treat them as evidence. However, even if we accept religious experiences as evidence, we must acknowledge that we are much better in identifying under what conditions our visual experiences are reliable than we are in recognizing under what conditions religious experiences are reliable. This marks a clear difference between ordinary visual experiences and religious experiences and thus weakens the argument by analogy.

Food for Thought

In a famous passage Bertrand Russell once wrote: "From a scientific point of view, we can make no distinction between the man who eats little and sees heaven and the man who drinks much and sees snakes. Each

Continued

Continued

is in an abnormal physical condition, and thus has abnormal perceptions."[5] Russell suggests here that religious experiences occur frequently
in extraordinary situations, which undermine the reliability of these
experiences. Do you agree with Russell on this point?

A final worry about appeals to religious experiences is that they seem to
support contradictory claims about God. People in different religions experience the supreme being in different ways: A Muslim has experiences that seem
to be of Allah; a Christian has experiences that seem to be of Jesus; and a
Hindu has experiences that seem to be of Krishna. If the argument from religious experience works with one religious tradition, it is hard to see why it
would not work in other religious traditions as well. This means that the argument from religious experience—if accepted—does not establish the existence
of one supreme being with attributes that reflect one particular religious tradition. On the contrary, if we accept this argument, we have just as much reason
to believe in the existence of Krishna as in the existence of Allah or any other
supreme being. In order to respond to this difficulty, one might conclude that
the argument from religious experience does not establish that a supreme
being exists but perhaps only that some form of ultimate reality exists. This
result, however, does not offer much help in our attempt to determine whether
there are good reasons for thinking that classical theism is true.

There can be no doubt that religious experiences are a powerful element
in the lives of many believers, but our discussion shows that they probably
cannot provide any decisive and intersubjective ground for establishing the
existence of God. William James expressed the situation well when he wrote:
"[Religious experiences] have the right to be absolutely authoritative over
the individual to whom they come . . . [but] no authority emanates from
them which should make it a duty for those who stand outside of them to
accept their revelations."[6]

The Cosmological Argument

An alternative strategy for trying to establish the existence of God is to infer
the existence of God from the existence of the universe, or cosmos. The cosmological argument, which has a long history that reaches back to the writings
of Plato and Aristotle, can be presented either as a deductive or as an inductive
argument. Deductive versions of the argument have been more popular, but we
will focus on an inductive version that I believe provides the most attractive
version of the argument. In order to understand the basic thrust of the cosmological argument, we need to understand two philosophical ideas: the concept
of a **necessary being** and the **principle of sufficient reason**, which we encountered in our discussion of free will.

Let us start by reviewing this principle. Consider the following example:
Suppose that you are walking through a remote forest and come across the

ruins of a huge ancient city.[7] You do not know what civilization created this city, and you certainly do not know why they created a city in this particular place, but you are sure that there is some explanation for why the city exists. This seems true not only for cities in remote forests but also for things in general; I might not know why I have a terrible headache, but I am sure that there is an explanation for the throbbing pain in my skull. Or I might not know why President Kennedy was shot in 1963, but I am certain that an explanation exists. This is the principle of sufficient reason—that for anything that exists there must be an explanation (i.e., a sufficient reason) of why it exists.

Let us now turn our attention to the concept of a necessary being. In order to understand this concept, it might be useful to explore its antonym—namely, the concept of a contingent being. I myself am a good example of a contingent being. I was born in the year 1965 and have been in existence ever since. However, I am acutely aware of that my existence is not necessary but contingent. At any given point something could happen that would put an end to my existence; I might have a heart attack, or a stray bullet might hit my head. Whether I continue to exist depends on many contingent factors, and what is true for me and my existence seems to be true for many other things as well. The tree outside my office window could burn, and the coffee cup on my desk could fall and break; the tree and the coffee cup are also contingent beings. Is there anything that exists with necessity? Are there beings that cannot be destroyed and that never have come into existence? Such necessary beings, if they exist, are very different from you and me. Necessary beings have always existed and are not brought into existence by anything else; they are self-sufficient and self-explanatory.

We are now in a good position to take a closer look at the logic of the cosmological argument. The basic structure of the argument can be presented as follows:

```
1.The world, or cosmos, exists.
2.There must be an explanation of why the world
  exists.
3.The best explanation of why the world exists is
  that the world was created by a necessary being.
```

```
Therefore:
4.A necessary being probably exists.
5.This necessary being is God.
```

```
Therefore: God probably exists.
```

Let us take a look at the various steps of the argument. The first premise is easy to accept: There can be no doubt that the cosmos exists—that's a fact! The second premise is supported by the principle of sufficient reason. If there must be an explanation for everything, it seems to follow that there must be an explanation for the existence of the world. The third premise is more difficult to justify. Why should we think that the best explanation of the existence of the world is that a necessary being created it? Clearly, there are other explanations available that should be compared in order to judge which is the best.

From a logical point of view, we can identify three possible explanations, as illustrated in the following chart:

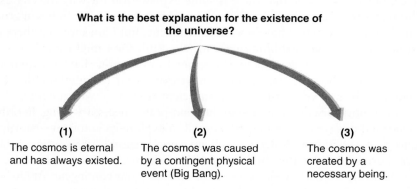

What is the best explanation for the existence of the universe?

(1) The cosmos is eternal and has always existed.

(2) The cosmos was caused by a contingent physical event (Big Bang).

(3) The cosmos was created by a necessary being.

Let us start by analyzing the first option. Even if we believe that our current cosmos originated with the big bang, it is still conceivable that the cosmos itself is eternal. We can imagine, for instance, that the currently expanding universe will at some point (by virtue of gravitational forces) start to contract. In this scenario, called the big crunch, the universe ultimately will collapse onto itself. After it has completely collapsed, the universe may restart itself with another big explosion and thus begin the cycle anew. We can imagine that this process has always been going on. If so, there may be no absolute beginning to the universe; in this endless state of renewal and destruction, it has always been around. Is there anything wrong with this idea?

To accept the idea of a universe that extends infinitely back in time, one must also accept that an infinite series exists. However, defenders of the cosmological argument argue that the idea of an existing infinite series is incoherent. Let me illustrate this with an example: Suppose that you come across an old man in the forest who is mumbling to himself. As you approach, you can hear that he is counting backwards; he says, "Five, four, three, two, one. Hooray, I am done! I have counted them all." You ask him what he has been counting, and he replies that he has counted all of the natural numbers. "Whoa," you exclaim, "that must have taken a long time. When did you start?" The old man replies, "You fool! There are infinitely many natural numbers, so obviously I never started."

This example illustrates that there is something suspicious about an existing process that extends backward into infinity; some philosophers argue that an existing infinite series is an incoherent idea. But even if we grant that the concept of an existing infinite series is coherent, we still face a serious problem: To grant that the universe has existed forever would still offer no explanation of why it exists. As the philosopher Richard Taylor has pointed out, giving the world an age—even if it is an infinite age—does not in any way answer the question of why the world exists.[8] This suggests that option 1 does not provide any explanation of why the cosmos exists.

The second option suggests that the universe started with the big bang. According to this hypothesis, the universe started with nothingness (i.e., a vacuum); prior to the big bang there was neither time nor space. I stress this point because people are prone to ask, "What caused the big bang?" The sensible answer to this question is that the question itself is flawed. The big bang cannot be caused by anything; it is a singular event that simply happened—that's all one can say! At first glance one might be suspicious of such an answer. Does it make sense to assume that physical events simply happen in the absence of any cause? Surprisingly, modern physics supports this idea—especially with respect to quantum phenomena. Take the example of radioactive decay: Although we know the time when a certain amount of uranium 239 has decayed by 50 percent to uranium 238 (the so-called half-life), we do not know when an individual molecule (i.e., atom) will lose its neutron—that process is due to chance. Defenders of the big bang hypothesis think that the big bang was a similar physical event without proper cause. There is a certain probability that a quantum vacuum produced the conditions for the rapid inflation that characterized the early stages of our universe. That is all we can say. But isn't there something terribly unsatisfactory about this picture—that there was nothing whatsoever, and then suddenly there was a rapidly expanding universe? The big bang hypothesis leads to the same quandary as the eternal cosmos hypothesis: It does not offer us a satisfactory explanation of the existence of the universe.

This situation leads supporters of the cosmological argument to conclude that the best explanation of the existence of the universe is the claim that it was created by a necessary being. But is not this explanation just as incomplete and deficient as the other two options? If we claim that a necessary being created the universe, don't we also have to ask how the necessary being came into being? Let us recall that a necessary being is eternal and uncreated, self-explanatory and self-sufficient. Only a necessary being is self sustaining and contains the reason for its existence in itself. Thus, a necessary being can provide an explanation of the existence of the universe that seems more complete and less puzzling than the alternative explanations.

If we accept this conclusion, we have good reason to think that premise 3 of the cosmological argument is true—that the best explanation of the world's existence is its creation by a necessary being. Premises 1, 2, and 3 together support the conclusion that a necessary being probably exists. And since any necessary being has many features that we normally attribute to the God of classical theism, it is tempting to think that the necessary being that provides the best explanation of the existence of the universe is identical with the God of classical theism. Thus, insofar as we have found good reason to believe that a necessary being exists, we have also found good reason to think that God exists.

Unquestionably, the cosmological argument is appealing, but in order to assess its significance, we need to explore the objections that have been raised against it. There are several that are worth our attention. First, premise 2 of the argument says that there must be an explanation of the existence of the cosmos, yet it is not entirely clear that we need to accept this premise. We have seen that the premise is supported by the principle of sufficient reason, but why do we have to accept this principle? Bertrand Russell once said in a famous debate with F. C. Copleston (1907–1994): "The universe is just there and that's it."[9] If we follow Russell, we might want to treat the existence of the universe as a "brute fact," that is, a fact that is true but that cannot be explained.

Moreover, even if we accept the principle of sufficient reason and demand an explanation of everything in the world, it is not clear that the world as a whole needs a reason as well. Advocates of the cosmological argument seem to commit the fallacy of composition. The Scottish philosopher David Hume (1711–1776) remarked on this topic: "Did I show you the particular causes of each individual in a collection of twenty particles of matter, I should think it very unreasonable should you afterwards ask me, what was the cause of the whole twenty."[10] It seems to follow that the principle of sufficient reason supports the idea that each individual entity in this world needs an explanation of its existence but does not support the idea that the world as a whole needs such an explanation.

Food for Thought

What is an adequate explanation? How we answer this question has important ramifications for the cosmological argument. Read the following debate between Bertrand Russell and Father F. C. Copleston, and decide which of the two thinkers is closer to your own thinking.

RUSSELL: So it all turns on this question of sufficient reason, and I must say that you haven't defined "sufficient reason" in a way that I can understand—what do you mean by sufficient reason? You don't mean cause?

COPLESTON: Not necessarily. Cause is a kind of sufficient reason. Only contingent beings can have causes. God is his own sufficient reason and He is not cause of himself. By sufficient reason in the full sense I mean an explanation adequate for the existence of some particular being.

RUSSELL: But when is an explanation adequate? Suppose I am about to make a flame with a match. You may say that the adequate explanation of that is that I rub it on the box.

COPLESTON: Well, for practical purposes—but theoretically, that is only a partial explanation. An adequate explanation must ultimately be a total explanation, to which nothing further can be added.

RUSSELL: Then I can only say that you are looking for something which can't be got, and which one ought to expect not to get.[11]

A further objection to the cosmological argument relates to premise 3, which asserts that explaining the existence of the cosmos in terms of a necessary being is better than explaining the existence of the cosmos in terms of the big bang. It is not clear that we need to accept this conclusion. According to Ockham's razor, we have reason to prefer a simpler hypothesis to a more complicated one. And the big bang hypothesis is certainly simpler than the creation hypothesis since it does not require any reference to necessary beings. The British Physicist Stephen Hawking[12] wrote in this context: "Spontaneous creation is the reason there is something rather than nothing, why the universe exists, why we exist. It is not necessary to invoke God to light the blue touch paper and set the universe going." If we follow Hawking's line of thought, we can make a good case that premise 3 might be false.

Finally, even if we accept the first three premises of the cosmological argument and thus accept that a necessary being brought the universe into existence, it is not clear that this necessary being is the God of classical theism. Although the cosmological argument might establish that a necessary being probably exists, it cannot show us that this necessary being is omnipotent, omniscient, omnibenevolent, and worthy of worship. Thus, the cosmological argument leaves the character of God undetermined and therefore cannot establish on its own that the God of classical theism exists.

The Design Argument

The design argument is one of the most popular theistic arguments. It has a long and complex history, but the basic idea behind it can be illustrated with this thought experiment: Suppose that you are a space explorer on a mission to find new intelligent life forms. At this moment you are the first human to walk on planet Alpha Nu, which is barren, and for hours you have seen only dust. There is no sign of water or vegetation, and you decide to radio back to your crew that there is no intelligent life on this planet and that it is time to move on. Suddenly you step on something in the dust. As you bend down to pick it up, you realize that it is a computer memory chip. At once this discovery puts planet Alpha Nu in a different category. Although the planet seems devoid of intelligent life now, the memory chip proves that some form of intelligent life must have been present in the past. Perhaps those who left the memory chip were visitors like you, or perhaps this chip is a remnant of a lost civilization. Regardless, the discovery of the memory chip supports the following kind of reasoning:

```
1.There are memory chips on planet Alpha Nu.
2.Memory chips are carefully arranged and orga-
  nized entities.
3.Carefully arranged and organized entities are
  most likely designed by an intelligent designer.
```
Therefore: An intelligent designer most likely has been present on planet Alpha Nu.

This is a strong inductive argument. A similar argument can be made with respect to Earth. This parallel argument goes as follows:

```
1.There are many plants and animals on Earth.
2.Plants  and  animals  are  carefully  arranged  and
  organized entities.
3.Carefully  arranged  and  organized  entities  are
  most likely designed by an intelligent designer.
```

```
Therefore: An  intelligent  designer  most  likely  has
been present on Earth.
4.This intelligent designer is God.
```

```
Therefore: God most likely exists.
```

This argument is immediately plausible, and for centuries it has been one of the most dependable bulwarks of rational theology. But does it stand up to closer scrutiny?

The crucial premise of this argument is the third premise. Is it reasonable to assume that the most plausible explanation for the apparent design of living organisms found on Earth is the presence and influence of an intelligent designer? There are obviously other possible explanations available. Broadly, we can identify three competing hypotheses, which are illustrated by the following chart:

There are Manifold Complicated and Well-Adapted Organisms on Earth.
This can be explained by reference to

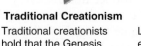

Traditional Creationism	**Theory of Evolution**	**Intelligent Design Creationism**
Traditional creationists hold that the Genesis account of creation is literally true, (e.g., God created the world in six days; all species were created at the same time).	Life on Earth started with extremely simple life forms, which subsequently, over millions of years, developed via the forces of natural selection into the manifold different species we see today.	An intelligent design creationist accepts the basic principles of the theory of evolution but maintains that God stands behind evolution and guides it to a preestablished end.

This brief overview is a bit simplistic, of course. There are, for instance, countless other accounts of creation besides the one in the Bible's Genesis. However, we do little harm if we group them together into one logical category, since the most potent arguments against the Genesis account of creation apply to other creation stories as well. Furthermore, by characterizing the theory of evolution as one theory, I do not want to imply that there are no theoretical differences among evolutionary biologists about the precise paths of evolutionary development or the relative importance of various evolutionary mechanisms. But for the purposes of discussing the design argument, we can characterize the theory of evolution as consisting of two main claims:

1. All living creatures have evolved from a few original simple life forms (the common descent hypothesis, which leads to the image of the tree of life).
2. The tree of life has been shaped by natural selection of randomly varying genetic differences among descendants.

The first claim is pretty easy to understand, but the second might require some further explanation. One of the key insights of evolutionary theory is that descendants of the same parents will vary from each other. For example, if I should happen to have four children, they would differ genetically from each other. These differences are due to random processes and would give my children differing probabilities of reproductive success. What is true for my descendants is true for all other living beings as well. Frog and beetle parents have genetically differing offspring, just as I do. And not all offspring will do well. According to the theory of evolution, genetic differences combined with the forces of natural selection slowly—over millions of years—add up and both create and shape the tree of life.

I have labeled the third possible explanation of the multiplicity and variety of living organisms as intelligent design creationism. Again, this is an oversimplification.[13] There are in fact several creation theories that differ substantially from traditional creationism—for instance, Old Earth creationism, theistic evolutionism, and progressive creationism. However, because intelligent design creationism seems to play the most central role in the current debate about the design argument, we will focus our discussion on this form of non-traditional creationism. The key idea of intelligent design creationism is to reject a literal reading of Genesis and to accept (to varying degrees) the results of modern science. Intelligent design creationists accept that the earth is billions of years old and that species have developed over time. These creationists insist, however, that God plays an important and necessary part in the creation of life and in the process of shaping the tree of life. Moreover, all intelligent design creationists reject the idea that a naturalistically interpreted theory of evolution provides a satisfactory explanation for life on Earth.

Let us now analyze how plausible these competing hypotheses are. Clearly, the theory of evolution is more plausible than traditional creationism, which involves too many claims that are at odds with our scientific knowledge of the world. First, according to our current understanding of chemistry and physics, the world is roughly five billion years old, not six thousand years as traditional creationists maintain. It is possible for a traditional creationist to dismiss all results of modern science, but this is an awkward move to make.

Food for Thought

Traditional creationists frequently insist that Darwin's theory of evolution is simply conjecture. It is certainly true that most evolutionary processes cannot be observed and verified by direct observation since they take too much time for direct observation—they often last millions of years. Does the fact that evolutionary processes are not directly observable justify the conclusion that the theory of evolution is only conjecture?

Second, we have plenty of paleontological evidence that many species (e.g., dinosaurs, saber-tooth tigers, Irish elks) existed in the past but do not exist any more. This suggests that the actual number of life forms on Earth changes constantly and is a result of dynamic processes. Traditional creationism supports the idea that the total number of species were all created at the same time and that each species has a unique function and role in creation as a whole. In light of the paleontological evidence, that claim appears implausible.

Third, we have plenty of evidence that many species are not designed in a perfect way. Many animals have rudimentary (i.e., vestigial) or atrophied

Why does the ostrich, a bird that cannot fly, have wings?

organs. For example, ostriches still have wings, although they cannot fly. Why would a perfect creator have given them wings? It is more plausible to explain these "imperfections" with natural selection. The ostrich, like all other flight-less birds, is likely a descendant of ancestors that could fly, but the ostrich developed stronger legs that enabled it to get by without flying. The wings are still useful to the ostrich but do not play the same role they played in the lives of its ancestors. These and similar observations provide strong evidence that species such as the ostrich have evolved from other species. The creationist claim that ostriches have been designed by a perfect designer seems contrived.

In addition, if we take a close look at different animals, as Charles Darwin did, we can discover many instances of cross-species patterns. Darwin wrote:

> What can be more curious than that the hand of a man, formed for grasping, that of a mole for digging, the leg of the horse, the paddle of the porpoise, the wing of the bat, should all be constructed on the same pattern, and should include the same bones, in the same relative positions?[14]

The existence of cross-species patterns (so-called homologies) is difficult to reconcile with the claim that an original designer created all species from scratch. What reason could the original designer have had for creating the wings of a bat or the leg of a horse from a common design? The functions of the organs are very different, so it would have been reasonable to make the designs different as well. The fact that the same design patterns can be found across very different species supports the idea that different species developed from the same ancestors, and thus supports the tree-of-life hypothesis. If we take all these points together, we can safely conclude that traditional creationism is a weak competitor to the theory of evolution.

Food for Thought

The Navajo creation story is quite different from the account in Genesis. According to the Navajos, the world where people first lived was deep within the world we inhabit now. It had no sun or moon and contained only dim clouds, which moved to tell the hours. Life began peacefully, but then lust and envy took hold. The people became violent. The Navajos fled, climbing through a hole in the sky to a world above. This world also began peacefully, but the same evils appeared, and the process repeated itself until finally the first man and woman emerged on the present Earth. The first man filled the world with the aid of a sacred bundle of medicine, transforming different items into mountains, animals, hours, and so on. Everything in this new world was balanced: four directions, four seasons, four basic colors of black, blue, amber, and white. An essential harmony, called *hozho*, prevailed. Is this creation story any more or less likely to be true than the creation story in Genesis?

Food for Thought

In some school districts in the United States, parents have insisted that traditional creationism should be taught in school alongside the theory of evolution. For example, in 2005 in Dover, Pennsylvania, the local school board voted to require teachers to read a statement about intelligent design prior to discussion of evolution in high school biology classes. The argument for this position is that schools have a duty to introduce a variety of different theories about one topic and let students themselves decide which of the theories they would like to adopt. What do you think about this proposal? Do you agree that traditional creationism should be taught in biology classes, along with the theory of evolution?

Things look a bit different if we compare intelligent design creationism with a naturalistic version of the theory of evolution. Intelligent design creationists accept the basic tenets of the theory of evolution: They believe in the tree-of-life hypothesis and also believe that natural selection is responsible for shaping the pool of living creatures. However, intelligent design creationists maintain that God still has a role to play in all of this. Is this a plausible idea? Well, there are some interesting reasons in defense of intelligent design creationism. First, the classical theory of evolution presupposes that during the early stages of life on Earth, there existed many, albeit primitive, life forms that competed with each other for the available resources on Earth. But this does not explain where life itself came from. How did the first protein, the first enzyme, or the first DNA or RNA molecule come to be? An intelligent design creationist maintains that only with reference to God can we explain how life originated in the first place. The Cambridge astrophysicist Fred Hoyle calculated that the probability of a small, typical enzyme forming randomly is comparable to the probability that a tornado whipping through a junkyard would stir up the scrap to form a Boeing 747. Intelligent design creationists thus conclude that it is unreasonable to believe that life originated as the result of random processes.

This is a tempting line of reasoning, but defenders of the naturalistic theory of evolution contend that no special explanation is needed for the fact that a certain highly unlikely event actually happened. After all, something or other had to happen. To illustrate this response, consider the following example: Suppose that you are in a building together with five hundred other people. Suddenly, there is a fire alarm, and all five hundred people leave the building, one after the other, through the front door. Because the chief of the fire department keeps track of the people who leave the building, at the end of the fire drill, the chief knows who left the building first, second, and so on. The probability that these five hundred people left the building in one particular sequence is very, very small. However, the fact that one particular sequence actually did obtain can be explained best with reference to random processes; it does not require any reference to supernatural forces. Defenders of the theory of evolution can say something very similar about how proteins or amino acids came to exist on Earth. Although the probability that random processes produced these macromolecules is very small, we cannot reject a possible explanation simply because it requires us to believe that events with a low degree of probability can happen. After all, some event had to take place, and it might as well have been one with a low degree of probability.

Food for Thought

The probability that life on Earth arose out of purely natural processes is very small. Does this fact entitle us to conclude that God must have had a hand in the creation of life? The following thought experiment by the philosopher Richard Swinburne should help you decide what to think about this:

> Suppose you are imprisoned by a mad scientist who locks you in a room with an automatic card-shuffling machine. He tells you that unless the card-shuffling machine draws ten aces of hearts from ten different decks, the machine will explode and kill you. To your amazement, the machine does indeed draw ten aces of hearts from ten different decks and you continue to live another day. Would you believe in this situation that your survival is due to pure luck, or would you conclude that the mad scientist must have manipulated the machine?[15]

A second reason that some thinkers prefer intelligent design creationism to the theory of evolution has to do with the fact that the fossil records found thus far are not complete. According to a naturalistic version of the theory of evolution, the development of new species is a gradual process. However, the fossil records sometimes simply show that during certain periods (e.g., the Cambrian era, 600 million years ago) lots of new species seem to have come into existence all of a sudden. Intelligent design creationists can interpret this as evidence that these sudden accelerated periods of evolution are signs that a conscious designer was at work. Defenders of naturalistic evolution will of course not be impressed by this argument. They can insist that an incomplete fossil record is not something surprising; not all periods of evolutionary development have necessarily left permanent traces. Moreover, sudden accelerated periods of evolutionary development can be well explained without reference to supernatural forces. Notice that the same piece of evidence can be interpreted as being compatible with both a naturalistic version of the theory of evolution and a modified version of creationism.

Defenders of the naturalistic theory of evolution have a different but powerful argument at their disposal: The principle of Ockham's razor favors the theory of evolution over intelligent design creationism. Since the naturalistically interpreted theory of evolution does not make reference to supernatural beings, it is a simpler theory than intelligent design creationism. However, use of Ockham's razor is similar to our experience with the principle of sufficient reason; although we use it frequently, it is uncertain whether we have to apply it in all cases.

The debate between intelligent design creationism and a naturalistic evolutionism has long been intense and is likely to remain so for quite some time. Even if we were to establish that the intelligent design creationist has the more plausible position, we would encounter the same difficulty that we faced previously in the context of the cosmological argument. For even if we are convinced that the complexity and beauty of life on Earth can be best explained with reference to a conscious designer, it is in no way evident that the designer resembles the God of classical theism. We are left to wonder whether the designer is omnipotent, all good, and worthy of worship.

The Ontological Argument

Among the various arguments for God's existence, the ontological argument is probably the most intriguing and puzzling. The first thinker to present a version of this argument was the theologian St. Anselm (1033–1109). The central tenet of the argument is the claim that those who think that God does not exist involve themselves in a contradiction.

This claim is not only questionable but outrageously bold. Why should it be the case that God's nonexistence involves a contradiction? This is by no means obvious and requires further explanation.

In order to understand the ontological argument better, it is useful to reflect on the logic of negative existential claims. Suppose somebody claims, "Goblins do not exist!" Suppose further that I ask that person what kind of creatures goblins are supposed to be, and he answers, "I have no idea what goblins are, but I know for a fact that they do not exist." In this case it seems obvious that the person's ignorance about goblins undermines the cogency of his claim that goblins do not exist. If one does not know what kind of creatures goblins are, one surely cannot have any reason to think that they do not exist. The same is true for atheists. An atheist who claims that God does not exist must have an idea of what kind of being God is supposed to be. If she does not, then her claim that God does not exist is undermined.

Anselm suggested that both atheists and theists should agree that the idea of God is the idea of the greatest being that we can think of. This is a plausible definition, and it is hard to see how atheists can deny it. We thus have made some progress in our quest to understand the ontological argument. The claim that God does not exist is equivalent to the claim that the greatest being that one can think of does not exist.

Let us analyze this claim a bit further. Suppose I tell you, "The best marriage that I can think of unfortunately does not exist." What this seems to say is that I have a clear idea in my mind, or understanding, of what a perfect marriage is, but that it is only an idea and not something that exists in reality. All real marriages, I might think, have at least some tiny flaw. Now let us apply this line of thought to the statement that the greatest being that one can think of does not exist. If we follow the same line of thought as we did before, we will understand this claim as follows: The greatest being that one can think of exists only in the understanding but not in reality. We are actually very close to grasping why supporters of the ontological argument think that the sentence is self-contradictory; all we need is one additional metaphysical principle.

The principle in question can be summarized as follows: Existence in reality is greater than existence only in the understanding. Let us consider an example: Suppose I have to choose between two steaks. One steak is grilled to perfection but exists only in my imagination, whereas the other one is a bit cold and tough but is sitting right in front of me. It seems clear that I would choose the steak that is sitting right in front of me. Imaginary steaks, even if grilled to perfection, are not very filling. What is true for steaks is also true for other objects. Anything that exists in reality, even if it is flawed, is much greater than the most wonderful fantasy. Nonexistence is a serious metaphysical shortcoming. It follows, therefore, that we have good reason to accept the following metaphysical principle. Existence in reality is greater than existence only in the understanding.

If we accept this principle, we can arrive at an intriguing insight: If something exists only in the understanding and not in reality, it is possible to think of something greater. A few more examples may help to clarify this: Suppose that a perfectly grilled steak exists only in the understanding and not in reality. In this case one can think of something greater, namely, a perfectly grilled steak that also exists in reality. The same is true for Santa Claus; since Santa Claus exists only in our imagination, we can think of something greater than Santa Claus—namely, a being like Santa Claus that also exists in reality. What is true for perfectly grilled steaks and Santa Claus is also true for all other things: If something exists only in the understanding and not in reality, it is possible to think of something greater than that thing.

Let us now go back to the ontological argument. We have seen that an atheist argues that God does not exist, and we now understand this claim in these terms: The greatest being that one can think of exists only in the understanding but not in reality. If we combine this sentence with the principle we have just established, we arrive at the following: It is possible to think of something greater than the greatest being that one can think of. This sentence is, of course, a blatant contradiction. We thus have shown that any atheist who asserts that God does not exist is involved in a contradiction, and therefore, that God must exist. Since the ontological argument is complex, we will summarize its most crucial steps:

```
1.The idea of God is, by definition, the idea of
  the greatest being one can think of.
```

2. If God does not exist, then the idea of God exists only in the understanding but not in reality.

Therefore:

3. If God does not exist, then the idea of the greatest being one can think of exists only in the understanding and not in reality.

4. If something exists only in the understanding and not in reality, then it is possible to think of something greater than this thing.

Therefore:

5. If God does not exist, then it is possible to think of something greater than the greatest being one can think of.

6. It is impossible to think of something greater than the greatest being one can think of.

Therefore:

7. It is false that God does not exist (i.e., God exists).

To most people, the ontological argument appears, at least at first glance, like a scam. The German philosopher Arthur Schopenhauer (1788–1860) observed that the ontological argument is, nothing more than a "charming joke."[16] However, the difficulty is in saying precisely where the argument goes wrong. As long as we cannot do that, the argument remains a potent force in defense of classical theism. We might, of course, object to defining God as the greatest being that one can think of, but it is hard to see anything that is glaringly wrong with defining God in this manner. David Hume pointed out that we can have clear ideas of dogs or cats since those ideas are derived from sense impressions, but that no comparable impressions are available for God. He concluded that we might define *God* as the greatest being we can think of but that this definition still leaves us with a fuzzy idea of what kind of being God is. If Hume were correct on this point, the very foundation of the ontological argument would be in doubt. However, Hume's criticism here is not decisive. He seems to think that we can have clear ideas of something only if we can produce a clear mental image of that thing. But having no precise image of God does not mean that we can have no clear idea of what kind of being God is. Consider the idea of the greatest natural number; I have no mental image of that number in my mind, but I can understand the idea very well. In fact, I understand the idea so clearly that I am able to deduce that such a number does not even exist. The case of God is similar: I have no mental image of God in my mind, but I clearly understand the concept of the greatest being one can think of. In fact, I understand it so clearly that I think it might be possible to deduce the actual existence of such a being.

However, David Hume raised a second, more powerful objection to the ontological argument. We have seen that the argument is based entirely on *a priori* considerations, which puzzled Hume and prompted him to reflect on the logical status of existence claims. Suppose somebody claims that polar bears exist. In order to understand this claim, we must understand the concept of polar bears. But more is involved—to say that polar bears exist seems to say that there are certain objects in the world that correspond to the concept of polar bears. The claim thus goes beyond the conceptual realm and requires access to the actual world. Hume concluded, therefore, that existence claims can never be analytic. We can analyze the concept of polar bears all we want, but we will never discover thereby whether polar bears in fact exist. Any existence claim seems to require access to matters of fact and can never be a mere analytic judgment.

Hume's conclusion that existence claims are always synthetic has been very influential, but it is perhaps less decisive than people have assumed it to be. Defenders of the ontological argument can grant Hume nearly everything he said about the logic of existence claims without undermining the plausibility of the ontological argument. It seems clear, for example, that ordinary existence claims like "Polar bears exist" must be synthetic and not analytic. However, the ontological argument does not deal with ordinary objects, and Hume gave us no reason to think that there might not be exceptions to the general rule. Although existence claims are nearly exclusively synthetic, it is possible that the case of God, the idea of the greatest being one can think of, confronts us with a unique case. It might be the one case in which the existence of a being can be deduced from the concept of that being alone. It is thus possible to maintain that the claim of God's existence can be analytic, even if one agrees with Hume that all ordinary existence claims are synthetic.

Historically, the most influential objection to the ontological argument has focused on our understanding of the term *existence*. If the ontological argument works, we need to maintain that existence is a perfection (i.e., a "great-making" property). Ever since Immanuel Kant (1724–1804), people have been suspicious about this claim that existence is a perfection. Let me illustrate Kant's objection with the help of an example: Suppose you are looking for a partner with the help of a computer-dating agency. Part of the process is to describe the properties you want your dream partner to have, such as the following:

- Athletic
- Intelligent and fun
- Rich
- Good-looking

One thing is clear: The more properties you add to this list, the smaller the pool of potential candidates. Properties have the "power" to exclude potential candidates. However, consider what would happen if you were to add the property of existence to the list:

- Athletic
- Intelligent and fun

- Rich
- Good-looking
- Existing

Notice that the new list does not exclude anybody who has not been already excluded. In other words, anybody who fulfills the first set of requirements will also satisfy the second list of requirements. This observation led Kant to suggest that existence is not a real property and thus not a perfection. If we accept Kant's position, we are able to raise a crucial objection to the ontological argument. We have seen that the argument depends on the principle that if something exists only in the understanding and not in reality, it is possible to think of something greater than this. If existence is not a real predicate, this principle becomes questionable. Kant wrote: "By whatever and by however many predicates we may think a thing—even if we completely determine it—we do not make the least addition to the thing when we further declare that this thing *is*."[17]

According to Kant, if I think about a perfectly grilled steak that exists in reality, I am thinking about the very same thing that I am thinking about when I think about a perfectly grilled steak that exists only in my mind. A perfectly grilled steak that exists in reality is, therefore, not a greater thing than a perfectly grilled steak that exists only in my mind. Thus, existence is not a "great-making" property of any object. We, therefore, have found reason to reject the metaphysical principle that existence in reality is greater than existence in the understanding alone. This is a pretty powerful objection to the ontological argument, and many philosophers have taken it to be fatal.

Perhaps the most famous objection to the ontological argument was developed by fellow monk Gaunilo shortly after Anselm published his version of the ontological argument. Gaunilo wondered whether the ontological argument might not establish too much. If it is possible to prove the existence of a greatest possible being, would it not also be possible to prove, in a similar way, the existence of other perfect entities, like perfect islands or perfect cars? Since we know that perfect islands and perfect cars do not exist, we can conclude that something fundamental has to be wrong with the ontological argument. At first glance Gaunilo seems to have a point. The same reasoning that helps us to establish the existence of the greatest being we can think of (i.e.,God), also seems to apply to the idea of the greatest island. If the greatest island we can think of does not exist, there could be an even greater island just like the greatest island but one that actually exists. Because this island would be greater than the greatest island we can think of, we end up with a contradiction. To avoid this contradiction, we have to admit that our initial assumption, that the greatest possible island does not exist, is false. So the greatest island must exist.

Initially, Gaunilo's objection seems a devastating reductio ad absurdum of the ontological argument, but further reflection raises concerns about the cogency of Gaunilo's counterexample. It seems clear that the ontological argument can be applied only to entities that have a maximum. For example, consider all beings that are morally good; it makes sense to say that among these beings there must be a best because the property of moral goodness has a maximum. However, the same cannot be said about islands. No single island is capable of being the greatest possible because one could always imagine a greater island. If this line of reasoning is correct, Gaunilo's criticism seems much less threatening. It seems false to claim that the ontological argument allows us to prove the existence of a great number of absurd nonexistent things.

Although Anselm's traditional version of the ontological argument has been subject to damaging criticism, the argument has made a comeback in recent years. Norman Malcolm (1911–1990) and Alvin Plantinga (1932–) are two philosophers who have presented so-called modal versions of the ontological argument. Because the details of the modal versions are rather technical, I will present only the basic outline of this type of argument. The basic idea is to focus the discussion on "necessary existence." It seems quite plausible to assume that God's existence is necessary and not contingent— that is, whether God exists is not dependent on any contingent feature of the world. If we grant this plausible assumption, we can present the argument in the following way:

```
1.God's existence is either necessary or logically
   impossible.
2.It is not impossible for God to exist (i.e.,
   there is no contradiction involved in assuming
   that God exists).
```
Therefore: God exists necessarily.

The argument is rather seductive and not obviously flawed. The discussion about modal versions of the argument is still in full swing, and it might be a while before universal consensus has been reached on whether and how this argument is fundamentally flawed.

Pascal's Wager

The wager argument is due to French mathematician and philosopher Blaise Pascal (1623–1662), who is best known in mathematics for his contributions to probability theory. In philosophy his most influential work is known as *Pensées*, or "Thoughts," which was not completed before his death and was subsequently edited by others. *Pensées* provides an exposition and defense of Christian beliefs. However, Pascal did not hold that the existence of God could be proven with the help of reason alone. According to him, what matters most is faith, not reason, and his wager argument should be understood as a springboard to embracing faith. However, the argument, if presented with care, is extremely effective and is worthy of closer analysis. The aim of the argument is not to establish that God exists, but rather that it is pragmatically prudent to believe that God exists. The argument is especially designed for agnostics—that is, those people who think that it is possible that God exists but who do not think that we can know this.

In order to understand the wager argument, we first need to understand the concept of **expected utility**, which allows us to measure the relative value of various possible but uncertain outcomes. Suppose that I offer you the following bet: If you pay me six dollars, I will let you roll a standard die. If you manage to get a three, you win and I will pay you twelve dollars; if you do not roll a three, you lose and I keep the six dollars you paid me. Is this a good game to play? You have the chance to win six dollars, but you also have the chance to lose six dollars. Decisions like these are quite frequently encountered in the real world and are called **decisions under uncertainty**. When we are facing decisions under uncertainty, we do not know what consequences we are going to face when we decide to perform certain actions. For example, if you choose to play the game just described, you do not know whether you will win or lose. If you win, you are better off, but if you lose, you are worse off. Both are possible outcomes of your decision to play the game. So what is the rational thing to do? In order to approach this decision clearly, it is useful to set up a decision matrix that summarizes the options and possible outcomes. The matrix would look like this:

Options	Possible Outcomes	
Play the game	Win	Lose
Don't play	No win or loss	

Obviously, if you refuse to play the game, you will neither win nor lose anything; the expected utility of this decision is zero. But what is the expected utility of playing the game? In order to calculate that, we need to take into account the probability of the various outcomes. The probability of rolling a three with a standard die is 1/6; the probability of not rolling a three is 5/6. Once we are clear on that, we can calculate the expected utility of playing the game.

$$\text{expected utility of playing the game} = (1/6 \times 6) + (5/6 \times -6)$$
$$= 1 - 5 = -4$$

This calculation shows clearly what you may already have suspected: You are much better off not playing the game, since the expected utility of playing the game is negative. The negative number shows that it is rational to expect a loss of four dollars if you play the game. The concept of expected utility is a great tool for making rational decisions under uncertain conditions. In general, we can formulate the following guiding principle: When faced with decisions under uncertainty, it is rational to choose the action that promises the highest expected utility.

Food for Thought

Blackjack, video poker, and roulette (i.e., all games offered in a casino) are unfair games; that is, those who play these games are faced with a negative expected utility. In spite of this reality, these games are very popular and make huge amounts of money for the people who own the casinos. Does this mean that all those who play these games are irrational decision makers?

But what does this principle of rational decision theory have to do with God's existence? Actually, there is a direct relationship. Pascal argued that many of us are not certain whether God exists or not. All we can say is that there is a certain probability that God exists and a certain probability that God does not exist. This situation suggests that we can approach the decision of whether or not to believe in God's existence as a decision under uncertainty. The matrix for this decision would look like this:

Options	Possible Outcomes	
Believe in God	God exists and you go to paradise!	God doesn't exist, and you waste some time and money.
Don't believe in God	God exists and you go to hell!	God doesn't exist, and you have saved money and time.

Based on this decision matrix, we can see that the expected utility of believing in God is much higher than the expected utility of not believing in God. For the value of going to heaven is of course infinitely positive, whereas the value of going to hell is infinitely negative. Notice that it does not matter how high the probability is for God's existence. Even if one believes that the probability of God's existence is very, very small, Pascal's wager nevertheless suggests that we should believe that God exists, since the potential gain of eternal life in heaven makes the expected utility of believing in God infinitely large.

What the argument shows is not that God exists, but that it is rational and prudent to believe in God's existence, since this belief promises a higher expected utility than not believing in God's existence. In day-to-day terms the argument might sound like this: "Come on and go to church. You have nothing to lose and infinitely much to gain!" Among all the arguments for the existence of God, this one is often most persuasive.

Critics of this argument normally point to two main issues. First, our beliefs are not always under our voluntary control. This point can be illustrated with the help of the following example: Suppose I have to take a calculus exam. I am nervous, but I know that if I believe that I am going to be successful on this exam, I will calm down and perform my best. In this situation I am better off if I believe that I am going to be successful on the test. However, in spite of the fact that it is prudent for me to believe this, perhaps I simply cannot make myself really believe that I am going to be successful. Without wanting to, I start thinking that I will fail this exam because I have always failed math exams. This example shows that what we believe is frequently not a matter of choice, and the same might be true for belief in God. Although Pascal's wager might convince me that it is prudent to believe in God, I might not be able to make myself believe it after all.

Food for Thought

What do you think? Is your belief in God or your belief in atheism under your voluntary control? Could you decide, at the drop of a hat, that God exists or does not exist? Or is it perhaps the case that no matter what happens, we would simply continue to believe what we have always believed?

The second objection to Pascal's wager is more serious. Suppose you are convinced by this argument and want to believe in God. What religion would you choose? Interestingly, a version of Pascal's wager can be presented in defense of a Jewish God, a Muslim God, a Christian God, a Hindu God, and so on. The only condition is that the God in question must promise eternal life to believers and eternal damnation to nonbelievers. Unfortunately, there seem to be infinitely many descriptions of God that can satisfy that requirement. This problem—normally referred to as the *many Gods objection*—shows that Pascal's wager is not as pragmatically useful as it might seem at first glance. For if there are indeed infinitely many possible descriptions of God available, the expected utility of believing in any one of them becomes rather small.

The Effect of These Arguments

None of the arguments for God's existence that we have discussed so far seem strong enough to establish the existence of an omnipotent, omniscient, and perfect being beyond all doubt. Objections can be raised to each one of them. Does this mean that belief in God cannot be justified by reason? It is too early to draw such a conclusion. Although none of the arguments alone has been able to prove that God exists, the arguments might have a cumulative effect. Together they might be seen as providing good reasons for belief in classical theism. However, even if the arguments together cannot move us to believe in a classical theistic God, it would be premature to conclude that no argument can establish the existence of such a being. The fact that human thinkers have failed to prove God's existence in the past does not establish that we cannot find such proofs in the future. We have seen that some of the arguments, especially the ontological and the design arguments, are continuously developed and refined. Thus, a more successful version of one such argument might emerge in times to come. We are therefore not justified to announce that it is impossible to prove the existence of God. But might we be able to establish the opposite result and prove that God does not exist? We will turn to this question in the following sections.

Arguments Against Classical Theism

On Saturday, March 23, 2002, Rodney P. was killed in a car accident, along with his children—Matthew, 8; Jordan, 9; and Rodney, Jr., 10. Their car, rear-ended by another driver, was smashed into the back of a Ford Bronco as they waited at a traffic light. Rodney P. had been a popular minister who spent most of his time helping others. The driver who rammed into his car suffered a medical emergency that caused him to lose control of his vehicle. Tragic events like this happen quite frequently in the world in which we live; people die in car accidents, they suffer diseases, they drown in floods, and they starve in famines. How can a good and benevolent God allow all of this to happen? It would have been so easy for God to spare the life of Rodney P. and his three young children; all he had to do was to prevent the driver who smashed into them from suffering a heart attack. Why did God not interfere in this situation? This question leads us to the heart of one of the most powerful arguments for atheism—**the problem of evil**. This problem can be presented either as a *logical problem* or as an *evidential problem*. We will start our discussion with the logical problem.

Food for Thought

On November 1, 1755, Lisbon, the capital of the Kingdom of Portugal, was struck by a powerful and devastating earthquake. Since November 1 was the Christian holiday All Saints Day, many churches in the city were packed with worshippers when the earthquake struck. Approximately forty minutes after the earthquake, an enormous tsunami engulfed the

Continued

Continued

city's harbor and downtown and drowned many of those who were lucky enough to have survived the collapse of nearly all the buildings in Lisbon. All in all, close to one hundred thousand people were killed in this natural disaster, which had a profound impact on the European intellectual culture. The eighteenth century understood itself as the Age of Reason; most thinkers in that era advocated that reason helps us to understand not only nature, but also an all-good creator of the universe. But the Lisbon earthquake was an event that seemed to go beyond reason. How could anyone make sense of the fact that thousands of people were killed on a Christian holiday while they were worshipping God? What do you think? Does the Lisbon earthquake defy reason? Is the fact that the earthquake happened good evidence for thinking that there is no omnipotent, all-good creator?

The Logical Problem of Evil

The Scottish philosopher David Hume succinctly expressed the questions that motivate the logical problem of evil:

> Is God willing to prevent evil, but not able? Then he is not omnipotent. Is he able, but not willing? Then he is malevolent. Is he both able and willing? Then whence cometh evil?"[18]

If God exists and if he is indeed all-good, all-knowing, and all-powerful, should we not expect the world to be much better than it seems to be? Should we not expect that the hungry will be fed, the needy will be sheltered, and the injured will be healed? Advocates of the logical problem of evil assert that there is a logical tension between these two claims:

1. Evil exists (i.e., innocent beings suffer terribly).

2. An all-good, all-knowing, and all-powerful God exists.

According to the problem of evil, these two claims are logically inconsistent with each other—that is, they cannot be true at the same time. However, since the existence of evil is a fact, we must accept that 1 is true, and we are, therefore, forced to conclude that 2 is false. If we refuse to draw this inference, we are irrational. The Australian philosopher J. L. Mackie observed: "[With the help of the problem of evil] it can be shown, not that religious beliefs lack rational support, but that they are positively irrational, that several parts of the essential theological doctrine are inconsistent with one another."[19] If Mackie is right, classical theists are in an uncomfortable position, of having to decide whether they want to be rational or whether they want to be theists; they cannot be rational and religious at the same time.

Is this tension between theism and rationality unavoidable? In order to answer this question, let us reflect with more care on the structure of the logical problem of evil. Note that assertions 1 and 2 do not form an explicit contradiction; that is, they do not assert that something both is and is not the case. For example, someone who asserts that Smith robbed the bank and yet did not rob the bank is asserting an explicit contradiction. Why then do so many people believe that assertions 1 and 2 are logically inconsistent and cannot be true at the same time? A further example might be helpful to illustrate the logical points at issue. Consider the following two assertions:

A. All humans are mortal.
B. Hercules is not mortal.

Can statements A and B be true at the same time, or are A and B logically inconsistent with each other? Strictly speaking, A does not assert the negation of B, but we can illustrate the logical tension between the two statements by adding a background belief C that is plausible but that allows us to derive an explicit contradiction. Consider background belief C:

C. Hercules is human.

If we add C to A and B, we can deduce the explicit contradiction that Hercules both is and is not mortal.

Something similar is true with respect to the earlier statements 1 and 2. In this case, too, we can try to add a background belief that allows us to derive an explicit contradiction. For example, we might add 3:

3. An all-good, all-knowing, and all-powerful God would eliminate all evil.

If we add 3 to assertions 1 and 2, we can deduce the explicit contradiction that evil exists and does not exist. Thus, with the help of background belief 3 we can show that 1 and 2 are logically inconsistent with each other and that the logical problem of evil is indeed a decisive refutation of classical theism. However, this strategy for strengthening the logical problem of evil requires that the statement we add as a background belief is an obvious and necessary truth. Is statement 3 an obvious and necessary truth? Probably not. It seems as if even an all-good and all-powerful God has no reason to eliminate all evil. Some evil (e.g., the suffering of innocents) might be necessarily linked to the existence of higher-order goods.

To illustrate this line of thought, let us consider an example: Suppose that my neighbor Helen is sick and is suffering terribly from a headache that prevents her from going to work. Helen might ask, "Why does God not cure my headache? Does God not care about my suffering? I thought he was all good and all-knowing." It might be possible that Helen's suffering will lead to some higher-order good. Perhaps I might decide to help Helen in this situation; I might go grocery shopping for her, and as a result a wonderful and long-lasting friendship might develop between Helen and me. Thus, perhaps God has no reason to eliminate Helen's suffering; although painful and undeserved, it has made the world better by leading to a higher-order good (our friendship).

An atheist might object at this point and argue that all higher-order goods could arise without suffering. Could Helen and I not have developed a beautiful friendship without her getting sick? In this case the answer might be yes, but in general it is hard to imagine how all higher-order goods could arise without the existence of some evil and suffering. How could compassion come to be if nobody suffered at all? How could courage appear if nobody got hurt or injured? It follows that it is unreasonable to think that an all-good God would eliminate all evil. God would have reason to eliminate only the evil that did not lead to higher-order goods. We thus cannot accept assertion 3 as an obvious and necessary background belief. Instead, a reasonable person might accept background belief 4:

4. An all-good, all-knowing, and all-powerful God would eliminate all evil that is not necessary for the development of higher-order goods.

However, if we accept 4 and add it as a general background belief to 1 and 2, we can no longer derive an explicit contradiction. In this case the existence of evil is logically compatible with the existence of God. As a result, classical theists are in a relatively strong position with respect to the logical problem of evil. They can argue that any attempt to derive an explicit contradiction from the claims that God exists and that evil also exists involves background assumptions that are neither obvious nor necessary.

A further response to the logical problem of evil was presented by the American philosopher Alvin Plantinga in his **free will defense**.[20] Plantinga argues not only that it is impossible to derive an explicit contradiction from the existence of evil and the existence of God but in addition that there are positive reasons to think that the existence of evil is logically compatible with the existence of God. According to Plantinga, even an omnipotent God would not have complete control over a creation that included genuinely free creatures. In short, Plantinga's free will defense asserts that it is not within God's power to eliminate all evil since God has given human beings the power to act freely on their own. And free humans do not always act for the good but inflict suffering on themselves and others. In other words, a world with free beings that contains no evil is not a logical possibility. It follows therefore that if we accept that (1) God exists and (2) humans are genuinely free creatures, then we can deduce that (3) evil exists. We thus should not be surprised to find that the world is full of evil; evil is a necessary and unavoidable byproduct of human freedom. The fatal accident of Rodney P. illustrates the logic of the free will defense: Rodney P., his three children, and the other driver were all free creatures, making their own decisions and thus determining the character of the world. If God had made sure that all their decisions and actions led to outcomes free of suffering, he would have eliminated their free will. Thus, it follows that God's existence is logically compatible with the fact that innocent beings suffer horribly.

Food for Thought

The American philosopher David Lewis (1941–2001) suggested an intriguing objection to the free will defense against the logical problem of evil.[21] Lewis pointed out that even if God had given some of his creatures free will, he could have avoided the existence of evil. Since God can foresee what humans will do with their freedom, he could have made it the case that only those humans who freely make the right choices are actually free. Thus, those good humans would use their freedom only to do good, and the others would find themselves unable to carry out their evil deeds. In this way there could be a world with free will that is free of suffering. Would not an all-good God create such a world rather than the one we live in? What do you think?

The Evidential Problem of Evil

As we have seen, the logical problem of evil does not provide a watertight case for atheism; it seems logically possible that an omnipotent God would not eliminate all evil in a world in which human beings have genuine free will. However, there is a more powerful version of the problem of evil available to the atheist—the so-called evidential problem of evil. According to an advocate of this line of thinking, God's existence is logically compatible with the fact that innocent beings suffer and experience evil, but the existence of evil makes God's existence highly implausible. Let us illustrate this line of reasoning with an example: Suppose you are a detective and you are investigating the death of a college student, Peter H., who has been found shot to death in his car. On the seat next to him, the police found a suicide note. His friends confirm that Peter had been very depressed prior to his death. Two of his best friends report that Peter spoke on more than one occasion about the possibility of committing suicide. In this situation it seems reasonable to conclude that Peter committed suicide; all the evidence seems to support this assumption. Notice, however, that this conclusion, although compelling, is not certain. It is logically possible that Peter has been murdered, in spite of the fact that all of the evidence points toward a suicide. It is, for instance, logically possible that all his friends are part of a plot to kill him and are therefore lying about his depressed state of mind prior to his death. It is similarly possible that the suicide note was fake, and so on. Although all of this is logically possible, it is extremely improbable and extremely hard to believe. In the absence of further evidence, nobody would seriously believe that Peter's death was murder.

The basic reasoning behind the evidential problem of evil applies the same kind of thinking to the relationship between God and the existence of evil. Although it is logically possible that the existence of evil is compatible with God's existence, it is highly improbable that God would allow so much evil to take place in his creation. The amount of pointless suffering in the world makes it irrational to believe that an all-powerful, omnibenevolent God is, in fact, operating behind the scenes. An advocate of the evidential problem of evil might say, "Yes, of course, God would not necessarily eliminate all evil, because some evil serves a purpose. However, we should expect an all-good God to eradicate all pointless suffering. If the world is full of pointless suffering, we have an excellent reason to think that God probably does not exist."

Food for Thought

The suffering of children seems to raise the evidential problem of evil most forcefully. In the following selection from Dostoyevski's novel *The Brothers Karamazov,* one of the main characters, Ivan Karamazov, explains to his religious brother Alyosha why the suffering of children makes him reject God:

> Listen! I took the case of children only to make my case clearer. Of the other tears of humanity with which the earth is soaked from its crust to its center, I will say nothing. . . . It's beyond all comprehension why the children should suffer, and why they should pay for the harmony. Why should they, too, furnish material to enrich the soil for the harmony of the future? I understand solidarity in sin among men, but there can be no such solidarity with children. . . . Some jester will say, perhaps that the child would have grown up and have sinned, but you see he didn't grow up, he was torn to pieces by the dogs at eight years old . . . and so I renounce the higher harmony altogether. It's not worth the tears of that one tortured child who beat itself on the breast with its little fist and prayed in its stinking outhouse with an unexpiated tear to "dear, kind God"! It's not worth it, because those tears are unatoned for. How are you going to atone for them?

Do you agree that the suffering of children raises the evidential problem of evil? Is the suffering of children necessarily pointless, or is it possible that the suffering of children is part of God's plan for the world?

In standard form we can present the evidential problem of evil as follows:

```
1.It is very likely that instances of pointless
  suffering exist.
2.If God exists, all suffering has a point.
```
Therefore: God probably does not exist.

Premise 2 is plausible in light of our discussion of the logical problem of evil. We have seen that it is unreasonable to expect that God would eliminate all evil and suffering from this world. If suffering is connected to the existence of higher-order goods, God has no reason to eliminate that suffering, or evil. However, if the only reason that God does not eliminate suffering is that it leads to higher-order goods, we have to conclude that all suffering that remains in the world must have a point—that is, no pointless suffering exists. Premise 2 is, therefore, very attractive. The problem in this argument is premise 1. Can we be sure that there are instances of pointless suffering? In order to show that there exist many instances of intense, pointless suffering that God could have prevented without thereby losing any greater good, the philosopher William Rowe wrote about a fawn trapped in a distant forest that has caught on fire during a lightning storm. The fawn is horribly burned, suffers for five days, and finally dies. If we agree with Rowe and think that this is an instance of pointless suffering, we have found good evidence for thinking that God probably does not exist.

Let us reflect more carefully on the structure of Rowe's thinking in this context. His argument can be presented as follows:

```
1.A fawn is caught in a bushfire and is burned
   badly. It suffers for five days and then dies in
   great pain.
2.This is one example of suffering that seems com-
   pletely pointless.
3.If something seems completely pointless, it
   probably is completely pointless.
```
```
4.Therefore: Completely pointless suffering proba-
  bly exists.
```

This inductive argument is attractive. However, it is easy to see that premise 3 can be challenged. How can we be sure that there is no hidden purpose to the suffering of the fawn that only God can see? The fact that we cannot see any point in the suffering of the fawn does not mean that no such point exists. Understanding God's purposes for all instances of suffering in the world might simply transcend our cognitive abilities.

This debate between theism and atheism cannot be resolved in a completely objective way. Our conclusions depend in part on how we experience and interpret the suffering that takes place in our universe. If we understand most of the suffering of innocent beings in this world to have purpose, then it seems quite plausible to believe that all suffering has purpose (even if we cannot see that purpose in all cases) and that the evidential problem of evil has no merit. If, on the other hand, we see this world as a place in which many innocent beings suffer without rhyme or reason, then belief in an all-good and all-powerful God appears foolish and irrational.

Food for Thought

An attempt to show that an omnipotent, all-good, and omniscient God might have good reasons for letting innocent beings suffer is called a **theodicy**. In the list that follows I describe—very roughly—a number of theodicies. Discuss with others in the class whether these theories are able to show that *all* suffering of innocent beings has a point:

1. *Big-Plan Theodicy:* All suffering of innocent beings is part of a big plan and has to happen. The whole plan, however, is completely good.
2. *Punishment Theodicy:* When we see innocent people suffer terribly, they have sinned; their suffering is a punishment for their sins. This solution can be well combined with the idea of original sin, which says that all human beings (including children) are sinners since they are descendants of Adam and Eve.
3. *Suffering-Builds-Character Theodicy:* This basic idea is that the suffering of innocents helps them to become stronger. All evil offers one the possibility to learn from it and to grow into a better human being. This theodicy is sometimes called soul-making theodicy.
4. *Limits-of-Human-Knowledge Theodicy:* The basic idea here is that we simply are too unintelligent to understand why God lets innocents suffer. God has reasons, but we humans cannot understand them.
5. *Contrast Theodicy:* This solution asserts that we need evil in the universe to know that there is good. If there were no evil and everything were good, we could not tell that all was good.
6. *Devil Theodicy:* Innocent beings suffer because the devil likes to let innocents suffer.
7. *Test Theodicy:* This basic idea is that this earthly life is just a test. God has thrown us into this world full of evil and pointless suffering in order to find out what kind of beings we are. Without pointless suffering, this test is not complete. If we pass the test, we are going to heaven; if we fail, some more sinister place awaits us.
8. *Free Will Theodicy:* God would like to eliminate all suffering of innocent beings but cannot do so without eliminating free will. A world with free beings and suffering is better than a world without suffering but also without free will.

Final Remarks on the Problem of God's Existence

Our discussion of arguments for and against the existence of God has shown that classical theists as well as atheists have reasons for their positions. Although none of the arguments are entirely successful, they are strong enough to show that neither of the positions is completely without merit. Where does this leave us? A few summarizing observations are in order: First, we might take the inconclusiveness of our discussion as a reason to embrace an **agnostic** position. By insisting that we cannot know whether God exists, an agnostic seems to keep all options open. However, agnostics face difficulties of their own. A person who holds that God might exist—without firmly believing that he does—avoids making any clear decision about God, even though our lives become worthwhile not by avoiding decisions but by making them. The American philosopher William James pointed out in his essay "The Will to Believe" that in real life we have to choose what seems most reasonable and promising even if we have insufficient evidence. A person who avoids making momentous decisions runs the risk of avoiding life as well. James illustrated this critique of agnosticism by quoting Fitzjames Stephen:

> In all important transactions of life we have to take a leap in the dark. . . . We stand on a mountain pass in the midst of whirling snow and blinding mist through which we get glimpses now and then of paths which may be deceptive. If we stand still we shall be frozen to death. If we take the wrong road we shall be dashed to pieces. We do not certainly know whether there is any right one. What must we do? "Be strong and of a good courage." Act for the best, hope for the best, and take what comes. . . . If death ends all, we cannot meet death better.[22]

This quotation suggests that we might be better off if we make a clear choice and embrace either theism or atheism. Making a decision, even if it is the wrong one, might be better than remaining in a state of indecision.

We have also seen that the evidential problem of evil makes a pretty strong case for atheism. However, even if we admit that there is no entirely successful theodicy available, we do not have to abandon belief in God. Instead, we might understand the problem of evil as a refutation of a certain *kind* of God, namely, the God of classical theism. Some theologians have taken this as a reason to change our traditional understanding of God's nature. Paul Tillich, for example, has suggested that we should not think about God as a being, but rather as Being itself. Whether such alternative conceptions of God are more promising and satisfactory in the light of religious experiences depends in part on how we understand the character of religious experiences. No general, universal answer seems to emerge.

Food for Thought

On Jan. 6 [2009] some 800 British red "bendy" buses carried the sign: "There is probably no God. Now stop worrying and enjoy your life." The Atheist Bus Campaign organizer, a young comedienne named Ariane

Continued

Continued

Sherine, took exception last June to several London buses swathed with biblical quotes, placed by Christian fundamentalists. Her idea to fund a few challenge ads took off; donors sent in $200,000 in two days. Ms. Sherine was joined by Oxford zoologist Richard Dawkins, a leading British atheist and author of "The God Delusion."

Much of the campaign's initial buzz centered on the assertion that God "probably" doesn't exist. Does this suggest a hedging of bets—a move past atheist dogma? Some organizers wanted a flat "there is no God" statement. Dawkins favored an "almost certainly no God" wording. But Ms. Sherine says that British advertising officials advised that a phrase less absolute and not subject to proof would ensure the ad did not run afoul of the advertising standards authority.

Dawkins predicted anger from believers. "They have to take offense, it is the only weapons they've got," Mr. Dawkins said as the first bus rolled through the streets of London. "They've got no arguments." But the response by most faith leaders isn't quite what was expected. Religious institutes, church pastors, and divinity school professors have not treated the ads with Old Testament wrath, but with a relatively open mind and even embrace of so important an issue.

"The campaign will be a good thing if it gets people to engage with the deepest questions of life," says the Rev. Jenny Ellis, Spirituality and Discipleship Officer of Britain's Methodist church. "Many people simply never think about God or religion as a serious question, and if this prods them a little bit, then that's great," says the Rev. Stephen Wang, of the Westminster diocese of the Roman Catholic Church.[23]

Do you agree with Rev. Stephen Wang? Is such an atheist campaign a good thing?

Study and Reflection Questions

1. We have seen that there are different ways to think about God. Even atheists must have a conception of God, for how else would they be able to claim that such a being doesn't exist? Describe various ways of thinking about a supreme being. Do you think that all these ways of thinking about God are equally meaningful?

2. Religious experiences play an important part in religion. It is, however, far from clear what should count as a religious experience. Is a religious experience equivalent to a miracle, or is it simply a feeling of joy, sinfulness, or dependence? Describe various examples that have been labeled as religious experiences, and try to distill what if anything is common to all religious experiences.

3. What is the difference between the logical problem of evil and the evidential problem of evil? Which of these problems poses a more serious threat to theism? How can a theist respond to these challenges?

4. Which of the arguments for the existence of God is the weakest, and which of the arguments is the strongest? Give reasons for your assessment.

5. What effect have the various arguments for and against the existence of God had on your position on religion? Has your perspective changed? If yes, how; if no, why not?

For Further Reading

Audi, R., and W. Wainwright, eds. *Religious Belief and Moral Commitment.* Ithaca, NY: Cornell University Press, 1986.

Coyne, Jerry. *Why Evolution Is True.* London: Viking, 2009.

Flew, Anthony. *God and Philosophy.* Amherst, NY: Prometheus Books, 2005.

Mackie, J. L. *The Miracle of Theism.* Oxford: Oxford University Press, 1982.

Penelhum, Terrence, ed. *Faith.* New York: Macmillan, 1989.

Peterson, M., W. Hasker, B. Reichenbach, and D. Basinger, eds. *Philosophy of Religion: Selected Readings.* Oxford: Oxford University Press, 1996.

———. *Reason and Religious Belief.* Oxford: Oxford University Press, 1997.

Plantinga, Alvin. *Warranted Christian Belief.* Oxford: Oxford University Press, 2000.

Rowe, William. *Philosophy of Religion.* Belmont, CA: Thomson-Wadsworth, 2007.

Ruse, Michael. *Darwin and Design: Does Evolution Have a Purpose?* Cambridge, MA: Harvard University Press, 2003.

Swinburne, Richard. *The Existence of God.* Oxford: Oxford University Press, 2004.

Endnotes

1. I do not want to assert here that our lives become meaningless if God does not exist. It is very possible to lead a meaningful life without God. Nevertheless, it seems correct to assert that our lives cannot have any "ultimate meaning" without God, for ultimate meaning seems to presuppose the existence of a necessary being.

2. The relationship between faith and reason is, of course, a matter of theological and philosophical controversy. However, for beginning students it might be most useful to understand the relationship between faith and reason in the way Thomas Aquinas understood it. For him, there are some religious statements that can be demonstrated to be true by reason alone—for example, "God exists" or "God is good." In addition, there are religious truths that "exceed all the ability of human reason." Among these truths is, for example, the claim that God, Jesus, and the Holy Spirit are one and three persons at the same time. In order to accept these latter beliefs, the believer needs faith. Aquinas concluded that faith completes and perfects human intellect. This is a useful picture for understanding the relationship between faith and reason because it explains why reason plays a crucial role in accepting religious beliefs and why we should not expect reason to answer and settle all religious questions we might have.

3. According to the Pew Forum on Religion and Public Life, 71 percent of Americans are absolutely certain that God exists, 17 percent are fairly certain that God exists,

and 4 percent are not certain. Only 5 percent of the American population does not believe in the existence of a higher being. For more details, see http://religions. pewforum.org/.

4. Richard Swinburne, *The Coherence of Theism* (Oxford: Clarendon Press, 1977), p. 2.

5. Bertrand Russell, *Religion and Science* (Oxford: Oxford University Press, 1935), p. 188.

6. William James, *The Works of William James: The Varieties of Religious Experience* (Cambridge, MA: Harvard University Press, 1979), p. 25.

7. This example is inspired by Richard Taylor, "A Contemporary Version of the Cosmological Argument," in *Philosophy of Religion: Selected Readings,* ed. Michael Peterson, William Hasker, Bruce Reichenbach, and David Basinger (New York: Oxford University Press, 1996), pp. 187–197.

8. Ibid, p. 192.

9. This debate between Russell and Copleston can be found in Bertrand Russell, *Why I Am Not a Christian and Other Essays on Religion and Related Subjects* (New York: Simon & Schuster, 1957).

10. David Hume, *Dialogues Concerning Natural Religion* (New York: Hafner, 1948), p. 59.

11. F. C. Copleston and Bertrand Russell, from "A Debate on the Cosmological Argument" in *Why I Am Not a Christian and Other Essays on Religion and Related Subjects* (New York: Simon & Schuster, 1957), pp. 292–294.

12. Stephen Hawking, *The Grand Design.* (London: Bantam Books. 2010).

13. For a good discussion of different versions of creationism, see Robert Pennock, *Tower of Babel* (Cambridge, MA: MIT Press, 2000).

14. Charles Darwin, *On the Origin of Species by Means of Natural Selection, or the Preservation of Favoured Races in the Struggle for Life* (London: Murray, 1859), p. 403.

15. Richard Swinburne, *Existence of God* (Oxford: Clarendon Press, 1979), p. 138.

16. The precise quotation reads, "Considered by daylight, however, and without prejudice this famous Ontological Proof is really a charming joke." From Arthur Schopenhauer, *On the Fourfold Root of the Principle of Sufficient Reason,* trans. Karl Hildeburg (London: Bell & Sons, 1902), p. 11.

17. Immanuel Kant, *The Critique of Pure Reason,* trans. N. K. Smith (London: Macmillan, 1929), p. 505.

18. Hume attributes this quotation to Epicurus. See David Hume, *Dialogues Concerning Natural Religion and The Natural History of Religion,* ed. J. A. C. Gaskin (Oxford: Oxford University Press, 1993), p. 100.

19. J. L. Mackie, "Evil and Omnipotence," *Mind* 64 (1955): 200–212.

20. Alvin Plantinga, *God, Freedom, and Evil* (Grand Rapids, MI: Eerdmans, 1977).

21. David Lewis, "Evil for Freedom's Sake," *Philosophical Papers* 22 (1993): 149–172.

22. William James, *The Will to Believe and Other Essays in Popular Philosophy* (Cambridge, MA: Harvard University Press, 1979).

23. *Christian Science Monitor,* January 16, 2009. Available at http://www.csmonitor. com/2009/0116/p01s04-woeu.html.

CHAPTER EIGHT

WHAT OUGHT WE TO DO?

Moral Intuitions and Moral Principles

On May 24, 2000, Robert Elliot and Kevin Smith were working their usual evening shifts in Ruby's Restaurant. When a fisherman came in and told them that somebody was drowning in the ocean outside, they didn't hesitate. Still wearing their white waiters' uniforms, the men ripped off their boots, jumped into the ocean, and kept the man afloat until lifeguards came to the rescue. When we hear this story, it immediately appears to us that Robert Elliot and Kevin Smith performed a morally good action. When actions appear to be morally good or morally wrong, philosophers say that we experience **moral intuitions.** When we hear in the news that a young child has been kidnapped from her bedroom, it immediately appears to us that this action is morally reprehensible. The same is true for stories about theft, arson, or murder. On the other hand, when we hear that somebody has risked his life to save a child from drowning, it immediately appears to us that this action is morally commendable.

Unfortunately, our moral intuitions are not always so clear. Consider the following story: On August 6, 1945, Lt. Col. Paul Tibbets took off from the American airbase on Tinian island in a B-29 Super Fortress. On board the airplane were twelve crewmen and one of the first nuclear bombs ever built. The bomb, nicknamed "Little Boy," was twelve feet long and twenty-eight inches in diameter and had an explosive power equal to twenty thousand tons of TNT. Seven hours later, Paul Tibbets and his crew dropped Little Boy on the Japanese city of Hiroshima. The explosion killed close to two hundred thousand people and contributed to Japan's decision to accept unconditional surrender a short time later.

When we consider the bombing of Hiroshima, most of us have the following moral intuitions:

1. Killing thousands of civilians in Hiroshima is morally wrong.
2. Ending the war sooner and saving the lives of many are morally good.

These two intuitions are in conflict with each other; we are torn between different ways of evaluating the same situation. This example illustrates that if we want to avoid moral confusion, we cannot be satisfied with evaluating situations simply in the light of our initial moral intuitions. When we experience conflicting moral intuitions, we need the additional help of general **moral principles,** which are rules that allow us to classify actions as morally good or morally wrong. In our example we might introduce the moral principle that it is always morally required to save as many lives as possible. If we accept this moral principle, we can evaluate the two conflicting intuitions about the bombing of Hiroshima and determine which of them ought to be abandoned.

Discovering general moral principles is one of the central goals of ethical theory. In this chapter we will discuss and evaluate some of the most important ethical theories that have been developed. We will try to discover what ethical theory is most compatible with the majority of our basic moral intuitions. A satisfactory moral theory will not only furnish us with moral principles that are in harmony with most of our basic moral intuitions, but will also help us decide what we are required to do when we are facing moral dilemmas.

Food for Thought

A good way to show that our moral intuitions are sometimes in conflict with each other is to consider the so-called Trolley Problem, which was first introduced by the British philosopher Philippa Foot[1]. Consider the following two situations:

Situation A: A trolley is running out of control down a track. In its path are five people who have been tied to the track. Fortunately, you can flip a switch that will lead the trolley safely down a different track. Unfortunately, there is a single person tied to that track. Should you flip the switch?

Situation B: As in situation A, a trolley is running down a track towards five people. You are on a bridge under which it will pass, and you can stop it by dropping a heavy weight in front of it. As it happens, there is a very fat man next to you; your only way to stop the trolley is to push him over the bridge and onto the track, killing him to save the five others. Should you push the man?

Most people who consider these two situations have different moral intuitions in the two scenarios. In situation A it seems that one is morally required to flip the switch. Although flipping the switch would bring about the death of an innocent person, it is much better to bring about the death of one person than to allow the death of five persons. In situation B, however, most people think that it seems morally wrong to push the fat man over the edge in order to save the five people on the track. Our moral intuitions seem to lead us directly into a logical contradiction: How is it possible that sacrificing one innocent person to save five others is morally acceptable in situation A but is not morally permissible in situation B? Are there morally significant differences between the two situations that would justify different moral intuitions? If yes, what are these moral differences?

A Fundamental Challenge: Relativism

Although all of us have moral intuitions, many people are very skeptical about whether moral intuitions are uniform enough to provide a solid starting point for the construction of objective ethical theories. There can be no doubt that different people differ in their assessment of the same moral question. Consider, for instance, the Food for Thought exercise that follows.

Food for Thought

Take a look at the following claims, and decide whether they appear true or false to you. After you have completed the exercise, compare your responses with those of a classmate.

1. Stealing is morally wrong.
2. Adultery is morally wrong.
3. Men and women should receive the same pay if they perform the same work.
4. If a baby is born with only a brain stem (which allows for breathing and heartbeat) and is missing all other major parts of the brain, it is morally permissible for the parents to volunteer the baby as an organ donor.
5. A person who is wealthy but who never gives any money to charity is an immoral person.
6. It is morally permissible to perform sexual activities in exchange for monetary compensation.
7. All members of a society have the right to receive equal educational opportunities.
8. Eating meat is morally wrong.
9. The right to get married should not be restricted to heterosexual couples; same-sex couples should have the right to marry as well.
10. People who have committed a felony in the past should have the right to vote after they are released from prison.
11. No government has the right to kill any of its citizens.
12. A terminally ill person has the right to insist that her doctor put her to death.

If you compare your answers to this exercise and the answers that some-one else has given, the chances are great that you will discover significant disagreements. Although most of us probably agree that men and women should receive the same pay if they perform the same work, many people dis-agree about whether it is immoral to eat meat or whether homosexual part-ners should have the right to marry. These disagreements have led some thinkers to suppose that ethics is a subjective affair; the philosophical posi-tion that makes this claim is called **ethical relativism.** An ethical relativist holds that there are no objective moral values. An ethical relativist might say, for example, that the bombing of Hiroshima will appear to American sol-diers to be morally good, but to Japanese people it will appear to be morally reprehensible. What the ethical relativist denies is that the bombing of Hiroshima in itself is either morally good or morally bad. According to the relativist, there is no neutral point of view that allows us to judge moral questions objectively.

Whether ethical relativism is true or false has important consequences for the study of ethics. If ethical relativism is correct, it is hard to see how there can be moral knowledge. I might believe, for example, that I am morally required to help homeless people, whereas you might believe that helping homeless people is a waste of money and therefore morally wrong. According to relativism, both of these intuitions can be correct; we cannot establish, from an objective point of view, whether it is true that helping homeless people is morally required. Thus, relativism supports skepticism about the truth-value of moral claims. On the other hand, thinkers who believe that we *can* obtain moral knowledge about ethical questions oppose relativism. Their denial of ethical relativism leads to a position called **ethical objectivism,** which holds that moral judgments are not dependent on our individual wishes, hopes, or aspirations. According to ethical objectivism, there are some universal moral truths that are true for all people at all times. Thus, the ethical objectivist believes that there are moral facts and that the crucial task of moral theory is to help us clarify what moral facts exist. The chart on the following page intro-duces some key terms used in the debate between ethical relativism and ethical objectivism:

If we decide that no objective moral values hold for all people at all times, it will be impossible in principle to find a universally satisfactory moral theory. Let us explore therefore whether there are any compelling arguments in sup-port of this position.

The Case for Ethical Subjectivism

An ethical subjectivist believes that ethical judgments depend on the tastes and preferences of each individual person. According to ethical subjectivism, all moral principles are justified by virtue of their acceptance by an individual agent. If we follow this line of thinking, personal conviction is the ultimate

Are there Universal Moral Values?

Ethical Relativism
An ethical relativist denies
that there are any objective
moral values.

Ethical Objectivism
An ethical objectivist
believes that there are
objective moral values;
that is, at least some
ethical norms are true for
all people, at all times.

Ethical Subjectivism
An ethical subjectivist
holds that moral claims
have to be assessed in
relation to an individual.
Rather than saying that
eating meat is wrong, one
should say, "Eating meat is
wrong for me."

Cultural Relativism
A cultural relativist holds
that moral claims have to
be assessed in relation to a
particular culture. Rather
than saying that female
circumcision is morally
wrong, one should say,
"Female circumcision is
wrong in the United States."

measure of morality. At first blush, this makes a good deal of sense; if we look around us, we can see that each person is unique in his or her preferences and tastes. I might like the music of Johann Sebastian Bach, while you might prefer the songs of Eminem. I like to play soccer, whereas you might like to play baseball. It would strike most of us as strange if somebody were to claim that he could establish objectively that playing soccer has no value. If I like to play soccer, then soccer has value for me. However, I am happy to grant you the right to say that playing soccer has no value for you. Thus, the value of soccer playing depends on the individual person. The ethical subjectivist argues that something very similar to the soccer debate is true for moral values. According to ethical subjectivism, we cannot establish whether eating meat is, from an objective point of view, morally wrong; it all depends on who makes the judgment. Eating meat might be wrong for me and morally right for you.

There are two main reasons that people are attracted to ethical subjectivism. First, it is compatible with our experiences of living in a pluralistic society. When we look around us, we see many different people with many different moral beliefs. Some people drink alcohol and smoke; others consider smoking and alcohol to be immoral activities. Some of us think that paying taxes is an important moral duty, whereas others feel perfectly fine when they cheat on their income tax returns. Ethical subjectivists can respond to this diversity by saying, "To each his own!" They are neither surprised nor annoyed by the fact that people make different moral judgments. According to ethical subjectivists, there are as many moral perspectives as there are different individuals. Second, ethical subjectivism seems very tolerant; its adherents will not try to change your mind about ethical questions. They expect you to do what is right for you, and they will do what is right for them. No one needs to convince anyone else that a particular moral belief is correct; each person has the right to determine what is morally right for him or her. In light of these considerations, it is no surprise that many people subscribe to ethical subjectivism.

Problems for Ethical Subjectivism

There are at least three fundamental problems with ethical subjectivism. First, it is in conflict with some of our most fundamental moral intuitions. Consider, for instance, the events of the Columbine High School shooting on April 20, 1999: Two students, Dylan Klebold and Eric Harris, walked into their high school and went on a shooting spree. Before they committed suicide, they had killed twelve students and a teacher. If ethical subjectivism is correct, we need to accept the following two statements about these shootings:

1. The actions of Dylan Klebold and Eric Harris considered on their own account are neither morally wrong nor morally right.
2. The actions were morally right for Dylan Klebold and for Eric Harris. The shooters felt that they were merely taking revenge for abuse and insults they had suffered in the past.

The emerging problem is obvious. Most of us would reject both statements as preposterous; they are not compatible with our moral intuitions. It appears to us that the actions of Dylan Klebold and Eric Harris were wrong on their own, not only wrong in relationship to what somebody thinks. To say that the actions of Klebold and Harris were wrong seems to be stating a moral fact. In addition, it seems absurd to claim that the shootings were right for Dylan Klebold and Eric Harris. An action does not become right for somebody just because the action appears justified to that person. Hitler might have felt justified to kill millions of Jews, but that seems to have no bearing on whether his actions were morally justified. What these examples show is that we often have clear and strong intuitions that specific actions are simply wrong, and the ethical subjectivist has no way to account for these moral intuitions.

A second problem is that, according to ethical subjectivism, it is impossible to disagree about ethical questions. Let me illustrate this with the help of an example: Suppose you and Tony are ethical subjectivists and Tony has borrowed twenty dollars from you. After Tony has failed to repay the money, you give him a call. Tony says, "I have changed my mind; I am not going to give you back that money. I have decided that you have too much money anyway." At this point you might say something like this: "I can't believe what you are saying. You borrowed twenty dollars, and you promised to pay it back. If you fail to do so, you are committing a moral wrong." Given that you and Tony are both ethical subjectivists, he might say, "Well, you are mistaken. You think that not paying back the money is morally wrong. However, I believe now that not paying back the money is morally right. Both of us have the right to our opinion, but neither of us has the right to impose an opinion on the other person."

As this conversation shows, ethical subjectivists cannot have meaningful disagreements and conversations about moral questions. They all have their own opinions about moral matters, and all opinions are equally correct. But this does not square well with our experience of moral conversations. When we disagree about moral questions, we tend to experience the conflict as a specific disagreement about objective subject matter. Genuine ethical conversations are not possible with ethical subjectivism.

The third weakness is closely related to the previous point. If ethical subjectivism is accurate, then our ethical judgments are always correct. If it appears to me that smoking is morally wrong, I am automatically justified in asserting that smoking is wrong for me. According to ethical subjectivism, I cannot go wrong in my ethical judgments, since my ethical judgments are merely the expression of my personal preferences. However, it seems rather strange to assert that we are all ethically infallible. In many situations it makes perfect sense to assert that somebody has a false moral belief. Consider the case of John, who sincerely believes that people who commit adultery should be stoned to death. Most of us probably agree that John is mistaken on this point; stoning does not appear to be an appropriate punishment for any wrongdoing. But if we accept ethical subjectivism, the belief that adulterers should be stoned to death is morally right for John as long as he sincerely believes it. These three arguments show why very few thinkers take ethical subjectivism seriously. Although it appears initially to be attractive, the theory is incompatible with some of our most fundamental moral intuitions and with our experience of meaningful moral conversations. If we want a plausible moral theory, we need to look somewhere else, perhaps to a more promising version of relativism.

The Case for Cultural Relativism

Cultural relativists[2] admit that individual persons can be mistaken about their moral judgments, According to cultural relativism, a given action is morally wrong if the given culture does not approve of it, and an action is morally right if the culture does approve. The culture in the United States, for example, does not approve of stealing. In the United States, therefore, it is morally wrong to steal any property that belongs to somebody else. In Saudi Arabia the culture expects men to have beards. It is therefore morally right for Saudi men to have beards. The overall motto of cultural relativism is this: When in Rome, do as the Romans do!

The idea that actions need to be morally evaluated in the context of the culture in which they occur is intuitively plausible, and there are several arguments that support cultural relativism. First, there can be little doubt that the culture in which we grow up has an impact on our moral intuitions. The fact that certain actions receive our approval while others strike us as reprehensible has a lot to do with our childhood and our education. We grow up hearing from our parents that taking the toys of our friends without permission is wrong but that helping an older person cross the street is morally good. Later on, teachers in school reinforce the same lessons. It is therefore plausible that our moral intuitions and feelings are not the result of objective, rational thinking, but rather the product of the culture in which we have been reared.

Second, different cultures endorse different moral and legal practices. In the United States it is perfectly fine for women and men to go to the beach in a small bikini or tight bathing suit. In Scandinavian countries it is acceptable to sunbathe naked, while most Muslim countries require women to cover most of their bodies in public. A cultural relativist is not surprised by these differences; different countries have different customs, and each country determines what is morally right in that country. Cultural relativism is therefore quite compatible with the great variety of differing moral rules that are followed in different countries.

Food for Thought

1. List five activities that are perfectly acceptable in the United States but completely unacceptable in another culture.
2. List five activities that are considered immoral in the United States but are perfectly acceptable in another culture.

Third, cultural relativism appears, at first glance, to be a tolerant and peaceable position. Suppose, for instance, that moral objectivism is true and that there is only one set of moral rules for all humanity. Suppose further that we discover two different cultures that embrace radically opposed sets of moral values. If moral objectivism is correct, we must conclude that one of these cultures is wrong and that the other is morally superior. Many people might feel uncomfortable drawing such a conclusion. What right do we have to elevate one culture over another? Cultural relativism can solve this dilemma by saying that both cultures are correct as long as they stay within their own spheres. This is a very attractive solution to an otherwise thorny problem. Thus, these three arguments show that cultural relativism is not only an intuitive but also a well-supported philosophical position.

Problems for Cultural Relativism

Cultural relativism is also open to several major objections. First, many cultural relativists are proud that cultural relativism seems to further cooperation and respect among different cultures because no culture has the right to assert that its cultural practices are superior to those of any other. Closer analysis reveals, however, that cultural relativism does not necessarily advance cooperation among cultures. Consider the case of the Vikings: The Vikings supported themselves for the most part by raiding, burning, and looting monasteries, cities, and farms all over northern Europe. If cultural relativism is correct, we cannot condemn the Vikings; they are simply following their own cultural practices, according to which raiding and plundering other cities is morally praiseworthy.

What this example shows is that cultural relativism does not necessarily lead to peaceful cooperation among cultures. It all depends on the cultures that interact; if one of the cultures is aggressive, cultural relativism sanctions war and oppression. Notice also that the losing cultures have no right to complain to the winning, aggressive culture because the more aggressive culture is simply following a different set of moral rules. Many people find this result unsettling; they believe that peaceful cooperation among diverse cultures is an important value. However, it appears that the best way to promote this value is to admit that peaceful cooperation among cultures is a moral value that applies to all cultures at all times. But this is tantamount to embracing a version of ethical objectivism.

Second, cultural relativism cannot explain the influence of moral critics. Consider the example of Martin Luther King, Jr., who grew up in a culture that practiced segregation. The overwhelming majority of his contemporaries believed that it was a good thing to keep the lives of black and white Americans separated. But King became an outspoken and influential critic of this practice, and now we praise him for his courage. We declare with a sense of pride that Martin Luther King, Jr., performed morally good actions when he opposed his own culture and fought for the equality of black and white Americans. Cultural relativists cannot explain this phenomenon easily. If cultural relativism is correct, we have to conclude that King's actions were morally wrong because he refused to accept what his culture told him was morally necessary. Thus, cultural relativism fails to provide an adequate explanation for the praiseworthy actions of moral critics.

Third, we have seen that cultural relativists support their position by pointing to the great variety of moral codes that can be found across different cultures. They argue that cultural relativism provides the best explanation of why different cultures embrace such different moral norms. Let us call their argument the anthropological argument in defense of cultural relativism. In standard form that argument looks like this:

```
1.Different cultures live according to very dif-
   ferent moral standards.
2.If there were a universal moral standard that
   held for all cultures, then different cultures
   would live according to similar moral standards.
```
```
Therefore: There are no universal moral standards
(i.e., ethical objectivism is false).
```

This argument is an instance of the argument form *modus tollens* and is, therefore, deductively valid. However, it is far from clear whether the premises of the argument are true. Should we accept the second premise? Suppose there *are* universal moral standards. Why would we expect every culture to accept these standards? It could very well be the case that some cultures fail to recognize universal moral truths. The cultural relativist overlooks the possibility that cultures can undergo moral development. For example, there was a time when the majority of Americans accepted slavery as a profitable and acceptable institution. But as time passed, the country realized that it was embracing and supporting a moral evil, and today it is rare to find defenders of slavery. Thus, the country has moved on and changed its moral perspective for the better. If we accept this idea that moral progress is possible, we can see that moral diversity among different cultures is compatible with the existence of objective moral norms. In other words, it is plausible that different cultures recognize and discover objective moral norms in different ways and that eventually, if the development goes on long enough, all cultures might embrace a similar set of moral norms. This is, however, a very slow process, and until it is completed, we should not be surprised to find great cultural and moral diversity among different cultures.

Food for Thought

Most people agree that it is a sign of moral progress that slavery was abolished in the United States. Can you think of other developments in American society that might be considered moral progress? What are some current cultural practices that future generations might consider barbaric and immoral?

Another weakness of the anthropological argument for cultural relativism is related to premise 1. Most cultural relativists take it for granted that there are great differences among the moral norms of different cultures. Closer examination seems to reveal, however, that different cultures may be much more similar in their ethical values than the cultural relativist believes. For example, it is quite plausible that all cultures share a certain basic set of core values—such as truth-telling and caring for children. Obviously, no culture can survive for long if it does not cherish certain practices: A culture full of liars is bound to sink into chaos, and a culture that does not care for its children is bound to disappear. Something similar can be said for many other core values: They are essential to the survival of any culture. This suggests that a core set of ethical beliefs may be shared across all cultures.

In addition, certain moral differences among different cultures are caused by nonmoral background beliefs and not by differences in moral values. Consider the example of an Inuit tribe that encourages older members to walk away from camp and subsequently freeze to death in the open.[3] At first glance we might suppose that this culture lives according to very different values from those of our own society; it appears that the Inuit culture is cruel and mean to its older members. However, suppose we find out that the Inuit people believe that it is necessary to die with a healthy body in order to have fun in the afterlife. Now, the fact that they encourage older members to die early seems like an act of kindness; they care about their older parents very much and want them to die with healthy bodies. This example shows that cultural differences are often caused not by differences in moral values, but by differences in nonmoral beliefs about the world and the afterlife. Cultural relativists may be too quick to conclude that different cultures embrace radically different value systems.

Food for Thought

Can you think of other examples of moral differences that are not caused by a difference in moral values but by a difference in factual beliefs about the world?

Final Remarks on Cultural Relativism

Although full-blown cultural relativism does not lead to a satisfactory ethical position, it would be unwise to dismiss cultural relativism as completely misguided. In some respects, cultural relativism is quite correct. Our upbringing and our cultural training do have a lasting effect on our moral intuitions, and it would be dangerous to assume that our thinking about moral questions is free of cultural bias. Cultural relativism rightly draws our attention to the fact that our moral intuitions are sometimes the result of cultural prejudice and must therefore be scrutinized carefully. Our moral intuitions are trustworthy only if they are in harmony with sound ethical principles.

Food for Thought

Can you think of some cultural practices that make most of us in the United States feel morally uncomfortable but that might be morally acceptable if we ignore our cultural prejudices?

Moreover, when we study and learn about other cultures, it is often helpful to ignore our own moral perspective and to accept other cultures as they are. As long as we are closely tied to our own cultural and moral perspectives, we tend to be biased observers. Thus, a dose of cultural relativism is often a necessary element in becoming a successful cultural anthropologist or sociologist. However, we can embrace these positive aspects of cultural relativism without accepting that there are no universal and objective moral values.

Some Important Ethical Theories

Our discussion so far suggests that there may exist some objective moral norms that apply to all people at all times, not because our cultures or societies claim that these norms are true, but because objective moral features of the world make these claims true. To say, for instance, that torturing babies is morally wrong is to express a moral claim that seems true for all people and all cultures. However, any endorsement of ethical objectivism remains shallow unless these objective moral facts can be specified in greater detail. We will explore here four mainstream normative ethical theories, which will help us identify what objective features of the world are morally relevant and will enable us to discover what moral norms are true for all people at all times.

The goal of a successful ethical theory is to provide a set of fundamental moral principles that is in harmony with our moral intuitions and that helps us to clarify what we should do when we face difficult moral decisions. It is quite challenging (if not impossible) to evaluate the merits of a given ethical theory from a completely objective point of view. Whether we find a given normative ethical theory cogent and compelling depends in part on the specific character of our moral intuitions. This does not mean that we have to embrace relativism, but it does mean that each person has to determine individually whether a given moral theory fits with his or her moral intuitions. The following discussion is designed to give readers the chance to explore some of the main ethical theories that have been developed in the past. The graphic here summarizes the various positions that we are going to discuss.

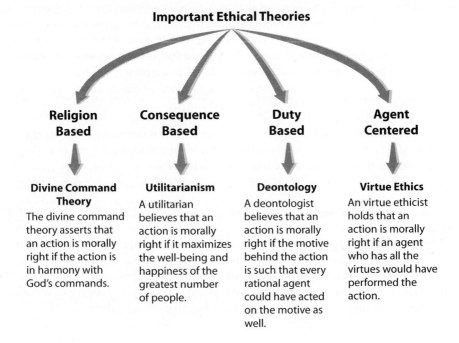

Important Ethical Theories

Religion Based	Consequence Based	Duty Based	Agent Centered
Divine Command Theory	**Utilitarianism**	**Deontology**	**Virtue Ethics**
The divine command theory asserts that an action is morally right if the action is in harmony with God's commands.	A utilitarian believes that an action is morally right if it maximizes the well-being and happiness of the greatest number of people.	A deontologist believes that an action is morally right if the motive behind the action is such that every rational agent could have acted on the motive as well.	An virtue ethicist holds that an action is morally right if an agent who has all the virtues would have performed the action.

Divine Command Theory

To many people it seems obvious that morality and religion are closely related. God is commonly understood not only as the creator of the universe, but also as the source of rules that guide humans and the universe as a whole. Just as God is often portrayed as the creator of the laws of nature, so God can be seen as the author of the rules of morality. Ivan Karamazov, a character in Dostoevsky's novel *The Brothers Karamazov,* articulates this idea well when he argues that if there is no God, everything is permitted. For those who see such a close relationship between God and morality, it is natural to adopt a position that philosophers tend to refer to as **divine command theory.**

The Case for the Divine Command Theory   The basic idea of divine command theories is that an action is morally right if it is in accordance with God's commands, and an action is morally wrong if it is in conflict with the commands of God. Let us illustrate the effect of the divine command theory with an example: Suppose Hajo is a professional bank robber who has evaded the authorities and who now lives pleasantly in a villa on the Côte d'Azur. He asks us what we think of his life and his accomplishments. If we accept the divine command theory, we will probably tell him that his past actions were morally wrong. If he wants to know why, we can reply that he has failed to follow God's commands—specifically God's command not to steal. Moreover, God commands us to give to the poor. So instead of spending all his money on luxuries, Hajo should share it with the poor.

Our words might have little impact on Hajo, but the situation shows why the divine command theory is attractive. It can explain clearly why there are objective and universal moral values—because a divine being has uttered universal commands that hold for every human being. Moral rules are therefore independent of subjective preferences and cultural norms. No matter what Hajo might think about his actions, his actions are wrong. In addition, the divine command theory provides a compelling motivation to be moral. Bank robber Hajo might think that his life of crime has paid off handsomely, but he has no chance to escape his just deserts. For God is an omniscient and infallible enforcer of moral rules. Furthermore, the divine command theory gives us a certain sense of security. It is often difficult to decide on our own whether a specific action is morally acceptable or not. Religious traditions have been around for a long time, and embedded within them are clear prescriptions of how we should live our lives. These prescriptions make it easier for us to recognize what is morally required.

Problems for the Divine Command Theory   Although the divine command theory has its appeal, it also leads to some serious difficulties. First, according to this theory, universal moral values require that there be universal divine commands, but how can we determine what these universal divine commands are? If God were to speak to us directly, we would have no difficulty understanding his commands. But most of us are not in this position; we have to rely on the testimony of established religions. And unfortunately, different religions disagree about what God wants us to do. Jews, for example, think that God does not want us to eat pork and that he requires us to keep the Sabbath holy. Muslims also eat no pork, but they believe that God requires us to pray five times a day. Hindus consider the cow to be sacred and refuse to eat beef, whereas the Christian God is indifferent to the eating of pork and beef. Is there any plausible way to decide which religion has the correct understanding of God's commands? If not, the divine command theory faces a serious epistemic problem. Although the theory tells us that morality requires us to follow God's commands, the theory fails to provide a method to determine what God's commands actually are.

Food for Thought

Different religions have different understandings of what God commands us to do. List ten actions that are demanded of us according to one religion but not demanded of us according to a different religion.

Second, for the sake of argument, let us assume that we can establish clearly what God has commanded. In order that these commands turn out to be useful guides for our lives, we have to interpret them. Suppose, for example, that we can establish with absolute certainty that God commands us not to kill. Should we conclude that it is morally wrong to become a soldier or to defend ourselves? Does the command mean that the killing of animals is wrong? If the command is to offer any help in guiding our lives, we need a precise interpretation and explanation of it. But such an interpretation can be given only by somebody who already has substantial moral knowledge. And if we are to avoid circular reasoning, this moral knowledge cannot be derived from God's commands.

Third, it seems clear that God's commands cannot be arbitrary. Few people would think that torturing babies would become morally right if God were to command it. Thus, God cannot command whatever strikes his fancy but must command us to perform those actions that are intrinsically right. If we agree with this conclusion, however, then we admit automatically that moral norms are prior and more fundamental than God's pronouncements. It follows, therefore, that God's commands are insufficient to provide a complete explanation of why actions are morally right or wrong.

Food for Thought

A good illustration of this difficulty for the divine command theory is found in the biblical story of Abraham and Isaac. According to the Bible, God commands Abraham to kill his son Isaac. Although God eventually intervenes and prevents Abraham from killing his son, the question arises of whether killing a child can become morally right when God commands it to be done. What do you think? How would you have responded if you were in Abraham's situation?

Utilitarianism

The Basic Idea The term **utilitarianism** does not refer to one single and uniform ethical theory, but rather to a group of ethical theories that center around two key ideas:

1. Human happiness is the ultimate moral good.
2. Actions should be evaluated in the light of their consequences.

Both principles are intuitively plausible. Let us start with the first principle: Why should we think that happiness is the most important good? At first glance it might seem as if people disagree about what kinds of things are desirable and good; one of us wants fame, another money, and a third person a quiet farm life in North Dakota. John Stuart Mill (1806–1873), one of the best-known advocates of utilitarianism, pointed out that in spite of the apparent variety of desires among different people, all of us ultimately seek only one thing—namely, happiness. The person who desires a quiet farm life in North Dakota expects this kind of life to make him happy. The same is true for the person who desires money; she expects money to make her happy. Thus, happiness is the common ultimate goal. If somebody asks me why I want to be happy, it is reasonable to reply that the question makes no sense. Although I can desire money or fame for the sake of happiness, happiness cannot be desired for the sake of anything else. Happiness is an ultimate, intrinsic good that is desired for its own sake.

Food for Thought

Is it possible to desire something even though we do not think that it will make us happy? If yes, give an example. If no, does this establish that happiness is not the most important good in life?

Once we establish that happiness is indeed the ultimate, intrinsic good in our lives, it makes sense to argue that all other goods have value only insofar as they contribute to happiness. When I say, for example, that George has a good job, I mean to assert that George has a job that makes him happy. A job that leads to misery cannot be good. This general idea that things have value insofar as they contribute to happiness can be applied to our thinking about morality as well, and here the second principle of utilitarianism originates. Utilitarian thinkers argue that an action is morally right insofar as the action contributes to general happiness. John Stuart Mill explained this central point as follows:

> The creed which accepts as the foundation of morals "utility" or the "greatest happiness principle" holds that actions are right in proportion as they tend to promote happiness; wrong as they tend to produce the reverse of happiness.[4]

Let us illustrate this central principle of utilitarianism with the story of Robin Hood. You might recall that Robin Hood was an outlaw who lived in Sherwood Forest and fought against the sheriff of Nottingham. Robin and his men stole from the rich and gave to the poor. Were Robin's actions morally right? Some people might condemn Robin Hood because he broke laws, but a utilitarian would not agree with such a response. From a utilitarian perspective what counts is whether his actions contributed to general happiness. And in this respect Robin Hood fares well: Although he stole, he shared the proceeds with the poor and thereby contributed to the happiness of the people around him. A utilitarian would conclude therefore that Robin Hood's actions were morally right.

The example of Robin Hood raises a crucial issue. Although Robin and his men contributed to the happiness of the poor, they made the rich quite miserable. The sheriff and other noblemen would have been much happier if Robin had stopped stealing. So was Robin Hood morally justified to make some people happy but others miserable? In order to answer this question, utilitarian thinkers introduce strict egalitarianism. When we calculate the consequences of our actions, we need to take into account the happiness of everybody affected. In these calculations everybody counts as one, and nobody counts as more than one. Thus, we cannot pay special attention to our own happiness or to the happiness of the people we like. Even if Robin disliked the sheriff, he needed to keep the sheriff's unhappiness in mind; stealing from the rich and giving to the poor was morally justified only if it produced more "net" happiness than any alternative action that Robin could have performed. The net happiness of an action is the happiness it causes minus the unhappiness it causes. And since more poor people than rich people were affected by Robin Hood's actions, it is plausible to suppose that Robin Hood's robbery produced a positive amount of net happiness and was therefore morally justified. Notice, however, that utilitarians might change this assessment if Robin Hood were to steal from many different rich people and distribute the money only among his few best friends. The moral status of Robin's actions depends on how many people's lives are happier as a result of his stealing.

Food for Thought

Utilitarianism looks out for the well-being and happiness of the majority. However, utilitarian thinking does not always go hand in hand with majority rule. There are situations in which a utilitarian would advocate making the majority of people slightly unhappy in order to save a few people from great misery. Can you think of some policies that affect most people negatively but maximize overall net happiness?

Pleasure and Happiness   The Robin Hood example shows that we need to be able to measure and compare the degree to which our actions make people happy. To do that, we need to know more about what happiness is. Traditionally, utilitarian thinkers have explained happiness in terms of pleasure and pain. If I come across a person who is experiencing intense pain, it seems natural to describe the person as unhappy. On the other hand, if I come across a person who is experiencing many pleasant sensations, it seems reasonable to call the person happy. Philosophers who believe that happiness is a result of how much pleasure and pain we experience are called **hedonists**. It is important not to misunderstand the basic message of hedonism. When we talk about pleasures and pains, we are talking not only about physical pleasures like having sex or eating a good steak. Many other activities are pleasant as well and might offer longer lasting and more fulfilling pleasurable experiences. Raising a child, writing a book, or going on vacation are all activities that can lead to long-term pleasures. The first philosophers who advocated hedonism, the Epicureans, argued that the greatest pleasures in life are friendship and peace of mind.

Food for Thought

A person who believes that happiness is a result of how much pleasure and pain we experience in our lives is called a hedonist. Are you a hedonist, or do you believe that there is more to happiness than maximizing pleasure and minimizing pain? If yes, what is the hedonist missing? Can you give a description of a happy life that is not also a pleasant life?

The two main advocates of utilitarianism, Jeremy Bentham (1748–1832) and John Stuart Mill, were both hedonists. However, they advocated different forms of hedonism. Bentham advocated a strict quantitative version of hedonism. According to him, we can measure all pleasures and pains on one scale. For example, watching a favorite TV show might produce three units of pleasure, but spending an evening with a good friend might produce twenty units of pleasure. So if you have to choose between watching TV and going out with your friend, you should choose the evening with your friend. Bentham called these kinds of calculations **hedonistic calculus.**

John Stuart Mill agreed with Bentham that we need to calculate happiness in terms of pleasure and pain, but Mill insisted that there are qualitative differences among different pleasures. In order to understand the difference between Bentham's and Mill's thinking, let us consider a specific example: Suppose that you are a very lonely person who has no friends. That means that you will never spend a pleasant evening with a good friend and so can never get those twenty units of pleasure. However, according to Bentham's theory, the lonely person can still lead a happy life. Since watching your favorite TV show produces three units of pleasure, you can simply watch seven episodes of your favorite TV show instead of going out with a good friend. Thus, your life can be just as happy as the life of the person who spends an evening with a good friend.

John Stuart Mill disagreed on this point. According to Mill, not all pleasures are commensurate with each other, and a life full of simple pleasures may not amount to a happy human life. He wrote: "Few human creatures would consent to be changed into any of the lower animals for a promise of fullest allowance of a beast's pleasures."[5] Mill's point seems plausible; it is difficult to imagine that any human would be satisfied and happy with a life that permitted us only to eat and sleep, even if the food was excellent and the bed very comfortable. Mill introduced this idea that pleasures differ not only in quantity, but also in quality. Some activities, like playing a musical instrument, can lead to such a high qualitative pleasure that no amount of lower pleasures can match it.

Although Mill's position initially appears more plausible than Bentham's, Mill's approach to hedonism raises some serious questions. If we agree with him that there are important qualitative differences among pleasures, how can we measure these qualitative distinctions? Mill thought that people with sufficient life experience would ultimately agree about what kinds of pleasures are qualitatively higher and which ones are lower. But this expectation seems overly optimistic. Even refined and well-educated people might disagree about whether reading a good book is a qualitatively higher pleasure than watching a favorite football team win the Super Bowl.

Food for Thought

Do you agree with John Stuart Mill that some activities are of such high qualitative character that they are essential to a happy human life? Take a look at the following activities. Which of these activities, if any, do you think are most essential for leading a happy human life? If possible, produce a qualitative ranking.

1. Exercising regularly
2. Working in a job that pays well
3. Eating in good restaurants
4. Owning a big expensive house
5. Having friends
6. Helping people in need

7. Having children
8. Getting drunk
9. Writing letters or a diary
10. Watching TV
11. Being politically active in one's community
12. Watching movies
13. Having a lover
14. Having a good sense of humor
15. Listening to good music
16. Talking about philosophical problems

Moreover, Mill's qualitative ranking of pleasures seems to imply that pleasure and pain are not the only possible values, but this idea seems incompatible with the hedonistic tenets of utilitarianism. The graphic that follows summarizes some key elements of utilitarianism.

Key Principles of Utilitarianism

1. Human well-being (happiness) is the ultimate moral good.
2. Actions should be evaluated in light of their consequences.
3. The happiness of each person is equally important to that of another.
4. We must consider the consequences of our actions on all sentient beings (including sentient animals) who are affected by them.
5. Actions are right to the degree that they promote the greatest amount of happiness for the greatest number of sentient beings.

Advantages of Utilitarianism   Although there is no general consensus among utilitarian thinkers about how pleasure and happiness are related, utilitarianism is nevertheless an attractive moral theory. In most circumstances it is pretty clear what kinds of actions promote or diminish general welfare. Utilitarianism is, therefore, a moral theory that produces clear and direct suggestions of what is morally required of us. This is especially helpful when we are confronted with difficult ethical dilemmas. In his book *Justice: What Is the Right Thing to Do?*[6] Michael Sandel describes just such a moral dilemma: In June 2005 a special forces team made up of Petty Officer Marcus Luttrell and three other U.S. Navy SEALs set out on a secret reconnaissance mission in Afghanistan. Their target was a close associate of Osama bin Laden who was staying in a remote village and was in command of 140 heavily armed fighters. Shortly after the special forces team took up a position on a mountain ridge overlooking the village, two Afghan farmers with about a hundred bleating goats came upon them. With them was a fourteen-year-old boy. The Afghans were unarmed. The American soldiers trained their rifles on them and then debated what to do. On the one hand, the goatherds appeared to be unarmed civilians. On the other hand, letting them go would risk their informing the Taliban in the village below of the presence of the U.S. soldiers. As the four soldiers contemplated their options, they realized that they did not have rope, so tying up the Afghans to allow time to find a new hideout was not feasible. The only choice was to kill them or let them go free.

The four soldiers did not agree on what to do. One of them argued that they should simply kill the goatherds, but Marcus Luttrell was conflicted about this. He reported later: "My Christian soul was crowding in on me and kept whispering in the back of my mind that it is wrong to kill these unarmed men in cold blood." In the end he cast the deciding vote that it would be better to let them go. An hour and a half after the release, the four U.S. soldiers found themselves surrounded by eighty Taliban fighters, and a fierce firefight ensued. All three of Luttrell's fellow soldiers were killed. In addition, the Taliban fighters managed to shoot down a U.S. helicopter that sought to rescue the SEAL unit, killing sixteen soldiers on board. Luttrell managed to survive the firefight by falling down the mountainside and crawling seven miles to a Pashtun village.

Isn't it clear that Marcus Luttrell made a mistake in this situation? After his rescue, he himself said that this was the "stupidest, most southern-fried, lamebrained decision"[7] he had ever made. If Marcus Luttrell had been raised as a strict utilitarian moral thinker, he might have acted differently. But Luttrell thought that it was morally wrong to kill three unarmed innocent persons. From a utilitarian perspective no type of action is always morally right or wrong—it all depends on the consequences! In this situation a utilitarian would have recommended killing the three goatherds, even though they had done nothing wrong, because killing them would have produced better consequences. This example illustrates a central strength of utilitarianism: Consequences matter and utilitarianism allows us to take them into account. Utilitarianism gives us the flexibility to bend moral rules; it can explain why moral guidelines that work well in ordinary life must be broken when we are confronting extraordinary circumstances. This is a great advantage.

Utilitarianism also explains well why moral thinking must be impartial. Utilitarian calculations take into account the well-being of everybody to an equal degree; thus, any form of egoism is incompatible with a moral point of view. In addition, utilitarianism has a good answer to the question of why we should be moral. According to utilitarianism, we care about morality because we are interested in making people happy. Increasing general well-being and happiness is a natural human endeavor, and the demands of morality are a natural part of our existence.

Problems for Utilitarianism   Although utilitarianism is an attractive moral theory, it faces a number of well-known problems. First, it seems as if maximizing general happiness requires us in certain situations to perform immoral actions. Consider the following example: Suppose you are a doctor in a remote hospital in the Andes. One day, three very important people of the village get seriously sick (the priest, the only teacher, and the mayor). The priest has kidney failure, the teacher has lung cancer, and the mayor needs a new liver. If all three die, the village will be in serious trouble. As an experienced surgeon, you know that you could save the three lives if you had the necessary organs. Suddenly you realize that Freddie, a friendless but very healthy young man who is disliked by everybody in the village, happens to be in the hospital to have his tonsils removed; he could provide the necessary organs. Since Freddie is an antisocial loner, he would never volunteer his organs to save the three important people. However, you realize that you could simply take Freddie's organs during his tonsil surgery without his permission and save the priest, the teacher, and the mayor. What should you do?

This is, of course, an artificial example, but it illustrates that utilitarianism can get us into trouble. Removing Freddie's organs without his permission seems to be morally wrong, but the action nevertheless seems to maximize general happiness. It follows, therefore, that utilitarianism does not always go hand in hand with our intuitions about what is morally required. A good utilitarian might respond that our moral intuitions are not always reliable and should be revised in light of utilitarian considerations. But many draw different conclusions; the British philosopher A. C. Ewing (1899–1973) wrote, for example, that "utilitarian principles, logically carried out, would result in far more cheating, lying and unfair action than any good man would tolerate."[8]

Food for Thought

Can you think of other situations in which maximizing general welfare requires us to perform actions that according to commonsense morality are immoral?

A closely related objection to utilitarianism charges that utilitarian thinking cannot explain why we should respect people's rights. The American philosopher James Rachels (1941–2003) gave the example of a Peeping Tom who secretly took pictures of his undressed neighbor Ms. York:[9]

> Suppose that he does this without ever being detected and that he uses the photographs entirely for his own amusement, without showing them to anyone. In these circumstances it is clear that the only consequence of his actions is an increase in his own happiness. No one else, including Ms. York, is caused any unhappiness at all. How, then, could utilitarianism deny that the Peeping Tom's actions are right? This example shows that utilitarian thinking is not fully compatible with our thinking about moral rights. Most of us would agree that everybody has the right to privacy and that the Peeping Tom has violated Ms. York's right to privacy. Thus, for those who take moral rights to be a central element in their moral thinking, utilitarianism seems unacceptable.

The third major objection to utilitarianism has to do with promise making. Suppose that I have promised to pick Susan up from the airport, but on the way to the airport, I stop at a convenience store and run into a homeless man with severe stomach pains who is walking to a hospital. If I offer him a ride to the hospital, I will not be able to meet Susan at the airport. What should I do? From a utilitarian perspective, taking the homeless man to the hospital has priority. After all, it is possible that the homeless man will experience severe health problems if he is not treated soon, whereas Susan's well-being will not be so seriously affected by my failure to show up at the airport.

These examples show that utilitarianism requires us to keep promises only if doing so will maximize general happiness. In all other cases, it is not only morally permissible but actually morally required to break the promise. Many philosophers find this result problematic. The American philosopher John Rawls (1921–2002), for example, wrote: "What would one say of someone who, when asked why he broke a promise, replied simply that breaking it was best on the whole? Assuming that his reply is sincere . . . one would question whether or not he knew what it means to say 'I promise.'"[10]

Food for Thought

Many objections to utilitarianism have to do with promise making. William Shaw describes a version of a deathbed promise in his book *Contemporary Ethics: Taking Account of Utilitarianism*:

> An elderly woman living alone in poor circumstances with few friends or relatives is dying, and you are at her bedside. She draws your attention to a small case under her bed, which contains some mementos along with the money she has managed to save over the years, despite her apparent poverty. She asks you to take the case and to promise to deliver its contents, after she dies, to her nephew living in another state. Moved by her plight and by your affection for her, you promise to do as she bids. After a tearful good-bye, you take the case and leave. A few weeks later the old woman dies, and when you open her case you discover that it contains $50,000. No one else knows about the money or the promise that you made. . . . Now suppose further that the nephew is a compulsive gambler and heavy drinker and that you know that, if you were to give him the $50,000 as promised, he would rapidly squander the money.[11]

What would a utilitarian do in this situation? What would you do? What is morally required?

Furthermore, utilitarianism seems to be too demanding by requiring us to maximize general happiness constantly. If you would choose to spend a lazy Sunday in bed, it would seem clear that this action would not be maximizing general happiness. Instead of lying in bed, you could visit a nursing home and play cards with its elderly residents, or you could at least call your mother or write a letter to your uncle. All of these activities would contribute more to general happiness than lying in bed. Thus, it seems to follow that spending a lazy Sunday in bed is an immoral action. But that is a very curious conclusion, and most of us would reject it. Commonsense morality draws distinctions between **obligatory actions,** that is, actions that are morally required, and **supererogatory actions,** that is, actions that are praiseworthy but are not strictly required. Going to a nursing home on your free Sunday to play cards with the elderly residents appears to be a supererogatory action, not an obligatory one. Utilitarianism makes it difficult, if not impossible, to distinguish clearly between obligatory and supererogatory actions. There seems to be no realm of moral indifference; all acts are either required or forbidden. There also seems to be no space to show partiality to one's own projects or one's family, friends, and fellow citizens. The British philosopher Bernard Williams (1929–2003) concluded therefore that utilitarianism is a "profoundly alienating" moral theory.[12]

Food for Thought

Practice your understanding of the difference between obligatory actions and supererogatory actions by identifying which of the following actions are morally obligatory and which are supererogatory.

1. Not parking in a handicap parking spot.
2. Studying as hard as you can for your final exams.
3. Being honest on your income tax report.
4. Giving at least some money to charity.
5. Spending time with your parents.
6. Making sure that your children receive the best possible education.
7. Supporting your own country in times of war.

Food for Thought

Utilitarianism also has problems incorporating our special obligations as parents, siblings, or relatives into our moral thinking. The following example illustrates this problem:

> Suppose you are the parent of a three-year-old son. This summer you are cruising the Atlantic on an expensive cruise ship, and disaster strikes—the ship sinks. You somehow manage to get on a lifeboat with a motor. All around you people are drowning and crying for help. Suddenly you see your son a hundred yards away. He is frantically trying to stay afloat. In order to save your son, you must drive the lifeboat to him. However, just as you are about to do that, you see that two children are about to drown ten yards away in the opposite direction.

What would you do? What would utilitarianism require you to do? What do you think is the morally right thing to do?

Duty-Based Theories

In light of the fact that consequence-based moral thinking leads to serious difficulties, some prominent thinkers have tried to find a foundation for morality that does not focus on the consequences of our actions. Might it be possible to ground morality on freedom or a good will or human flourishing? We will explore this question in this and the next section.

The Importance of a Good Will   The German philosopher Immanuel Kant (1724–1804) developed one of the main alternatives to consequence-based moral thinking. Kant's moral theory is often referred to as **deontology**, since the concept of duty plays an important role in it. Kant rejected the idea that morally good actions always lead to good consequences. According to him, consequences cannot explain why our actions are morally good or morally bad. An example will help to clarify his position: Suppose Amelia is a twenty-one-year-old college student who is a bit short on money. She thinks to herself, "If I go home next weekend and surprise my mother with an unannounced visit, I am sure she will give me some money." So Amelia takes off early Saturday morning and drives for three hours to her mother's house. To Amelia's surprise, it turns out that it is her mother's birthday, and her mother is so moved by Amelia's surprise visit that she calls her daughter the "most thoughtful daughter in the world." It is obvious that Amelia's decision to visit her mother led to good consequences: Her mother is happy, and Amelia ends up with some additional money. However, Kant would argue that all of these positive consequences do not make Amelia's decision to drive to her mother's house a morally praiseworthy action. Something is missing. Amelia's motive for visiting her mother is too self-centered and too egoistic to make her action morally good.

Food for Thought

We have seen that an action that leads to good consequences might nevertheless be morally wicked. But Kant also thought that an action that leads to bad consequences might be morally good. Can you think of examples of actions that lead to terrible consequences but that one might nevertheless consider to be morally good?

Kant suggested that moral judgments must focus on the motives behind our actions. It is the **will** that determines whether our actions are morally good or bad. Kant wrote:

> There is no possibility of thinking of anything at all in the world, or even out of it, which can be regarded as good without qualification, except a good will.[13]

Kant's idea that a good will is the key factor in moral judgments is plausible. It makes sense to say that we should not be judged on the basis of what we achieve, but rather on the basis of what we try to achieve. We are good, not because we succeed in our efforts, but rather because we try as hard as we can.

However, Kant's concept of a good will raises a crucial question: When exactly can we be sure that our will is good? According to Kant, we have to realize that our will is constantly threatened by potentially overwhelming alien forces. Suppose I wake up one morning and feel a strong desire to eat a freshly baked bagel with cream cheese. Consequently, I get dressed and eat a bagel at the closest bagel shop. What should we say about this action? I had a will to eat a bagel, and I acted on that will. Was my will a morally good will? Kant would say no, not because there is something wrong with my decision to eat a bagel, but because my action is not worthy of moral praise. The problem is that my will and my action were determined by my desire to eat a bagel. My desires, however, are not something I control; I cannot determine whether I will wake up with a desire for a bagel. As far as I know, I might wake up with a desire for toast with jelly. Desires come and go, and as long as my will is determined only by my desires, my will is subject to forces that I do not control. For this reason, Kant thought that animals cannot be moral agents. The will of animals is always controlled by their desires, and they are, therefore, unable to freely determine their own will. Thus, animals are puppets of nature and not moral agents.

But how can we humans escape the fate of animals and become free moral agents? Kant argued that a good will is a will that stands on its own. It must determine itself in a manner that is independent of all outside forces. If we accomplish that, our will becomes **autonomous,** which makes our will good and worthy of respect. Let us take a closer look at how the autonomy of our will can be achieved. Suppose you have promised to help your friend Joe with his move to a new apartment. On Saturday, the day you have promised to help him, you wake up with a terrible headache and feel a strong desire to stay in bed. You are not sure what you should do. One possibility is to do what you feel like doing and stay in bed. In this case your will is neither free nor autonomous, and your action has no moral worth because it is shaped by your feeling of discomfort. How else could you approach this decision? Rather than focusing on how you *feel,* it would be much better if you were to *think* of how you would want others to act if they were in your situation. You might imagine what a person with a good will would do if he or she had a headache but had promised to help. Would not such a person fulfill the promise even if he or she did not feel like doing so? Suppose then that you pull yourself out of bed and get dressed in order to help your friend. You do this not because you feel like doing it (on the contrary!) but rather because you have come to the realization that any decent human being would act in this way. In this case your will is starting to be shaped in the right way. Kant suggested that our will becomes free, autonomous, and worthy of respect if it is shaped according to principles that are acceptable to all moral agents. He expressed this idea as follows:

> Act only according to that maxim whereby you can at the same time will that it should become a universal law.[14]

Kant called this the **categorical imperative;** it offers a procedure that allows us to evaluate whether a principle should be allowed to shape our will. In order to understand this more clearly, consider the following two principles:

1. Always keep your promises even if you do not feel like fulfilling them.

2. Keep your promises unless you have a headache.

The categorical imperative shows us that we should not allow the second principle to shape our will. This principle cannot be adopted by all rational agents, for if all rational agents broke their promises if they had a headache, nobody would trust anybody else's promises. And then promise making would not really be possible. So if one understands principle 2 as a universal law, it turns out to be self-defeating. But the same is not true for principle 1. If we imagine a world in which all rational agents adopt principle 1, we do not end up with any contradictions. Thus, principle 1 passes the categorical imperative and is therefore an acceptable moral principle.

Kant suggested that the more we shape our will according to universal principles and the more we act on reasons that can be reasons for everyone, the more our will becomes autonomous and worthy of respect. Clearly, this is a demanding project. Nobody will succeed in making the categorical imperative the lone power that shapes the will in every situation. But this is beside the point. The categorical imperative is not a description of how we do act but an ideal of how we ought to act. In real life we will at times act on mere impulses and inclinations, but the categorical imperative shows us a way in which we can rise above the brute forces of nature. It is our ability to shape our will according to universal principles that makes us moral agents who deserve dignity and respect.

Food for Thought

Test your understanding of the categorical imperative by deciding whether the following principles can be consistently universalized:

1. Give money to people in need.
2. Be faithful to your spouse unless you suspect that your spouse is not faithful to you.
3. Be friendly to someone only if that person was friendly to you.
4. Never steal from anybody.
5. Always do what is in your best interest.
6. If you want to perform an action and the action does not harm anyone, go ahead and do it.
7. Tell lies only if you have to.
8. Never break a promise.
9. If you feel like it, drink a shot of tequila.
10. Treat people with respect.

This Food for Thought exercise illustrates that it is not always easy to tell whether a principle can be universally adopted by all rational agents. For this reason Kant offered an alternative formulation of the categorical imperative. Keep in mind that the main purpose of the categorical imperative is to shape the will such that it becomes autonomous. And it is the autonomy of will that makes it possible to become a moral agent. It seems obvious that it would be wrong to prevent others from developing an autonomous will. Kant put it this way:

> Act in such a way that you treat humanity, whether in your own person or in the person of another, always at the same time as an end and never simply as a means.[15]

In this so-called second formulation of the categorical imperative, Kant expressed the same idea: We need to act on principles that are universally acceptable to all rational agents. But a principle cannot be universally accepted if it prevents a rational agent from becoming autonomous. Consider this example: Suppose Dennis and Anna have been dating for six months. Dennis is very much in love with Anna, but last weekend, after having too much to drink, he had sex with somebody else. He does not care for that other person, and since he truly loves only Anna, he decides to keep this whole unfortunate event secret. What is wrong with this action? Notice that Dennis's decision to keep his affair secret is an attempt to influence and manipulate Anna's decisions. He wants Anna to stay with him but is afraid that she might leave him if he told her the truth. In this situation it is clear that Dennis is not respecting Anna as an autonomous agent; he is thinking only about his own interests, and his silence prevents Anna from making a well-informed decision about whether she wants to continue to go out with him. Her not knowing makes it impossible for her to make a free and rational decision. By keeping his actions secret, Dennis is treating Anna as a mere means to his own ends. If he had genuine respect for her autonomy, he would tell her everything—regardless of the consequences. The second formulation of the categorical imperative explains why Kant thought that lying is always and everywhere an immoral action. Lying, by definition, involves treating another rational agent as a mere means to an end, and that is never acceptable.

Food for Thought

The second formulation of the categorical imperative stresses that we should never treat others as a means to an end. Give some examples of situations in which people are treated only as a means to an end.

A good test to clarify whether you understand Kantian ethics is to apply his concepts to concrete situations. Let us return to the story of Robin Hood to see what Kant would have to say. Let us start by analyzing Robin Hood's actions in the light of the first version of the categorical imperative. Robin Hood seemed to be acting on the following principle (i.e., maxim): If I can help many poor people, it is acceptable to steal from the rich. Would we want this principle to become a universal law? The answer is a clear no. If we were to universalize this principle, everyone would feel justified to steal. And if that were the case, there would be no personal property, which would make stealing conceptually impossible. So the principle in question, if universalized, would be self-defeating. Thus, the principle does not pass the first version of the categorical imperative, and we must conclude that Robin Hood's actions were morally wrong.

We reach the same result if we apply the second formulation of the categorical imperative to this situation. Robin Hood was treating rich people as a mere means to an end; he did not respect their autonomy, and his actions were therefore morally wrong. We see in this example that the two versions of the categorical imperative work hand in hand. We can choose either formulation in order to help clarify what we should do in specific situations. The key principles of deontology are summarized in the graphic that follows.

Key Principles of Deontology

1. Freedom (autonomy) is the ultimate moral good.
2. Each and every rational being has infinite moral worth.
3. We must respect the dignity and autonomy of all human beings in all situations (all human beings have inalienable rights).
4. It is never permissible to treat a human being as *a means to an end only,* (e.g., torture is always wrong even if it might lead to good consequences).
5. All human beings have to fulfill certain absolute duties (e.g., the duty not to lie, the duty not to commit suicide, the duty to develop one's talents).

Food for Thought

Utilitarianism and deontological thinking frequently lead to conflicting recommendations of what we should do in difficult moral situations. In the following situation a committed utilitarian would act differently than a full-blown deontologist. Explain the differences.

> Suppose you are a famous anthropologist, and one day you find a remote tribe in the middle of the Amazon rain forest. The tribe is really surprised by your visit. After all, you are the first stranger they have ever seen. The tribe is in the middle of a religious ritual, preparing to execute twenty prisoners from a neighboring tribe as a gift to the sun god. However, since they also want to honor you, they offer you the honor of strangling one of the prisoners with your own hands. If you do that, they will let the others go back to their tribe. If you refuse to accept the honor, they will sacrifice all twenty people. You try to tell them that your god does not allow you to strangle people, but the tribal leader is unwilling to make any deals. He is very clear: Either you strangle one of the prisoners, or all twenty will be killed.

Advantages of Kant's Ethics Kant's moral philosophy has a number of advantages. First, Kant derives moral principles simply on the basis of rational and a priori reasoning; thus, the principles are independent of time and place and are binding for all human beings. Second, deontological ethics tells us that we have a number of strict duties: We must tell the truth, we must develop our talents, we cannot commit suicide, we have to give to charity. This categorical and rigorous advocacy of duties helps us when we face difficult moral decisions by providing clear and unambiguous moral directions. Third, Kant's theory of ethics shows us that human beings have infinite worth. Most of us have probably always suspected that there is something morally wrong with putting a price on a human life—is it worth one million dollars or perhaps ten million dollars? Deontological thinking demonstrates that each of us is worth an infinite amount, for each of us has to be seen as an ultimate end and not just as the means to some other purpose. Finally, deontological ethics is compatible with the idea that we have fundamental moral rights. According to Kant, we must respect the autonomy of others in all situations; we are all born with fundamental rights (e.g., the right to life, the right to be treated as a rational and autonomous agent) that nobody can take away from us. Such rights-based moral thinking is familiar to most of us, and Kant's ethics provides a good foundation for it.

Problems for Kant's Ethics The biggest weakness of deontological thinking is that it does not allow the consequences of our actions to be of ethical significance, and this neglect of consequences can lead to paradoxical results. Suppose that your friend Susan has an argument with her husband, Felix, and decides that it is better to spend the night at your house away from her husband. Two hours later, Felix stands at your door and is carrying an axe. He breathes heavily and seems very angry as he asks you whether Susan is staying with you. What do you do? Most of us would probably choose to tell Felix a lie because the consequences of telling the truth might be terrible. A deontologist would insist, however, that we tell the truth; we have a duty never to tell a lie, and consequences do not matter. That recommendation seems crazy! In some situations, obviously, consequences do matter a great deal and should therefore influence our decisions. Clearly, deontological thinking is too restricted, and Kant's insistence that a good will is sufficient for moral goodness seems misguided.

Food for Thought

Can you think of other situations in which telling a lie is not only morally permitted but even morally required of us?

A closely related problem with Kant's ethics is caused by situations in which duties conflict with each other; for example, in certain situations our duty to respect the autonomy of others can conflict with the duty to save as many lives as possible. Kant's ethics gives us no recipe for prioritizing duties when they conflict, and this lack of clarity makes it difficult to apply deontological thinking in challenging ethical situations.

There are further weaknesses of deontological ethical theories, but the two discussed here make it clear that deontology faces some serious challenges. In response, some deontological thinkers—for example, W. D. Ross (1877–1971)—have tried to refine deontological ethical thinking, but a completely different approach might fare better.

Virtue-Based Theories

The Importance of Moral Character   Although utilitarianism and deontology are often presented as opposing ethical theories, they have something in common: Both try to develop general and universal criteria that allow us to classify actions as either morally good or morally bad. Utilitarianism and deontology are therefore considered action- and rule-centered ethical theories. Virtue ethics takes a different approach, by drawing our attention to the role of agents in moral deliberations. Let us illustrate this difference with the help of an example: Suppose you have to explain to a child why lying is morally wrong. According to utilitarianism, lying is wrong because it tends to lead to bad consequences. A deontologist would say that lying is wrong because it involves treating others as a mere means to our ends. A virtue ethical thinker, on the other hand, prefers a different type of explanation: Lying is wrong because it tends to corrupt our character. In other words, a virtuous person—that is, a person who is honest—realizes that habitual lying leads to the development of bad character traits. From a virtue ethical perspective, judgments about character are more fundamental than judgments about rules, duties, and obligations. Virtue ethics replaces the question What ought I to do? with the question What sort of person ought I to be? In other words, we should focus our energies on improving our moral character rather than finding abstract moral rules that allow us to classify actions.

This moral theory introduces a new direction in our thinking about ethics—attempting to clarify what type of moral character is praiseworthy, and virtuous. Virtues are character traits that enable agents to act well habitually. Honesty, for example, is a virtue. People who are honest are people who have, among other traits, a strong disposition to speak the truth in all situations. Many people lack this virtue; some people have a character that tempts them to exaggerate constantly, which is a vice. Compassion is another virtue. Persons with compassion can relate well to people who suffer and thus are motivated to help people in need. In addition to honesty and compassion, many other positive and praiseworthy character traits are considered to be virtues. However, it is important to realize that virtues are not simply habits; a person who, out of habit, never steals is not necessarily a virtuous person. A true virtue requires having the right kind of inner attitude and the right kind of motivation.

Imagine that I am faithful to my spouse because nobody else is interested in having an affair with me. That kind of faithfulness would not make me a virtuous person. A virtuous person would think about faithfulness in the right way and would not be motivated to cheat even if the opportunity arose. For this reason we cannot tell from the outside whether somebody is truly virtuous; we would need to know the motivation behind the person's actions.

Having a particular virtue involves many aspects of personality, emotions as well as intellect. Being generous, for example, involves more than sharing money and resources with others. A generous person also feels pleasure and joy while sharing and understands when generosity is appropriate. These types of judgments require practical wisdom, which is the knowledge more experienced persons have acquired and younger people normally lack. Practical wisdom comes from observing human affairs carefully and remembering how our actions and the actions of others have played out. Since virtues are rather complex, multitrack character traits and since possessing a virtue completely also requires practical wisdom, it seems natural to understand virtue possession as a matter of degree. Very few of us are always fully courageous and loyal, for example, and even if we are, we might lack the practical wisdom to choose the right response. In real life it is therefore more appropriate to make comparative judgments about virtues—saying that someone is more courageous or loyal than somebody else. A virtue ethical thinker claims that the more we develop a virtuous character and acquire practical wisdom, the greater the chance that we will act well in life. Good actions flow from a good character and a good character is an essential part of any flourishing and happy human life.

The ancient Greek philosopher Aristotle was the first to provide a systematic account of virtues. In the *Nicomachean Ethics* he argued that moral virtues are character traits that are the mean between two vices. Courage, for example, is the mean between cowardice and rashness: Cowardice causes a person to feel fear too strongly (a state of excess), whereas rashness causes the person to feel fear insufficiently (a state of deficiency). Only the courageous person has the character to feel fear to the right degree and at the right time. The nature of other moral virtues—such as temperance, generosity, anger control, friendliness, and modesty—can also be analyzed as a character state that lies between two vices. Generosity, for instance, is the mean between stinginess and wastefulness; modesty is the mean between shamelessness and bashfulness. With his doctrine of the mean, however, Aristotle pointed out that finding the mean cannot be accomplished by theoretical reflection alone.

Over time, Aristotle's virtue theory became the dominant account of the virtues. In medieval discussions the main virtues described by Aristotle and the ancient Greeks became known as the cardinal virtues, but medieval writers like Thomas Aquinas added the Christian virtues of humility, chastity, obedience, faith, and love to the list of important virtues. In the eighteenth century it was common to add frugality, industry, cleanliness, and tranquility to the list. These various lists of virtues highlight the fact that there is no general agreement regarding how many virtues there are.

Food for Thought

Although it is relatively easy to list various virtues and vices, it is much more difficult to describe in detail what these virtues or vices actually are. Take a look at each of the following virtues, and explain to a classmate what you think these virtues entail. Give some concrete examples, and determine whether both of you understand the virtues and vices in a similar fashion.

Virtues: civility, courage, compassion, courteousness, dependability, fairness, friendliness, generosity, good temper, honesty, justice, loyalty, moderation

Vices: envy, lust, cruelty, gluttony, anger, covetousness, sloth, greed, selfishness, impulsiveness, insensitivity, recklessness

The absence of a definite list of virtues can actually be seen as an advantage of virtue ethics. It means that it is perfectly fine for different agents to focus on different virtues if they happen to live in different societies. In other words, it is appropriate that a person in ancient Athens aimed to develop a different character from that of a person who lives in present-day New York City. Moreover, a person's occupation can be taken into account; a good nurse has to develop a different character from that of a banker or a university professor. Virtue ethical thinkers stress the importance of role models, persons of excellent moral character who habitually act well and who feel pleasure when exercising their virtues. Role models can help us to decide what we should do in difficult situations. If the role models are close by, we can ask them for advice, or we can simply imagine what they would do.

Food for Thought

Role models are important in virtue ethical thinking. From the following list of persons, decide which is the best role model and which is the worst.

1. Socrates
2. Buddha
3. Oprah Winfrey
4. Jesus Christ
5. Abraham Lincoln
6. Mahatma Gandhi
7. Martin Luther King, Jr.
8. Mohammed
9. Mother Teresa
10. Alan Greenspan
11. Tom Hanks

A good test to see whether you are beginning to understand the basic thrust of virtue ethics is to analyze a specific situation in the light of virtue ethical considerations. Let us turn to the story of Robin Hood one last time: Would a virtue ethical thinker approve of Robin Hood's actions? In order to answer this question, we must do more than look at what Robin Hood did; we have to understand what kind of person Robin Hood was. According to most portrayals of Robin Hood in movies and books, he was motivated by a sense of loyalty to King Richard. This is one reason that he was opposing the new king, John. From a virtue ethical perspective, loyalty is a virtue and a praiseworthy character trait. Notice how different our assessment of Robin Hood would be if his disobedience toward King John were simply caused by youthful rebelliousness. Robin Hood also seemed to be very compassionate toward poor people, and he was not cruel or inhumane when he robbed the rich. Just the opposite, he was often portrayed as humorous and gentle, even when he had to fight against wicked men. In addition, Robin Hood was a good friend and a courageous leader. It seems then that Robin Hood's actions flowed from a praiseworthy and excellent character, which made his actions morally good. The key principles of virtue ethics are summarized in the graphic that follows.

Key Principles of Virtue Ethics

1. Human excellence is the ultimate moral good.
2. When contemplating what to do, ask yourself this question: Would a morally virtuous person perform the action?
3. Try to shape your own character by doing good acts habitually.
4. Try to imitate the behavior of virtuous role models.
5. Perform actions that are an expression of core virtues like honesty, courage, compassion, justice and loyalty.
6. Do not perform actions that are an expression of vice, such as laziness, greed, anger, or cruelty.

Advantages of Virtue Ethics   Virtue ethics has a number of attractive features. By concentrating on moral character rather than on abstract rules, virtue ethics stresses that becoming a moral person is mostly a matter of receiving the right education and upbringing. Utilitarianism and deontology make it appear that becoming morally good is simply a matter of applying the right moral principles, which suggests that being moral is a theoretical matter rather than a practical affair. By stressing the importance of role models, practical wisdom, and moral education, virtue ethical thinking provides a practical moral framework that squares well with common sense. However, it is important not to conclude that moral rules do not matter in virtue ethics; in fact, moral rules still play an important part in moral education. Aristotle pointed out that a young person who wanted to learn how to become a navigator of a ship initially would need to rely on firm rules in order to navigate the ship from one port to another.

However, with time, an expert navigator would know when to bend the rules. And what is true of navigation seems also true of moral education. When we are young, we need firm moral rules, but later in life, as we become more experienced, we are able to see that moral rules can have exceptions.

Another advantage is that virtue ethics allows us to draw attention to the important role of emotions in our moral life. This is especially true with respect to moral motivation. To illustrate this, it will be useful to consider an example: Suppose three adult sisters call their mother on her birthday. The oldest daughter is a deontologist, who calls her mother because it is the right thing to do. The second daughter is utilitarian, and she calls her mother because it maximizes the general welfare. Both of these motives seem artificial and even a bit callous. The third daughter is a virtuous person who calls her mother because she has developed the kind of character that finds it pleasant to call one's mother on her birthday. She does not ask herself whether it is her duty to do this or what the consequences of her actions are apt to be; she simply acts out of a *feeling* of affection for her mother. This example shows that according to virtue ethical thinking, our emotions play an important role in causing us to act. Utilitarianism and deontology, on the other hand, provide an unrealistic and shallow account of moral motivation.

Furthermore, virtue ethics makes it possible to give weight to special relationships within our ethical deliberations. Classical ethical theories like utilitarianism and deontology require us to adopt a position of strict impartiality, which requires that we care as much about the well-being of strangers as about the well-being of our children. In many situations this absolute impartiality seems forced and inhumane. Virtue ethics allows us to pay attention to the special moral obligations that arise in the context of being a lover, a parent, or a good friend.

Food for Thought

Can you describe situations in which we might be morally required to violate a strict sense of impartiality? For example, is it morally acceptable to prefer the well-being of one's own country over that of other countries? Is it morally permitted to give more weight to the well-being of one's own children than to the well-being of other children?

Finally, virtue ethics provides a more flexible moral framework than competing ethical theories do. We have seen in prior discussion that utilitarian thinking and deontological thinking are both confronted with counterexamples, because both theories demand that we apply one theoretical principle to all situations. Virtue ethics does not face such a problem. According to virtue ethics, we should perform those actions that a completely virtuous person would perform, but this opens up the possibility that our role models will sometimes think in terms of consequences and sometimes in terms of strict duty. We thus are able to incorporate the best recommendations of the two main competing theories within a virtue ethical framework.

Problems for Virtue Ethics   We have seen that virtue ethics moves away from the question of what we ought to do and focuses instead on the analysis of moral character traits. However, we study and develop moral theories in order to find answers to specific moral questions—whether it is morally right to execute dangerous criminals or whether we are morally required to help terminally sick patients to die, for example. It is difficult to see how virtue ethics can provide much help in answering such questions. Virtue ethics recommends that we do what a completely virtuous person would do, but this recommendation raises two crucial epistemic questions:

1. How can we identify a completely virtuous person?
2. How does the role model know what to do in difficult ethical situations?

The first question might be answered in a pragmatic way; we might simply accept someone as a role model if the society around us accepts the person as a role model as well. Aristotle, for instance, told us that Pericles and men like him had practical wisdom.[16] But this recommendation made sense only in the context of the Athenian community. If we today adopt this approach, virtue ethics seems to require that we accept the moral judgments of our society and thus seems to embrace a form of cultural relativism. On the other hand, if we reject this pragmatic solution, we need to develop some objective and timeless criteria for recognizing and identifying completely virtuous persons—a difficult if not impossible task.

As for the second question, what does guide the virtuous person when different virtues are in conflict with each other? The honest thing to do is not always the most prudent or the most courageous. How are we to weigh the different virtues against each other? The role model must appeal to some general moral rules that are provided by classical ethical theories. But this suggests that virtue ethics cannot stand completely on its own. Thus, it might be best to regard virtue ethics as part of an overall theory of ethics rather than as a complete theory itself.

Final Remarks on the Problem of Morality

We started our discussion of ethics by criticizing moral relativism. There are good reasons to think that at least some moral norms apply to all people in all cultures at all times. However, our discussion of important moral theories did not produce a unanimous winner. Divine command theories, utilitarianism, deontology, and virtue ethics offer different accounts of morality, but we were not able to identify one superior theory. This is puzzling. If moral objectivism is correct and an objective moral reality truly exists that is independent of our moral judgments, shouldn't we be able to recognize one ethical theory that provides a better description of moral reality than all the other theories? A moral relativist would count this quandary as evidence against moral objectivism. However, we do not have to reach that same conclusion. We can agree with Plato and argue that moral values are the most difficult entities to be clearly grasped by human intellect—and hope that in the future, philosophers who are smarter than we are will find an ultimate, unified moral theory. Or we could embrace a form of moral pluralism, which holds that moral reality consists of multiple and competing moral values. If we accept this view, we can understand each internally consistent moral theory as explaining a part of moral reality and contributing something to our moral understanding. But no one theory can claim that it is entirely accurate.

Study and Reflection Questions

1. Are there some moral norms that are shared by all cultures? If yes, what are these norms?

2. Describe some objections to the divine command theory. How could a defender of the divine command theory counter these objections?

3. Do you agree with John Stuart Mill that there are qualitative distinctions among pleasures? If yes, give an example of a high-quality pleasure and an example of a low-quality pleasure. If no, clarify how you would argue that Mill's view is mistaken.

4. Utilitarianism and deontology agree that morality requires us to be impartial, that is, from a moral point of view treating all people as being of equal value. Is it possible to be moral but give greater moral weight to one's own children and friends? What do you think?

5. Take a look at the list of virtues and vices. Is there a virtue that is especially praiseworthy? Is there a vice that is especially heinous?

For Further Reading

Allison, Henry. *Kant's Theory of Freedom.* Cambridge: Cambridge University Press, 1991.

Driver, Julia. *Ethics: The Fundamentals.* Oxford: Blackwell, 2006.

Ellin, Joseph. *Morality and the Meaning of Life: An Introduction to Ethical Theory.* Orlando, FL: Harcourt, 1995.

Frankena, William. *Ethics.* Englewood Cliffs, NJ: Prentice Hall, 1973.

Rachels, James. *The Elements of Moral Philosophy.* 6th ed. New York: McGraw-Hill, 2009.

Shafer-Landau, Russ. *The Fundamentals of Ethics.* Oxford: Oxford University Press, 2010.

Shaw, William. *Contemporary Ethics: Taking Account of Utilitarianism.* Oxford: Blackwell, 1998.

Singer, Peter, ed. *A Companion to Ethics.* Oxford: Blackwell, 1993.

Swanton, Christine. *Virtue Ethics: A Pluralistic View.* Oxford: Oxford University Press, 2003.

Timmons, Mark. *Moral Theory.* New York: Rowman & Littlefield, 2001.

Endnotes

1. Philippa Foot, *The Problem of Abortion and the Doctrine of the Double Effect* (Oxford: Blackwell, 1978).
2. It is important to keep in mind that I treat the term *cultural relativism* exclusively as a normative theory, that is, as a theory that makes claims about what ought to be done. It is possible to treat the term as merely a descriptive theory, that is, as a theory that describes differences in moral judgments among different cultures. I thank Will Heusser for pointing out the need to draw attention to this distinction.
3. This story is probably factually false; Inuits probably never treated elders in this way. However, it does not matter whether the story is historically accurate or not; it illustrates well that certain drastic behavioral differences among different cultures can be caused by nonmoral background beliefs and not by differences in moral values.
4. John Stuart Mill, *Utilitarianism* (Indianapolis, IN: Hackett, 1979), p. 32.
5. Ibid., p. 9.
6. Michael Sandel, *Justice: What Is the Right Thing to Do?* (New York: Farrar, Straus & Giroux, 2009), pp. 24–27.
7. Ibid., p. 25.
8. A. C. Ewing, *Ethics* (London: English Universities Press, 1953), p. 40.
9. James Rachels, *The Elements of Moral Philosophy,* 4th ed. (New York: McGraw-Hill, 2003), pp. 112–113.
10. John Rawls, "Two Concepts of Rules," *Philosophical Review* 64, no. 1 (January 1955): 3–32.
11. William Shaw, *Contemporary Ethics: Taking Account of Utilitarianism* (Oxford: Blackwell, 1998), p. 24.
12. Bernard Williams, "A Critique of Utilitarianism," in *Utilitarianism: For and Against,* J. J. C. Smart and B. Williams (Cambridge: Cambridge University Press, 1973), pp. 77–150.
13. Immanuel Kant, *Grounding for a Metaphysics of Morals* (Indianapolis, IN: Hackett, 1981), p. 7.
14. Ibid., p. 30.
15. Ibid., p. 36.
16. Aristotle, *Nicomachean Ethics,* 1140b8–10 (Indianapolis, IN: Hackett, 1999).

Credits

Chapter 2: *p. 15:* Michael Tooley, "The Problem of Evil," *Stanford Encyclopedia of Philosophy* (Spring 2010 Edition), Edward N. Zalta (ed.), URL = http://plato. stanford.edu/archives/spr2010/entries/evil/index.html#SomImpDis.

Chapter 3: *pp. 48–49:* From *White Noise* by Don DeLillo, copyright © 1984, 1985 by Don DeLillo. Used by permission of Viking Penguin, a division of Penguin Group (USA) Inc.

Chapter 5: *p. 104 (photo):* Richard Drew/AP Wide World Photos.
p. 107 (photo top left): Anwar Hussein/Getty Images Inc.
p. 107 (photo top middle): Frank Edwards/Getty Images–Hulton Archive Photos.
p. 107 (photo top right): Frazer Harrison/Getty Images Inc.
p. 107 (photo bottom left): Alamy Images.
p. 107 (photo bottom middle): Frans Lanting/Alamy Images.
p. 107 (photo bottom right): Peter Frischmuth/Argus/PhotoLibrary/ Peter Arnold Inc.
pp. 121–122: Practical Guide to Past Life Memories: Twelve Proven Methods, © 2001, Llewellyn Publications. pp. 1–3.
pp. 122–123: M.E.N. magazine, February 1995.

Chapter 6: *p. 132:* George Graham, *Philosophy of Mind: An Introduction* (Oxford: Blackwell, 1998).
pp. 145–146: John Searle, *The Rediscovery of the Mind* (Cambridge, MA: MIT Press, 1992), p. 65.
p. 149: Reprinted with permission. Copyright © *Scientific American*, a division of Nature America, Inc. All rights reserved.

Chapter 7: *p. 168:* Bertrand Russell, *Why I Am Not a Christian and Other Essays on Religion and Related Subjects* (New York: Simon & Schuster, 1957). Copyright of The Bertrand Russell Peace Foundation Ltd. and Taylor & Francis.
p. 172 (photo): EyeWire Collection/Getty Images-Photodisc-Royalty Free.

Chapter 8: *p. 218:* William, Shaw, *Contemporary Ethics: Taking Account of Utilitarianism* (Oxford: Blackwell, 1998).

Index